Street by Street

BLACKBU… N
BURNL…

ACCRINGTON, CLITHER… RWEN,
NELSON, RAWTENSTALL

Bacup, Barrowford, Brierfield, C… -le-Moors, Great Harwood, Haslingden, Osw…ldtwistle, Padiham, Rishton, Sabden, Whalley, Wilpshire

2nd edition December 2005

Original edition printed May 2002

Published by AA Publishing (a trading name of Automobile Association Developments Limited, whose registered office is Fanum House, Basing View, Basingstoke, Hampshire RG21 4EA. Registered number 1878835).

Mapping produced by the Cartography Department of The Automobile Association. (A02417)

A CIP Catalogue record for this book is available from the British Library.

Printed by GRAFIASA S.A., Porto, Portugal

The contents of this atlas are believed to be correct at the time of the latest revision. However, the publishers cannot be held responsible or liable for any loss or damage occasioned to any person acting or refraining from action as a result of any use or reliance on any material in this atlas, nor for any errors, omissions or changes in such material. This does not affect your statutory rights. The publishers would welcome information to correct any errors or omissions and to keep this atlas up to date. Please write to Publishing, The Automobile Association, Fanum House (FH12), Basing View, Basingstoke, Hampshire, RG21 4EA.

Ref: ML204z

Key to map pages ii-iii

Key to map symbols iv-1

Enlarged map pages 2-5

Main map pages 6-65

Index – towns & villages 66

Index – streets 66-79

Index – featured places 79-81

Acknowledgements 81

National Grid references are shown on the map frame of each page.
Red figures denote the 100 km square and the blue figures the 1km sqaure.
Example, page 5 : Anchor Retail Park 384 433

The reference can also be written using the National Grid two-letter prefix shown on this page, where 3 and 4 are replaced by SD to give SD8433

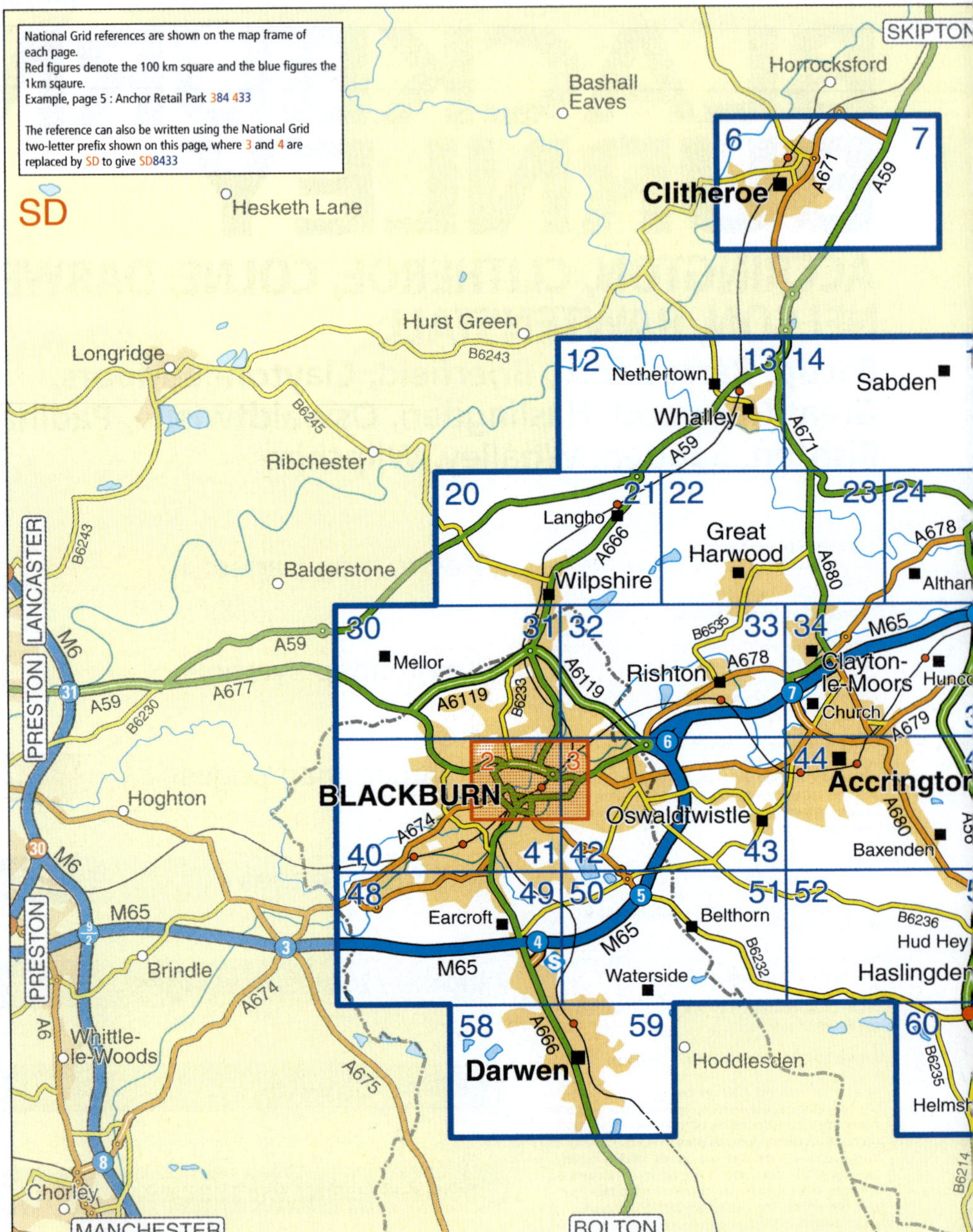

Scale of enlarged map pages 1:10,000 6.3 inches to 1 mile

0 1/4 miles 1/2

1/4 1/2 kilometres 3/4 1

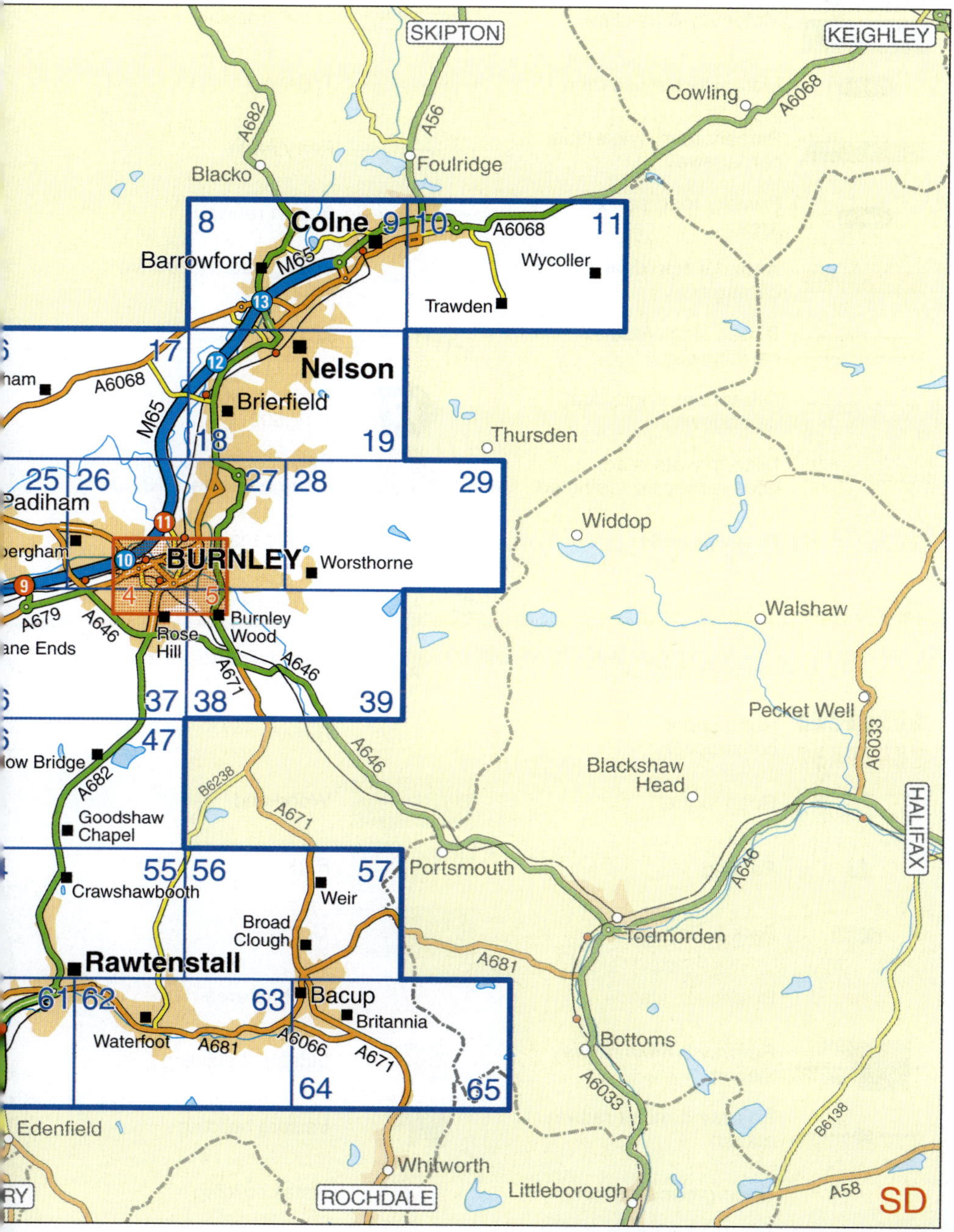

3.6 inches to 1 mile

Scale of main map pages 1:17,500

0 1/2 miles 1

0 1/2 1 kilometres 1 1/2

- Junction 9 — Motorway & junction
- Services — Motorway service area
- Primary road single/dual carriageway
- Services — Primary road service area
- A road single/dual carriageway
- B road single/dual carriageway
- Other road single/dual carriageway
- Minor/private road, access may be restricted
- One-way street
- Pedestrian area
- Track or footpath
- Road under construction
- Road tunnel
- P — Parking
- P+ — Park & Ride
- Bus/coach station
- Railway & main railway station
- Railway & minor railway station
- Underground station
- Light railway & station
- Preserved private railway
- LC — Level crossing
- Tramway
- Ferry route
- Airport runway
- County, administrative boundary
- Mounds
- 17 — Page continuation 1:17,500
- 3 — Page continuation to enlarged scale 1:10,000
- River/canal, lake, pier
- Aqueduct, lock, weir
- 465 Winter Hill — Peak (with height in metres)
- Beach
- Woodland
- Park
- Cemetery
- Built-up area
- Industrial building
- Leisure building
- Retail building
- Other building

	City wall
A&E	Hospital with 24-hour A&E department
PO	Post Office
	Public library
	Tourist Information Centre
	Seasonal Tourist Information Centre
	Petrol station, 24 hour Major suppliers only
	Church/chapel
	Public toilets
	Toilet with disabled facilities
PH	Public house AA recommended
	Restaurant AA inspected
Madeira Hotel	Hotel AA inspected
	Theatre or performing arts centre
	Cinema
	Golf course
	Camping AA inspected
	Caravan site AA inspected
	Camping & caravan site AA inspected
	Theme park
	Abbey, cathedral or priory

	Castle
	Historic house or building
Wakehurst Place NT	National Trust property
	Museum or art gallery
	Roman antiquity
	Ancient site, battlefield or monument
	Industrial interest
	Garden
	Garden Centre Garden Centre Association Member
	Garden Centre Wyevale Garden Centre
	Arboretum
	Farm or animal centre
	Zoological or wildlife collection
	Bird collection
	Nature reserve
	Aquarium
V	Visitor or heritage centre
	Country park
	Cave
	Windmill
	Distillery, brewery or vineyard

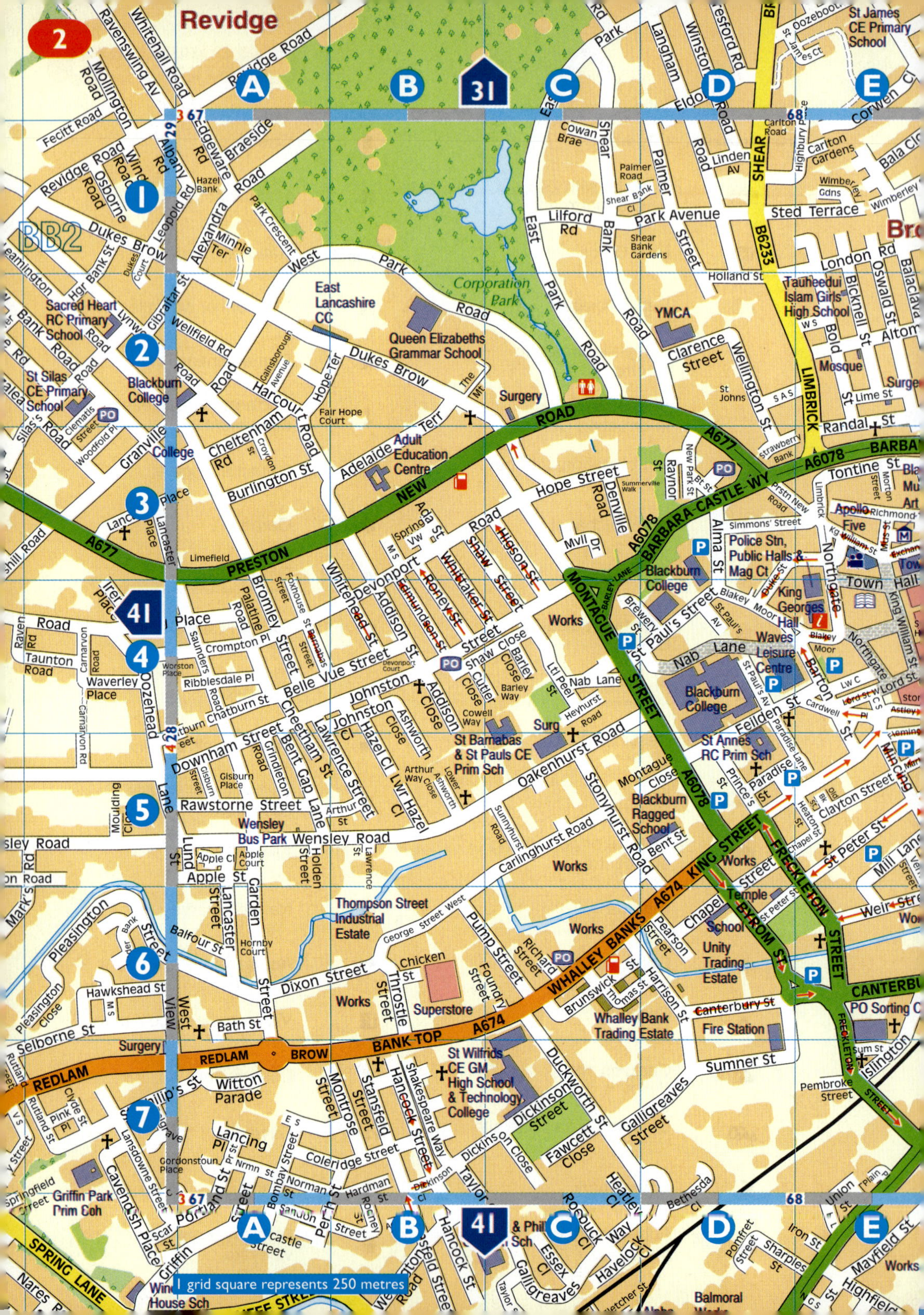
2
Revidge
31
41
A
B
C
D
E
1
2
3
4
5
6
7
67
68
BB2
1 grid square represents 250 metres
Corporation Park
East Lancashire CC
Queen Elizabeths Grammar School
Sacred Heart RC Primary School
St Silas CE Primary School
Blackburn College
Adult Education Centre
Surgery
YMCA
Tauheedul Islam Girls High School
Mosque
St James CE Primary School
St Johns
Police Stn, Public Halls & Mag Ct
King Georges Hall
Town Hall
Waves Leisure Centre
Apollo Five
St Barnabas & St Pauls CE Prim Sch
St Annes RC Prim Sch
Blackburn Ragged School
Wensley Bus Park
Thompson Street Industrial Estate
Superstore
Chicken
Works
Unity Trading Estate
Temple School
Fire Station
PO Sorting Office
Whalley Bank Trading Estate
St Wilfrids CE GM High School & Technology College
Griffin Park Prim Sch
Balmoral
Revidge Road
Whitehall Road
Ravenswing Av
Mollington Road
Fecitt Road
Osborne Road
Wind Road
Albany Rd
Edgeware Rd
Braeside
Alexandra Road
Minnie Ter
Park Crescent
West Park Road
Dukes Brow
Leopold Rd
Gibraltar St
Wellfield Rd
Harcourt Road
Hope Ter
Cheltenham Rd
Croydon St
Burlington St
Adelaide Terr
Preston New Road
A677
Granville Road
College
Lancaster Place
Limefield
Bromley Street
Palatine Road
Whitehead St
Addison St
Devonport Road
Shaw Street
Higson St
Hope Street
Denville Road
Barbara Castle Wy
A6078
A6078
Montague Street
St Paul's Street
Nab Lane
Limbrick
Northgate
Tontine St
Simmons' Street
Richmond Ter
King William St
Lord St
Feilden St
Paradise Lane
Clayton Street
St Peter St
Mill Lane
Weir St
Freckleton Street
Byrom St
King Street
Whalley Banks
A674
Bank Top
Redlam Brow
Redlam
Spring Lane
Selborne St
Pleasington Close
Hawkshead St
West View
Bath St
Dixon Street
Throstle Street
Foundry Street
Pump Street
George Street West
Balfour St
Lancaster Street
Garden Street
Apple St
Lund St
Wensley Road
Rawstorne Street
Downham Street
Belle Vue Street
Johnston St
Oakenhurst Road
Stonyhurst Road
Carlinghurst Road
Ozzehead
Waverley Place
Taunton Road
Raven Road
Crompton Pl
Ribblesdale Pl
Chatburn St
Cheetham St
Grindleton Road
Bent Gap Lane
Lawrence Street
Hazel Cl
Ashworth Close
Holden Street
Duckworth St
Dickinson Street
Fawcett Close
Galligreaves Street
Sumner St
Canterbury St
Harrison St
Pembroke Street
Islington
Witton Parade
Lancing Pl
Coleridge Street
Norman St
Hardman St
Montrose Street
Stansfeld Street
Hancock Street
Shakespeare Way
Taylor St
Heatley Cl
Havelock St
Bethesda Cl
Pomfret Street
Sharples St
Iron St
Mayfield St
Highfield
Union St
Lansdowne Street
Cavendish Place
Portland St
Castle Street
Perth St
East Park Road
Lilford Rd
Park Avenue
Shear Bank Road
Palmer Street
Clarence Street
Wellington St
Holland St
Sted Terrace
London Rd
Bicknell St
Oswald St
Balaclava
Limbrick
Randal St
Lime St
Strawberry Bank
Alma St
Raynor St
Summerville Walk
Mvll Dr
Cowan Brae
Langham
Winston Road
Eldon Road
Linden Av
Shear Brow
B6233
Carlton Road
Carlton Gardens
Wimberley Gdns
Corwen Cl
Bala Cl
St Oozebooth

F
G
H
J
K
32
42
69
I
2
3
4
5
6
7
BLACKBURN
Higher Audley
Whalley New Rd
Lark Hill A666
Castle Way
Eanam A6078
HGR Eanam
Copy Nook A678
Audley St
Higher Audley St A6078
Lower Audley Street A6078
Park Road
Grimshaw Pk A6077
Brookhouse Business Centre
Brookhouse Lane
Shearwater Drive
Med Cen
St Albans RC Prim Sch
St Michael with St John CE Prim Sch
Daisyfield Swimming Pool
Daisyfield Primary Sch
Daisyfield Business Centre
Fort Street Industrial Estate
Science Park
Furthergate Industrial Estate
Orient Works
St Thomas CE Primary School
Market
Brewery
Superstore
Cathedral
Radio
Blackburn Station
Surgery
Works
Ghousia Mosque
Primary School
Audley Sports & Neighbourhood Centre
Mosque
Council Building
Al-Islah Private School
Lower Audley Industrial Estate
Blackburn Arena (Ice Rink)
Grimshaw Retail Park
Audley Junior School
Audley Inf School
St Mary & Josephs RC Prim Sch
Merchants Landing
Dickens Street
Pringle Street
Queen's Road
Queen's Park
Walter Street
Nottingham Street
Ripon Street
Temple Street
Stanley Street
Hutton Street
Appleby Street
Dock Street
Cicely Lane
Salford
Brown St
Penny Street
Starkie Street
Pendle Street
Addington St
William Hopwood Street
Copperfield Street
Audley Range
Leeds Close
Sussex Drive
Stirling Dr
Whitendale Cresent
Harrow Dr
Lincoln Street
Harwood Street
Moss Street
Pelham St
Church Hill Rd
Plane St
Ash Street

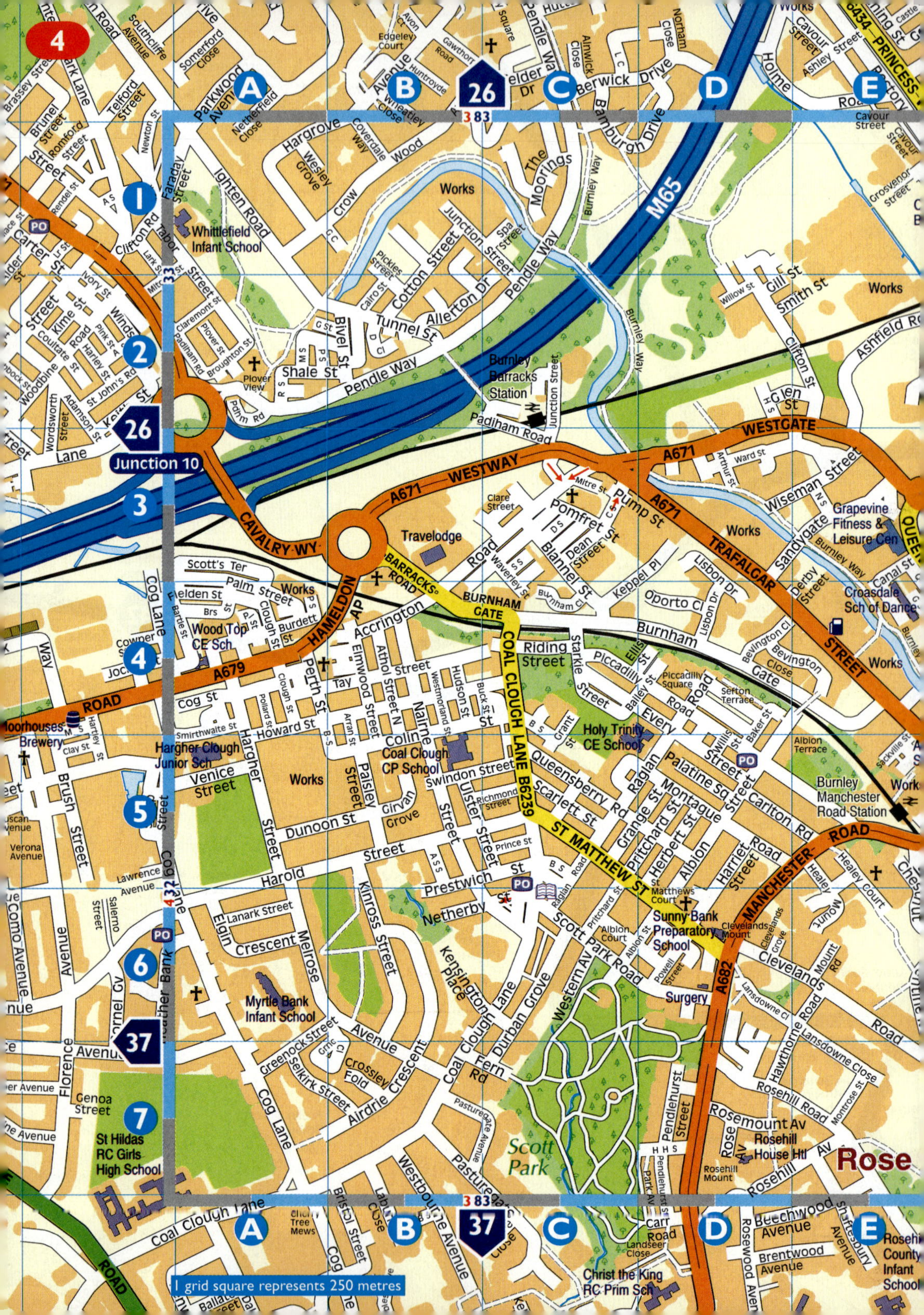
A
B
C
D
E
26
383
M65
Works
Hargrove
Wesley Grove
Coverdale Way
Wood
Crow
The Moorings
Bamburgh Drive
Berwick Drive
Norham Close
Alnwick Close
Pendle Way
Parkwood Avenue
Netherfield Close
Somerford Close
Southcliffe Avenue
Telford Street
Brunel Street
Romford Street
Newton St
Faraday Street
Clifton Rd
Whittlefield Infant School
Junction Street
Spa Street
Cotton Street
Pickles Street
Allerton Dr
Tunnel St
Bivel St
Shale St
Plover View
Pendle Way
Burnley Barracks Station
Junction Street
Padiham Road
Burnley Way
Willow St
Gill St
Smith St
Works
Clifton St
Ashfield Rd
Glen St
Cavour Street
Holme Street
Grosvenor Street
Carter St
Ivory St
Kime St
Coultate St
Woodbine
Adamson St
St John's Rd
Wordsworth Street
Lane
1
2
3
4
5
6
7
Junction 10
26
Cavalry Wy
Westway
A671
Westgate
Ward St
Arthur St
Wiseman Street
Grapevine Fitness & Leisure Cen
Mitre St
Pump St
Pomfret St
Clare Street
Travelodge
Barracks Road
Burnham Gate
Blannel St
Dean Street
Keppel Pl
Oporto Cl
Lisbon Dr
Trafalgar Street
Sandygate
Derby Street
Burnley Way
Canal St
Croasdale Sch of Dance
Works
Scott's Ter
Palm Street
Fielden St
Works
Burdett St
Wood Top CE Sch
Cog Lane
Hameldon Ap
Accrington Road
A679
Road
Moorhouses Brewery
Cog St
Howard St
Perth St
Elmwood Street
Athol Street
Street
Hudson St
Buck St
Coal Clough Lane B6239
Riding Street
Starkie Street
Piccadilly Road
Piccadilly Square
Sefton Terrace
Bevington Close
Burnham Gate
Hargher Clough Junior Sch
Hargher Street
Venice Street
Works
Colin
Coal Clough CP School
Nairne
Holy Trinity CE School
Every Street
Raglan Road
Albion Terrace
Burnley Manchester Road Station
Works
Queensberry Rd
Scarlett St
Palatine Sq
Montague Street
Carlton Rd
Swindon Street
Richmond Street
Girvan Grove
Dunoon St
Ulster Street
Paisley Street
Brush Street
Verona Avenue
Street
Harold Street
Prince St
Prestwich St
St Matthew St
Grange St
Pritchard St
Herbert St
Albion Street
Harriet Street
Road
Manchester Road
Healey Court
Lawrence Avenue
Salerno Street
Como Avenue
Avenue
Lanark Street
Elgin Crescent
Melrose
Kinross Street
Netherby
Kensington Place
Sunny Bank Preparatory School
St Matthews Court
Albion Court
Clevelands Mount
Clevelands Grove
Clevelands
Mount Rd
Heather Bank
Myrtle Bank Infant School
Greenock Street
Selkirk Street
Crossley Fold
Avenue
Airdrie Crescent
Coal Clough Lane
Durban Grove
Western Av
Scott Park Road
Surgery
A682
Lansdowne Cl
Hawthorne Road
Lansdowne Close
Rosehill Road
Montrose St
Florence Avenue
Genoa Street
37
St Hildas RC Girls High School
Cog Lane
Fern Rd
Pasture Avenue
Scott Park
Pendlehurst Street
Rosemount Av
Rosehill House Htl
Rose Av
Rosehill Mount
Rosehill Av
Rose
Coal Clough Lane
Cherry Tree Mews
Bristol Street
Westbourne Avenue
Pastureg Close
Carr Road
Landseer Close
Beechwood Avenue
Brentwood Avenue
Shaftesbury Avenue
Rosewood Aven
Rosehill County Infant School
Christ the King RC Prim Sch
Road
1 grid square represents 250 metres

BURNLEY
BB11
Burnley Wood
Golf Course
Thompson Park
Burnley Central Station
Retail Park
Superstore
Burnley College Higher Education Centre
Burnley College
Anchor Retail Park
St Peters CE Prim Sch
Sparrow Hawk Hotel
Royal Mail Sorting Office
Burnley Business Centre
Charter Walk Shopping Cen
Market Square
Market Promenade
The Mall
Howe Walk
Fleet Walk
Clinic
Town Hall
Cncl Bldg
Pol Stn and Mag Cts
William Thompson Recreation Centre
St Nicholas Health Cen
Weavers Triangle Vis Cen
AMF Bowling
Healey Wood Rd Ind Est
Hollywood Park Cinema
Healey Wood Infant School
Leeds & Liverpool Canal
Fire Station
St Theodores RC School
Burnley Lawn Tennis Club
RC Primary School
Burnley Cricket Club
Burnley FC (Turf Moor)
Yorkshire Street Medical Cen
Med Cen
Springfield Community Prim Sch
Burnley Wood Health Cen & CP School
Towneley High School
CE School
Atrium Court
Travel Inn
ACTIVE WAY
CENTENARY WAY
COLNE ROAD
CHURCH STREET
YORKSHIRE ST
BELVEDERE ROAD
TODMORDEN ROAD
Ormerod Road
Harry Potts Way
Manchester Road
Parliament Street
Oxford Road
Hollingreave
A679
A682
A6114
A671
B6434
F
G
H
J
K
27
38
84
85
1
2
3
4
5
6
7

1 grid square represents 500 metres

Chatburn Road
A671
PIMLICO LINK ROAD
Clitheroe Hospital
Deanfield
Salthill Industrial Estate
Green Drive
Clitheroe Royal Grammar School
Lincoln Way
LINK ROAD
A671
Salthill Industrial Estate
Up-Brooks
Up-Brooks Industrial Estate
Hawthorne Industrial Park
Bracken Hey
Middlewood
A59
Worston
Hall Foot
Meadows Farm
Mearley Brook
Fields
Lane Side
Mearley Hall
Knowl Top
Pendle Road
Pendle Rd
Brett Cl
A59
Pendleton Hall
Howcroft Barn
Pendleton
F
G
H
J
K
76
77
43
42
41
440
1
2
3
4
5
6

A
B
C
D
E
1
2
3
4
5
6
384
85
86
41
40
39
438
18
Blacko Foot
Pendle Way
Pendle Water
Hollin Top
Middlewood
Stone E
Higherford
Roughlee
BB9
Pasture House
Pasture Lane
Crow Trees
Ribblesdale Place
Barleydale Rd
Middleton Dr
A682
ROAD
Roughlee Junior School
Lowerford
Ridgaling Farm
Oaklands
Works
Appleby Drive
Lipton Dr
Mint Av
Church St
GISBURN
Pendle Heritage Centre
Cemetery
BARROWFORD
St Thomas CE Primary School
Barrowford CP Sch
Rushton St
Oaklands Avenue
Harry St
Back Harry St
Victoria St
Wheatley Lane Road
Daleswav
Higher
Surgery
Burnsall
Ridgeway
Wilkinson St
Pendle Street
Lee Street
Mosman Pl
St Michael's Court
Clinic
Wilton St
Romney Av
Cadogan St
Roughlee Street
Sandy La
Calder St
Nelson & Colne College
Sandyhall Lane
Forest Lane
Carr Hall
Laund
Newbridge
Holy Saviour RC Primary School
Holland Pl
Charles Street
REEDYFORD ROAD
Canal Side
Hodge Bank Bus Park
Boothman Place
Throup Place
Bradley Primary School
Seedhill Athletics Stadium
BARROWFORD ROAD
Surrey Rd
Junction 13
M65
Gill St
Parrock Road
Applegarth
Linden Cl
Chevassut Cl
North Park Av
Lwr Parrock Rd
Nelson Bowling & CC
Willow Cl
Carr Hall Gdns
Hamilton Rd
A6068
B6249
CARR
ROAD
Churchill Road
Carr Hall Rd
Park Avenue
Clayton St Ind Est
Pendle St
Mosque
Superstore
Norfolk St
Scott St
SCOTLAND RD
NEW SCOTLAND RD
Fleet St
Riverside Business Cen
Derby St
Fire Sta
Hosp
Health Centre
Crawford St
Cooper St
Fountain St
Dalton St
WHEATLEY LANE ROAD
Carr
Hall
Cemetery
Mallet
Admiral Shop Cen
BROADWAY
Lomeshaye Business Village
Sun St
Kirby Road
Craven St
Victoria St
Macleod St
Netherfield Rd
Pendle
Nelson
Philips Prim Sch
1 grid square represents 500 metres

Red Lane
Colne Edge
Sacred RC Primary School
Alkincoats
Colne & Nelson RUFC
COLNE
Blakey Hall
White Gv
Rimington Av
Harrison Dr
Alkincoats Road
Park Way
Harrison Drive
Birtwistle
Slater Av
Keats Cl
Coleridge
Judge Fields
Ruskin Av
Talbot Street
Burrell Av
Glenroy Avenue
Belgrave
Keighley Avenue
North Street
Road
Tennyson Rd
Milton Rd
Stanley St
Derby St
NORTH VALLEY ROAD A6068
North Valley Retail Park
Argyle St
Hiers House Lane
Barrowford Lock House
Priestfield Av
Barcroft St
Parker St
Milford St
Reginald St
Selby St
Haverholt
Lord Street Prim Sch
Health Cen
Church St
Mkt Hall
Town Hall
West St Prim Sch
CHURCH A56
Nelson & Colne College
BARROWFORD ROAD B6247
Netherheys
Ing Dene Av
VIVARY WAY A6068
CROWN WY
RIGBY ST
QUEEN ST
LORD ST
North Va Rd
Colne Station
Pendle Leisure Cen
A56 ALBERT ROAD
Shaw Street
Exchange Street
Dam Side
ROAD
B6247
Greenfield Road
Colne Water
Peel Road
Cross St N
Bolton St
Road
PRIMET HILL
PRIMET BR
Holker Business Cen
Primet Business Cen
Greenfield
Garden Vale Business Cen
Knotts La
Green Road
Works
Garden St
Spring Gdns
Atkinson St
Lenches Fold
10
WHITEWALLS DR
A6068
Sewage Works
White Walls Close
Works
Medical Centre
BURNLEY ROAD
Primet Prim Sch
Grindlestone Hirst
Valley Drive
Dewhurst Street
Knotts Mount
South Drive
Regent Street
Superstore
Corporation St
Whitewalls Industrial Est
Junction Street
Colne Primet High School
Knotts Lane
Lenches Road
Birchenlee Lane
Kiln Hill
Edward Street
Progress
BURNLEY ROAD
Hereford Road
Clare Av
Works
Bott House La
Briercliffe Avenue
Briercliffe Av
SS John Fisher & Thomas More High Sch
Colne Gibfield School
Hill End
Regent Street
Norwood Av
Lee Road
A56 ROAD
Bott House La
Oxford Road
Hollins Road
Sweet Clough
Southfield Lane
Sansbury Crs
Castercliff
Works
Walton Lane
Cemetery
Marsden Hall Rd N
Merclesden Av
Thursden Pl
Gib Hill Rd
Works
LEEDS
Waterford Street
Glenfield Rd
Brentwood Rd
Nelson Castercliff City School
Shelfield Road
Boulsworth Crs
Cock Leach
Walton Lane
Glenfield Park Ind Est
Marsden Hall
Townhouse Special School
Hallam Road
Woodlands Rd
Golf Course
19
Park Golf Course
Barkerhouse Rd
Avenue
Rowland
Marsden Crescent
Ringstone Crescent
Hazelwood Road
Town House
Barkerhouse
Walverden Sec
Shelfield
Southfield Lane
Chur Clou
F G H J K
1 2 3 4 5 6
87 88 89
38 39 40 41

10
9
Upper Reservoir
Colne Golf Club
Skipton Road
Castle Road
Manor Rd
Brown Hill
Park High School
SKIPTON ROAD
Hill Lane
Heyroyd
A6068
KEIGHLEY ROAD
Bent Lane
Christ Church CE Primary School
Colne Water
WINDSOR STREET
LANGROYD RD
BYRON ROAD
Favordale Rd
North Valley Retail Park
Norfolk Street
Works
Standroyd Drive
Ball Grove Dr
COTTON TREE LANE
B6250
KEIGHLEY RD
Colne CC
Cemetery
Health Cen
MARKET ST
CHURCH ST
Mkt Hall
CRAD RD
Superstore
Town
Waterside Industrial Estate
Newtown St
Carry Lane
Old Mill Drive
Coal Pit Lane
Rosley St
Hawley St
TRAWDEN ROAD
Works
Bankfield Street
New Row
Winewa
Mire Ridge
Far Laithe Farm
Church Clough
Lenches Road
Birchenlee Lane
Kiln Hill
Foulds Road
Colne Road
Lachman Rd
Leyland Close
Bannister Close
Holme Crs
SKIPTON ROAD
Works
Surgery
Hall Road
River Street
Keighley
Stunstead Road
Dean St
Trawden CP School
CHURCH STREET
Back La
Bright Ter
Green Meadow
White Lee Av
Sweet Clough
Fox Clough
New Laith
Burnley Road
Lane House Lane
Hol Hal
Doughty Farm
Slack Laithe
A B C D E
1 2 3 4 5 6
89 90 91
41 40 39 38
1 grid square represents 500 metres

Flass
Lane
Monkroyd
F
G
H
J
K
Lane Head
Emmott
92
Laneshaw Bridge
93
A6068
94
41
Laneshawbridge Primary School
Emmott Ct
Sheridan Road
Vernon Rd
Lane
Works
River Lane
I
KEIGHLEY ROAD
PO
School
Lane
Emmott
Carrier's Row
Pendle
Way
Keighley
Road
Ing Heys
2
Far Laith
40
Bronte Way
Slack
3
Thorn Edge
BB8
Wycoller
4
Foster Leap
Trawden
39
Copy House
Bronte Way
Raven Rock Farm
5
Bronte Way
Wanless
Little Laith
Great Hill
6
Alderbarrow
38
92
93
94
F
G
H
J
K

St Josephs RC Primary School
WHALLEY B6243 ROAD
Cross Gills
Fox Fields
Jumbles
Ribble Way
Mitton Wood
River Ribble
Brockhall Farm
Works
Tuscany Gv
Provence Av
St Andrews Rd
The Winds
Brockhall Village
Cherry Dr
Damson Close
Highwoods Park
Bradyll Court
Pendle Vw
The Drive
Nwd Gdns
Mansfield Cl
Gleneagles Drive
Larkhill
The Avenue Hotel
Highwoods Pk
Elm Tree Gv
Highwoods Pk
Potter Ford House
Elker La
Old Langho Road
Cravens
Aspinalls
Brookside
Dinckley Brook
Old Langho
Dinckley
Lower Elker
Hillock Farm
Road
Wardfall
Old Langho Road
Northcote Road
A59
Lower Fold Farm
St Leonards CE Primary School
Northcote Manor Hotel
Chapel La
Longsight Road
Whalley Rd
A666
LONGSIGHT ROAD
Hall
Dinckley
21
1 grid square represents 500 metres
369
70
71
38
37
36
435

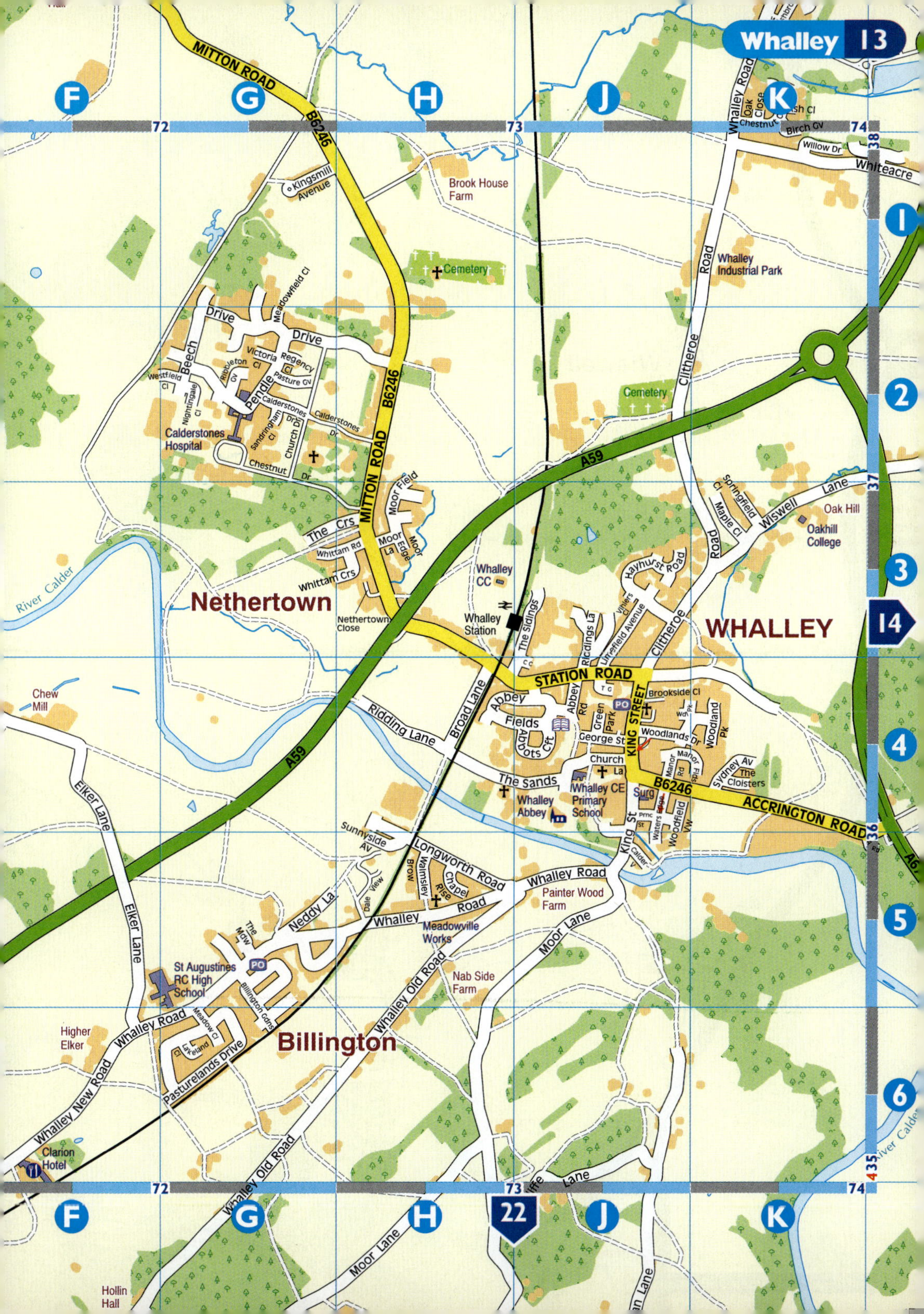
F
G
H
J
K
72
73
74
38
37
36
435
1
2
3
4
5
6
14
22
MITTON ROAD
B6246
Kingsmill Avenue
Brook House Farm
Cemetery
Whalley Road
Oak Close
Chestnut
Birch Gv
Willow Dr
Whiteacre
Whalley Industrial Park
Meadowfield Cl
Drive
Beech
Victoria Cl
Regency Cl
Pasture Gv
Ribbleton Gv
Westfield Cl
Nightingale Cl
Pendle
Calderstones Dr
Calderstones Dr
Sandringham Cl
Church Dr
Calderstones Hospital
Chestnut Dr
Clitheroe Road
Cemetery
A59
Moor Field
The Crs
Moor La
Moor Edge
Whittam Rd
Whittam Crs
River Calder
Nethertown
Nethertown Close
Whalley CC
Whalley Station
The Sidings
Springfield Cl
Maple Cl
Wiswell Lane
Oak Hill
Oakhill College
Hayhurst Road
Villiers Cl
Limefield Avenue
Riddings La
WHALLEY
Chew Mill
STATION ROAD
Abbey Fields
Abbey Rd
Abbots Cft
Green Park
KING STREET
Brookside Cl
Woodland Pk
Woodlands Dr
George St
Manor Rd
Church La
Sydney Av
The Cloisters
Ridding Lane
Broad Lane
The Sands
Whalley Abbey
Whalley CE Primary School
Surg
B6246
ACCRINGTON ROAD
Elker Lane
Sunnyside Av
Longworth Road
Brow
Walmsley
Chapel Rise
King St
Waters Edge
Woodfield Vw
Calder V
Whalley Road
Painter Wood Farm
Neddy La
Dale View
Whalley Road
Meadowville Works
Moor Lane
The Maw
PO
St Augustines RC High School
Billington Gdns
Whalley Old Road
Nab Side Farm
Higher Elker
Whalley Road
Meadow Cl
Lakeland Cl
Pasturelands Drive
Billington
Whalley New Road
Clarion Hotel
Whalley Old Road
Lane
Moor Lane
Hollin Hall
River Calder

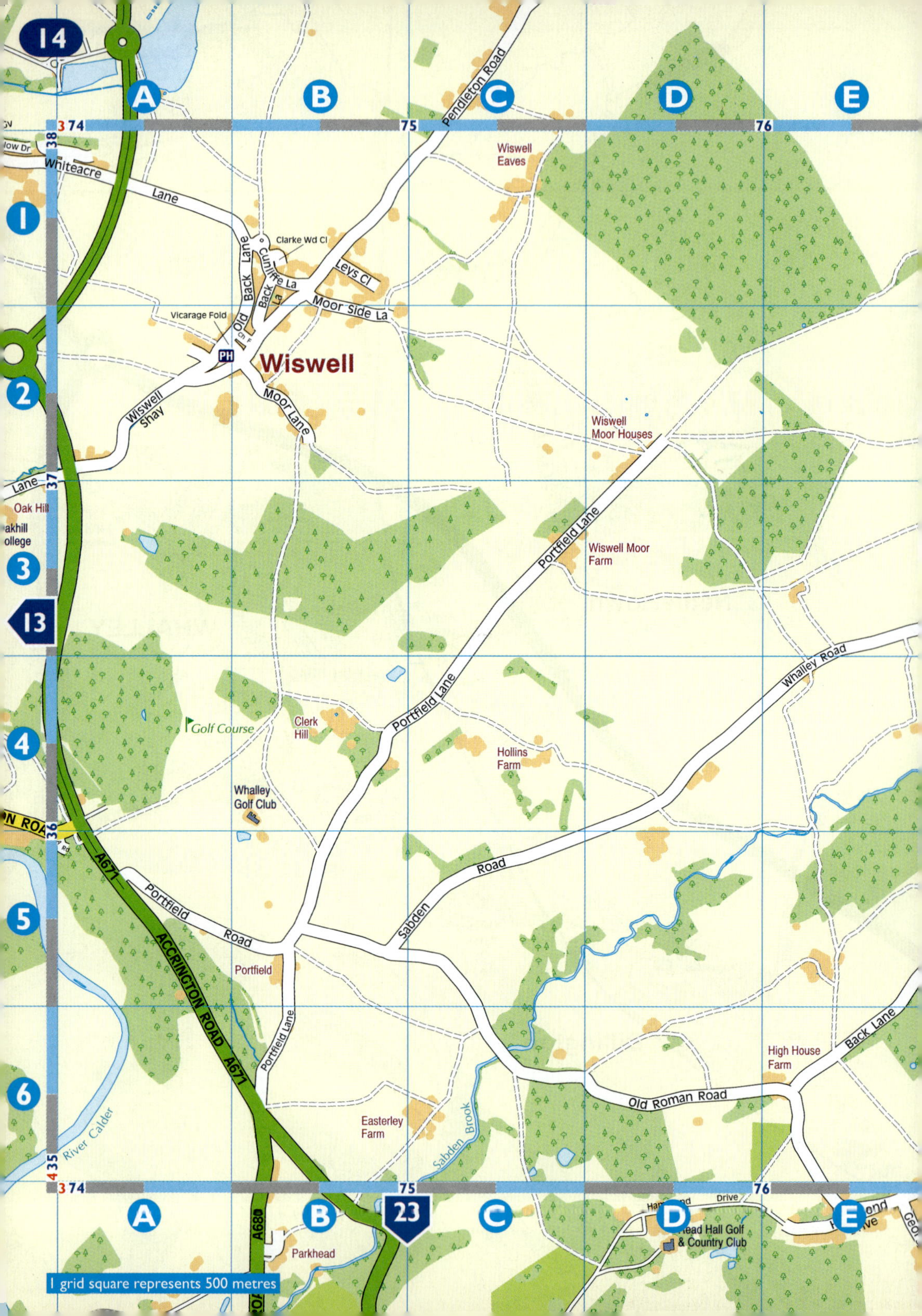
14
13
23
A
B
C
D
E
1
2
3
4
5
6
74
75
76
38
37
36
35
Wiswell
Wiswell Eaves
Pendleton Road
Whiteacre Lane
Clarke Wd Cl
Old Back Lane
Back La
Cunliffe La
Leys Cl
Moor Side La
Vicarage Fold
PH
Wiswell Shay
Moor Lane
Wiswell Moor Houses
Portfield Lane
Wiswell Moor Farm
Oak Hill
Whalley Road
Golf Course
Clerk Hill
Hollins Farm
Whalley Golf Club
A671
Portfield Road
Sabden Road
ACCRINGTON ROAD
Portfield
Portfield Lane
High House Farm
Back Lane
Old Roman Road
Easterley Farm
Sabden Brook
River Calder
A680
Parkhead
Drive
Head Hall Golf & Country Club
1 grid square represents 500 metres

Clough Reservoir
Parsley Barn
Clitheroe Road
F
G
H
J
K
77
78
79
Ratten Clough
38
Wilkin Heys
Timbrills Av
Crowtrees Rd
Dry Corner
I
Sabden Primary School
Wesley Street
Stubbins Lane
St Nchl Av
Sabden Brook Ct
Sabden
Gardeners Row
PO
The Whins
Surgery
Sabden Brook
2
Whins Av
Works
Pendle St East
Pendle St West
Watt St
Sabden RC School
Close
Pendleside
Thorn St
Whalley Road
Works
Heyhouse
37
Padiham Road
Simonstone Road
3
16
Cobden Farm
Back Lane
Sabden Road
The Cavaliers
White Hill
4
36
Priddy Bank Farm
Trapp Lane
5
New Hall
Whins Lane
Whins Lane
6
Whins Lane
Woodfields
Huntroyde
Law Farm
Lane
Straits
Turner Fold
35
Read
Buckingham Dr
Windsor Close
Berkeley Dr
Patrick Av
Woodhead Road
Read St Johns CE Primary School
Woodside Road
Dawson Avenue
Carleton
Harew
24
Trapp Lane
Huntroyde

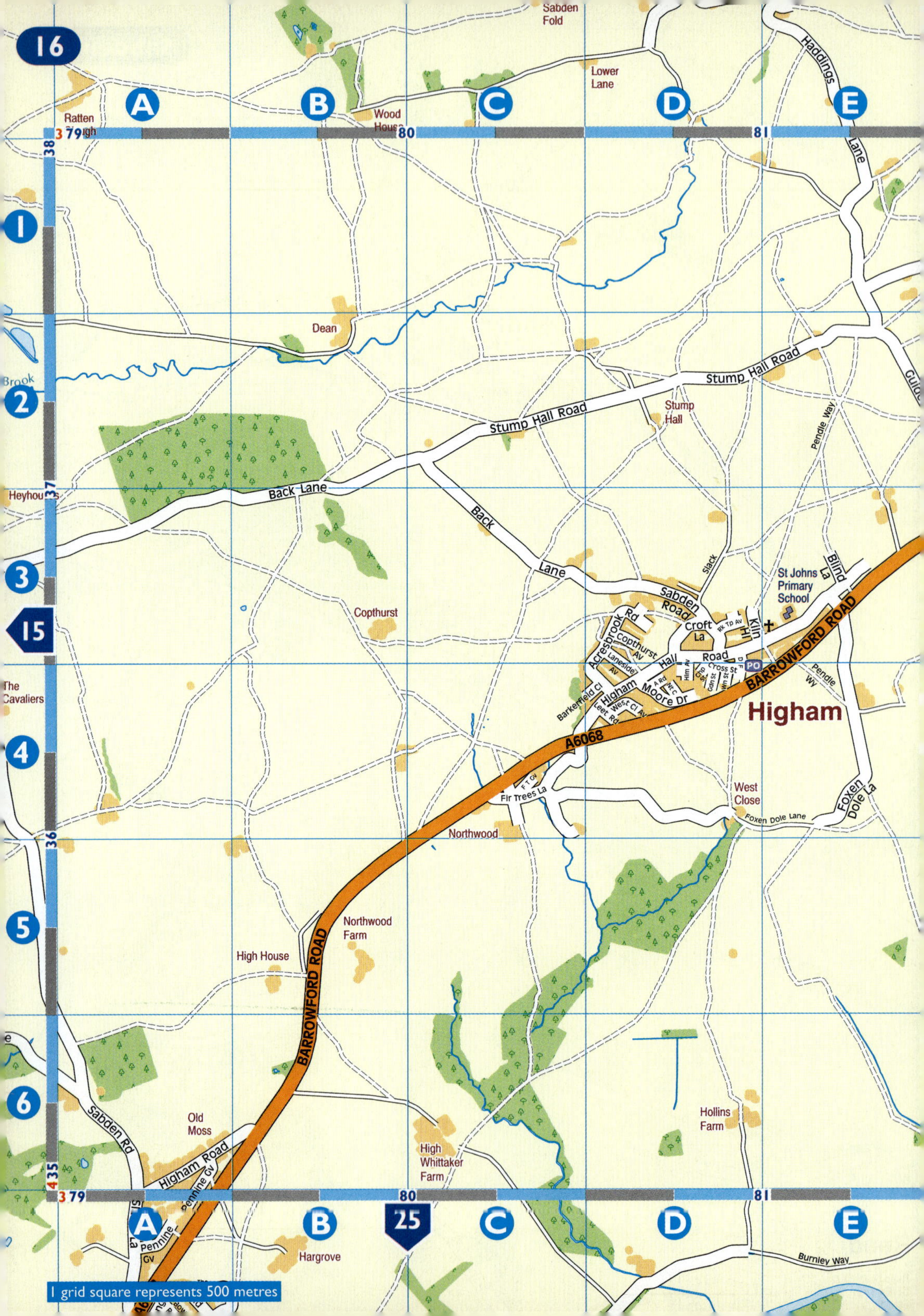
Sabden Fold
Lower Lane
Haddings Lane
Ratten
Wood House
Dean
Brook
Stump Hall Road
Stump Hall
Pendle Way
Back Lane
Heyhouses
Copthurst
Slack
Blind La
St Johns Primary School
Sabden Road
Croft La
Kiln Hl
Acresbrook Rd
Copthurst Av
Laneside Av
Hall Road
Cross St
Higham
Moore Dr
Barkerfield Cl
Leet Rd
West Cl Av
BARROWFORD ROAD
A6068
Pendle Wy
The Cavaliers
Fir Trees La
Northwood
West Close
Foxen Dole Lane
Foxen Dole La
Northwood Farm
High House
Hollins Farm
Old Moss
Sabden Rd
Higham Road
Pennine Gv
High Whittaker Farm
Hargrove
Burnley Way
A B C D E
1 2 3 4 5 6
15
25
379 80 81
438 437 436 435
1 grid square represents 500 metres

Wheatley Lane
Fence
Noggarth Road
BARROWFORD ROAD
A6068
Greenbank Dr
PO
Laund Gate
Harpers La
Deer Chace
Forester Drive
Wheatley La Road
Wheatley Lane Methodist Prim Sch
Pendle Forest Sports Club
Hoarstones
Heatherlea Road
Uplands Dr
Hoarstones Av
Cuckstool La
Works
St Anne's Drive
Pendle Fields
PH
Barrowford Rd
B6248
CUCKSTOOL LANE
Cuckstool Lane Top
Raven's Clough
Fence House
Ashlar House
Lower White Lee
Montford
Hill St
Montford Rd
CLITHEROE RD
Sykefield
18
M65
New Laund
Greenhead Lane
Green Head
Moor Isles
Pendle Way
Holme End
Wood End
Bronte Way
Barden Lane
Healdwood Dr
Wood End
Mnr Lane
Burnley Wy
Hunters Oak
River Calder
26
Lower Md
Garswood Cl
Bronte Wy
Leeds and Liv
F
G
H
J
K
82
83
84
1
2
3
4
5
6
38
37
36
435

1 grid square represents 500 metres

NELSON
Lane Bottom
Haggate
Cockden
Works
Waterford Street
Grafton St
Hildrop Rd
Glenfield Rd
Brentwood Rd
Glenfield Park Ind Est
Hallam Road
Nelson Castercliff City School
Walton Lane
Pinfold Pl
Shelfield Road
Boulsworth Crs
Cock Leach
Marsden Hall
Special School
Golf Course
Marsden Park Public Golf Course
Woodlands Rd
Barkerhouse Rd
Hendon Road
Whitehall St
Tavistock St
Earl St
Pine St
Marsden Hall Road
St John's Pl
Rowland Avenue
Marsden Crescent
Hazelwood Road
Ringstone Crescent
Town House Road
Linkside Av
Deerstone Road
Trent Rd
St Johns CE Primary School
Castle St
Larch St
Fir St
Bracewell Street
Walverden Sec Modern Sch
Walverden Prim Sch
York St
Squire Rd
Clough Rd
Manor St
Bath St
Fletcher Street
Vale Street
Southfield Street
J Nelson War Memorial Sports Club
Wickworth Street
Windsor St
Wenning St
Pendle Industrial Estate
Park Dr
Vaughan St
Clover Hl Rd
St Georges Rd
Sackville St
Pilgrim St
Lily St
Barnfield Business Centre
Boston St
Walverden Reservoir
Barkerhouse Road
Southfield Lane
Delves Lane
Shelfield Farm
Southfield
Pendle Way
Crawshaw Lane
Catlow Farm
Foulds House Farm
Burwains Farm
Walverden Rd
Coldweather Avenue
Halifax Road
Golf Course
Robin House Lane
Stirling Ct
Nelson Road
Chapel Ct
Briercliffe County Primary School
Tiverton Dr
Delamere Rd
Drive
Surgery
Burnley Road
Douglas Rd
North St
Duke St
Queen St
Jubilee St
Banks Street
Black House Lane
Todmorden Road
Burnley Way
Queen Street Mill
Queen Street
Cross St
F
G
H
J
K
I
2
3
4
5
6
9
28
87
88
89
38
37
36
435

1 grid square represents 500 metres

Lower Fold Farm
Langholme
Northcote Manor Hotel
St Leonards CE Primary School
Whalley Road
Longsight Road
Whalley Rd
A59 LONGSIGHT ROAD
A59
Chapel Lane
A666
WHALLEY RD
Langho Station
Golf Course
Home Farm
The Rydings
Clayton Row
Bushburn Drive
Moorland Road
Cronshaw Dr
Hacking Cl
Whitehalgh Lane
PO
Tudor Close
St Marys RC Primary School
St Mary's Drive
Whinney Lane
Rogersfield
Lowerfield
Midfield
Higher Fld
Kirkdale Rd
Portland Rd
Springdale Rd
Hillcrest Rd
York Lane
York
Whalley Old Road
Hawthorn Close
Langho
York Road
Snodworth Road
ping's Farm
Carr Hall
Dean Clough Reserv
Sunnyside Av
Ribblesdale Rd
Anderson Rd
Hollies
WHALLEY ROAD
Snodworth
Golf Course
Wilpshire Golf Club
WILPSHIRE
Rishton Road
Parsonage Reservoir
Blackburn Old Road
Harwood Road
New Inns
Warrenside
F
G
H
J
K
12
32
22
70
71
1
2
3
4
5
6
35
34
33
432

A
B
13
C
D
E
1
2
3
21
4
5
6
33
Whalley New Road
Pasturelands
Whalley Old Road
Moor Lane
Shawcliffe Lane
Dean Lane
Berrys Lane
Hollin Hall
Miles Hill
Heys Farm
Cronshaw
Sunny Bank
Dean Brook
Dean Farm
Whittle Hall
BB6
Cowden
Coldacre Lane
Allsprings
Dean Clough Reservoir
Blackburn Old Road
Great Harwood CC
North Cliffe School
Northcliffe
Westcliffe
Southcliffe
Blackleach
Ravenswood
GREAT HARWOOD
Cliffe
Hindle Fold
Kebb
Limers
Brantfeld Road
St Bartholomews Parish CE Prim Sch
PARK LA
Park Av
Premier Business Park
Windsor Rd
Lowerfold Road
B6535 CHURCH ST
Beaconsfield St
Gladstone St
Delph Road
Clinkham Road
Edge End
Belmont Road
Queen Street
Mercer Hall Leisure Centre
Surgery
Superstore
Works
Princess St
Russell Pl
St Wulstans RC Primary School
Great Harwood Prim Sch
Segar Street Mosque
Lomax St
Waverledge Business Park
Waverledge Rd
Shakespeare
Moss St
St Johns CE Prim Sch
Railway Ter
Meadow Street
Alan
Hameldon
1 grid square represents 500 metres

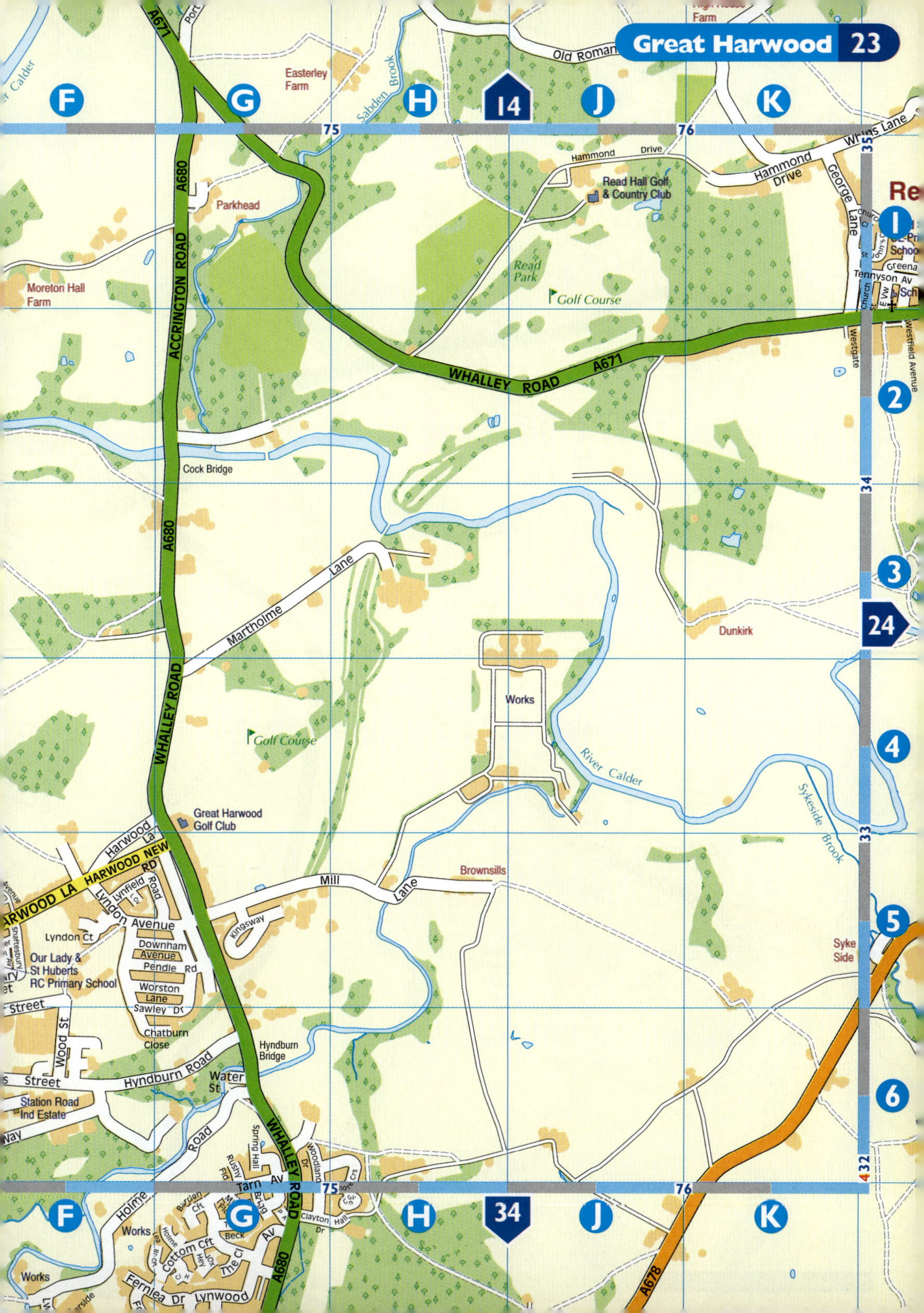
F
G
H
14
J
K
75
76
Old Roman
Easterley Farm
Sabden Brook
A671
A680
ACCRINGTON ROAD
Parkhead
Hammond Drive
Read Hall Golf & Country Club
Whins Lane
George Lane
Church Cl
St John's Cl
Greena
Tennyson Av
Church St
E Vw
Westgate
Westfield Avenue
1
2
3
4
5
6
35
34
33
32
Moreton Hall Farm
Read Park
Golf Course
WHALLEY ROAD
Cock Bridge
Martholme Lane
Dunkirk
24
Works
River Calder
Sykeside Brook
Golf Course
Great Harwood Golf Club
Harwood La
HARWOOD NEW RD
HARWOOD LA
Lynfield Rd
Lyndon Avenue
Lyndon Ct
Kingsway
Mill Lane
Brownsills
Downham Avenue
Pendle Rd
Worston Lane
Sawley Dr
Chatburn Close
Our Lady & St Huberts RC Primary School
Shaftesbury
Street
Wood St
Street
Hyndburn Road
Hyndburn Bridge
Water St
Station Road Ind Estate
Way
Road
Spring Hall
Rushy Fld
Tarn Av
Woodland Dr
Clayton Hall Dr
Syke Side
A678
Holme
Works
Cottom Cft
Beck
The Cl
Hey
Fernlea Dr
Lynwood
Works
34
F
G
H
J
K
75
76

1 grid square represents 500 metres

Old Moss
High Whittaker Farm
Hollins Farm
16
F
G
H
J
K
80
81
35
34
33
32
I
2
3
4
5
6
26
36
Higham Road
Pennine Gv
Sabden Rd
Slade La
Slade Lane
A6068
Hargrove
Burnley Way
Grove Lane
Langdale Road
Windermere Rd
Coniston
Rydal Cl
Hargrove Av
Garden St
Derwent Avenue
Bowness
The Shortlands
St Leonards CE Primary School
Adamson St
Moor La
Tinedale Vw
Town Bank
Ashendean Vw
Quarry St
High St
Guy St
East St
North St
Mill St
A671
Surgery
Wyre St
Mytton St
Lawrence St
Cobden St
Holmes Street
Fleetwood Road
Gothic Works
Lune St
Cornfield House
Cornfield
Gawthorpe Hall (NT)
Bronte Wy
Stockbridge Drive
Habergham Dr
Grove
PADIHAM
Victoria Works
River Dr
South Dr
Padiham County Primary School
Gawthorpe County High School
St Josephs Convent School
Padiham Leisure Centre
Town Hall
Station Road
Park Road
Works
Padiham Green CE Primary School
Burnley Way
Green La
Hill St
Thompson St
Hapton Rd
Elizabeth St
Waterside
WITTLEWOOD DR
BURNLEY ROAD
PADIHAM ROAD
A671
A646
PO
Padiham Cemetery
St John the Baptist RC Prim Sch
St John's Road
West View Ter
Wheat St
Coronation Av
Abingdon Rd
Dorset Av
Warwick Drive
Cambridge Drive
Norfolk Av
Victoria Road
Kingsley Av
Masefield Av
Dryden St
Ruskin Av
Whitegate Cl
Cowley Crs
Marlowe Av
Lytton St
Moore St
Byron Street
Poets Rd
Scott St
Habergham High School
Habergham
Burnley Sixth Form Centre
Ivy Bank Business & Enterprise College
Caernarvon Avenue
Sycamore
Cardigan Av
Avenue
Devon Gv
Middlesex
Cumberland Av
Rutland Av
KIDDROW LANE
Kiddrow Health Cen
Lowerhouse
Lowerhouse Crs
Lowerhouse Lane
Lowerhouse CC
Lowerhouse County Junior School
Rosegrove Inf Sch
Printers Fold
Bear St
Knotts Lane
Low Bank
High Cl
Merlin Gv
Harrow Cl
Kings Dr
Cambridge Dr
Malvern Av
Lancaster Drive
Balliol Cl
Greenbrook Road
Holyoake St
LIVERPOOL ROAD A646
Works
Swimsafe Swimming Pool
Rosegrove Lane
Molly Wd La Lower
M65
ACCRINGTON
Vulcan Works
A679
Magneta Works
Hapton
Simpson St
Manchester Rd
North Street
Water St
Cobden St
Whitefield St
Jun 9
Bentley Wood Way
Bridgewater Cl
Valley Gdns
Burnley Crem
Cemetery La
Burnley Cemetery
Hapton CE Methodist
Network 65
Drew St
Holmestrand Av
Sylvan Dr

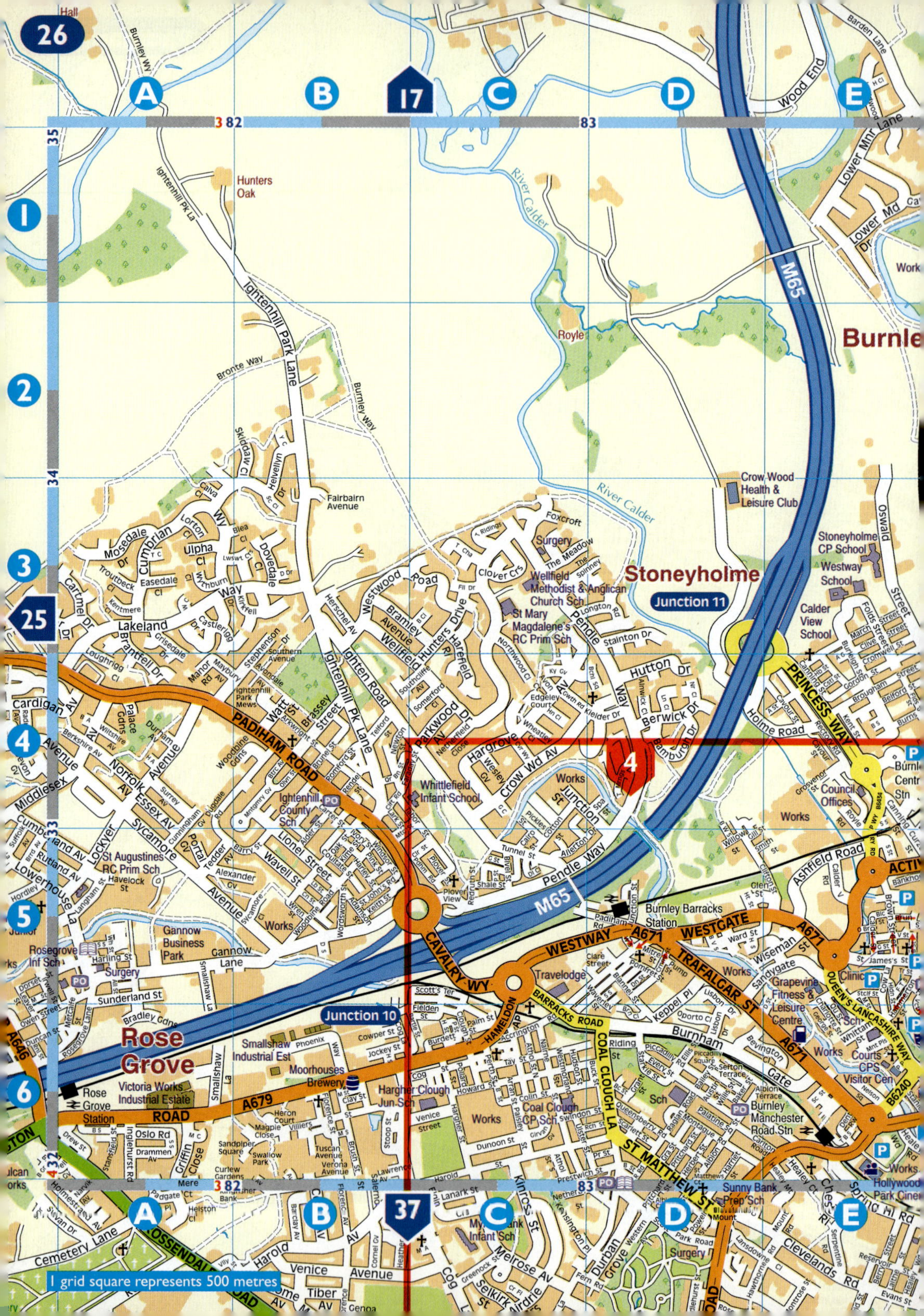
17
25
37
4
A
B
C
D
E
1
2
3
4
5
6
382
383
35
34
33
432
River Calder
M65
Burnley
Hunters Oak
Ightenhill Pk La
Ightenhill Park Lane
Bronte Way
Burnley Way
Royle
Crow Wood Health & Leisure Club
Stoneyholme
Junction 11
Stoneyholme CP School
Westway School
Calder View School
Foxcroft
Surgery
Wellfield Methodist & Anglican Church Sch
St Mary Magdalene's RC Prim Sch
Pendle Way
Hutton Dr
Berwick Dr
Princess Way
Holme Road
Council Offices
Works
Burnley Centr Stn
Ashfield Road
Mosedale Dr
Cumbrian Way
Ulpha Cl
Lorton Way
Dovedale Cl
Lakeland Way
Carmel Dr
Brantfell Dr
Fairbairn Avenue
Westwood Road
Bramley Avenue
Wellfield Hunters Drive
Harefield Rd
Ighten Road
Herschel Av
Padiham Road
Cardigan Av
Avenue
Middlesex Av
Norfolk Av
Essex Av
Sycamore Av
Durham Av
Palace Gdns
Lockyer Av
Cumberland Av
Rutland Av
Lowerhouse La
St Augustines RC Prim Sch
Woodbine Gdns
Ightenhill County Sch
Lionel Street
Wavell St
Tedder Av
Portal Gv
Alexander Gv
Whittlefield Infant School
Parkwood Dr
Hargrove Av
Crow Wd Av
Junction St
Tunnel St
Pendle Way
Plover View
Shale St
Gannow Business Park
Gannow Lane
Rosegrove Inf Sch
Surgery
Sunderland St
Bradley Gdns
Rose Grove
Junction 10
Smallshaw Industrial Est
Moorhouses Brewery
Victoria Works Industrial Estate
Rose Grove Station
A679
Road
Hargher Clough Jun Sch
Works
Coal Clough CP Sch
Cavalry Wy
Westway
A671
Westgate
Burnley Barracks Station
Travelodge
Barracks Road
Coal Clough La
Hameldon Ap
Trafalgar St
Burnham Gate
Grapevine Fitness & Leisure Centre
Clinic
Queen's Lancashire Way
Courts CPS Visitor Cen
B6240
Burnley Manchester Road Stn
St Matthew St
Sunny Bank Prep Sch
Sch
Oslo Rd
Drammen Av
Griffin Close
Sandpiper Square
Swallow Park
Curlew Gardens
Tuscan Avenue
Verona Avenue
Venice Street
Dunoon St
Kinross St
Mere
A646
Cemetery Lane
Rossendale Road
Harold Av
Venice Avenue
Tiber Av
Genoa
Mytholmbank Infant Sch
Melrose Av
Selkirk St
Airdrie
Durban Grove
Kensington Pl
Park Road
Surgery
Clevelands Rd
Lansdowne
Hollywood Park Cinema
Spring Hl Rd
Works
Wood End
Barden Lane
Lower Mnr Lane
Lower Mnr Dr
Oswald Street
1 grid square represents 500 metres

BURNLEY
Brunshaw
Pike Hill
COLNE ROAD
A682
CASTERTON AVENUE
QUEEN VICTORIA ROAD
A6114
EASTERN AVENUE
BELVEDERE ROAD
CENTENARY WAY
CHURCH ST
YORKSHIRE ST
Netherwood Road
Burnley Way
Ennismore Street
Briercliffe Road
Harrogate Crs
Red Spar Rd
Standen Hall Dr
Brunshaw Rd
Brunshaw Road
Ridge Av
Brownhill Avenue
Queen's Park Road
Ormerod Rd
Harry Potts Way
Athletic St
Heald Road
Pratt St
Disraeli St
Ruskin St
Keswick Rd
Windermere Av
Burnley General Hospital
A&E
Barden High School
Barden Junior School
Barden Lane Athletics Track
Walshaw High School
Heasandford Industrial Estate
Heasandford Prim Sch
Briercliffe Shopping Cen
St Andrews Bowling & CC
St Johns the Baptist RC Inf Sch
St Johns RC Jun Sch
Casterton County School
St James Lane Head CE Prim Sch
Primrose Hill School
Burnley Youth Theatre
Premier Travel Inn
Queens Park
Thompson Park
Burnley College
Fire Station
Burnley Lawn Tennis Club
St.Theodores RC Sch
St Marys RC Prim Sch
Burnley FC (Turf Moor)
Burnley CC
Med Cen
Superstore
Burnley Bus Cen
Shop Cen
Leisure Centre
Pol.Stn & Mag.Cts
AMF Bowling
Springfield Community Prim Sch
Towneley High School
St Stephens CE School
Burnley Wood CP Sch
Health Cen
Council
Sparrow Hawk Hotel
Rowley Hall
River Brun
Leeds & Liverpool Canal
Works
Surgery
Mosque
F
G
H
J
K
18
28
38
5
85
86
1
2
3
4
5
6
32
33
34
35

28
Haggate
19
Cockden
Burnley Road
Todmorden Road
Banks Street
Black House Lane
Burnley Way
Delamere Rd
Sandiway Drive
Surgery
Briercliffe Business Cen
Milton St
Talbot Street
Cross St
Harrison St
Church St
Queen Street Mill
Queen Street
Portsmouth Av
Shore Av
Talbot Dr
Lygate
Cuerdale St
Jubilee St
Duke St
Douglas Rd
River Don
Northbank Farm
Shay Lane
Todmorden Road
Bronte Way
Ing Hey
High Halstead
Swinden Reservoirs
Swinden
Bottin Farms
27
Brownside
Works
Riddings Av
Heckenhurst Av
Goldfield Av
Crookhaigh
Barnfield Avenue
Townfield Avenue
Copperfield Cl
Lindsay Pk
Brownside Rd
Worsthorne CP School
Lennox St
Gordon St
Heap St
Hope St
Water St
Smith St
Halstead St
Showfield
Extwistle Road
Inch Fld
Worsthorne
PO
Gorple Road
Gorple Green
Brownside Road
Lindsay Park
Duncan Cl
River Brun
Daisy Bank Crs
Buttermere Rd
Ullswater Rd
Thirlmere
Springwood Rd
Hollins Farm
Hall St
Clegg St
Wallstreams Lane
Wallhurst Cl
Raven Oak Lane
Ormerod
Saville Green
Brown Edge
A
B
C
D
E
1
2
3
4
5
6
35
34
33
32
387
88
39
Hurstwood
Hurstwood Reservoir
Dyneley Av
Hall Pk Av
Hill Crest Av
Red Lees Av
1 grid square represents 500 metres

Halifax Road
High Ridehalgh
Ridehalgh Lane
Ridehalgh Lane
Thursden
Halifax Road
Burnley Way
Thursden Brook
Burnley Way
Bronte Way
Halifax Road
Extwistle Moor
Swinden Water
Hameldon
Gorple Road
F
G
H
J
K
1
2
3
4
5
6
90
91
35
34
33
432

A
B
C
D
E
1
2
3
4
5
6
64
65
66
32
31
30
29
Commons Lane
Higher Commons Lane
LONGSIGHT ROAD
St Marys RC Primary School
Osbaldeston
Holmes Farm
Birley Fold
Abbott Brow
Saccary
Primrose Hill
Mellor Lane
Mellor Brook
Whalley Road
Myerscough Smithy Rd
The Willows
Fellgens Farm La
Woodfold Cl
Broadtree Cl
Mellor Brow
Mellor
The Millstone Hotel
PH
PO
Eiswick Gdns
Eiswick Lea
Brundhurst Fold
Mellor St Mary CE. Primary School
Yerburgh Rd
Church Lane
Church Close
Surgery
St Mary's Gdns
Brookfield
Glendale Drive
Arley Ri
Stanley Ga
Fouracre
Carter Fold
Hob Green
Nickey Lane
Lane
Whitecroft
Branch Road
Bosburn Drive
Intack La
Long Meadow
A677
Mire Ash Brow
Further Lane
Reaps
A677
PRESTON NEW ROAD
A6119
YEW TREE DRIVE
Edmonton Drive
Ontario Cl
Heatwood Cl
Stockwood Cl
The Pastures
Charnwood Cl
Country Ms
Wilton Cl
Eden Pk
T Spnny
T Brmbl
Beardwood
The Coppice
Acrefield
Hayfield
Beardwood
PRESTON NEW ROAD
Wyfordby Avenue
Arley Brook
Billinge Scarr
Beardwood Hos
Westholme School
Heathfield Park
Beardwood
Scarr
40
1 grid square represents 500 metres

F
G
H
20
J
K
67
68
69
Hagg's Hall
Ramsgreave Hall
Ramsgreave and Wilpshire Station
Salesbury Cl
Station Cl
Walden Road
Parsonage Road
York Crs
Lancashire Rd
Isle of Man
Waverley Rd
Paris Road
Moorfield Av
Mayfield Rd
Glengreave Av
Ramsgreave Road
Higher Ramsgreave Road
WHALLEY NEW RD
A666
Surgery
Brownhill
Brownhill Dr
Bank Hey Lane North
Newington Av
A6119
Pleckgate Rd
Ramsgreave Works
Barker Lane
Lancashire County
Blackburn
Whinney Lane
RAMSGREAVE DRIVE
Ramsgreave Dr
Blackburn RFC
St Gabriels CE Primary School
Holy Souls RC Primary School
Roe Lee
Roe Lee Industrial Est
Roe Lee Pk
Topaz St
Cornelian St
Emerald St
Emerald Av
Beryl Av
Amber Av
Peridot Cl
Gretna Walk
Douglas Pl
Highbank
Park Prim Sch
Wilworth Crs
Lower Wilworth
Campbell St
Pleckgate High School
Pleckgate Fold
Royal Oak Av
Haydock Street
Regents Vw
N Bank Av
Rosewood Av
Surgery
Sapphire St
Agate St
Pleckgate
Grasmere Av
Willow Trees Dr
Lammack Prim Sch
Barmouth Crs
Four Lane Ends
Knighton Av
Whinney Lane
Hudson Cl
Quebec Road
Calgary Avenue
Vancouver Crescent
Montreal Road
Lammack Road
St Lawrence Av
Alberta Cl
Close
Cranshaw Dr
Ottershaw Gdns
Briar Rd
Clarendon Rd
Swallowfields
Aspinall Fold
Pleck Farm Avenue
Openshaw Drive
Harrier Dr
Heron Cl
Harrier Drive
Petrel Cl
Kestrel Cl
Falcon Cl
Osprey Cl
Rhodes Avenue
PLECKGATE ROAD
Carham Rd
Royshaw Avenue
Cadshaw Cl
The Cedars Infant School
Sycamore Rd
Hawthorne St
Boxwood St
Cedar St
Lammack
Lammack Rd
West Leigh Rd
Cuckoo Brow
Paignton Rd
Road
Works
B6233
BLACKBURN
St Marys RC Sixth Form College
James St
Troy St
Holly Street
Logwood St
Euro Trading Estate
Golf Course
Colenso Road
East Pk Av
Park Ter
Conway Av
Deganwy Av
Snowdon Av
Rhyl Avenue
Tenby Close
Neath Close
Ruthin Close
Trevor Cl
Aberdare Cl
Wimberley Banks
Brookhouse Primary School
Poplar St
Walnut St
Baywood St
Red Rake
Revidge Road
Brantfell Road
Park Road
Langham Rd
Winston Rd
Beresford Rd
SHEAR BROW
Northfield Rd
Oozebooth Ter
St James CE Prim School
Calder Banks
Wimberley St
Calder St
Bangor St
Cowper St
WHALLEY NEW ROAD
Ravenswing Av
Mollington Rd
Whitehall Rd
Blackburn Golf Club
Revidge
East Shear
Eldon Rd
Corwen Cl
Earl Street
Cowan Brae
F
G
H
41
J
K
Brookhouse
Corporation Park
West Park Rd
East Lancashire CC
Sacred Heart RC Prim Sch
Dukes
Alexandra Road
Lilford Rd
Bank Rd
Park Av
Holland St
YMCA
Tauheedul Islam Girls High Sch
London Rd
Balaclava St
Oswald St
Mosque
Whalley St
Brookhouse Lane
Whalley Old Road
Pool
Notre Dame Gdns
Lynwood Road
Revidge Rd
1
2
3
4
5
6
32
31
30
29
Blackburn Cemetery
Masjid bilal

32
21
31
42
A
B
C
D
E
1
2
3
4
5
6
369
70
71
430
429
Rishton Road
Parsonage Reservoir
York Road
Wilpshire Road
Harwood Road
New Inns
Wilpshire Road
Warrenside Close
Balmoral Av
Belvedere Rd
Parsonage Road
Upper Mickle Hey
Old Road
Blackburn Old Road
Dunscar
Lower Cunliffe
Brownhill Drive
Lee Park Prim Sch
Highbank
Blackburn Cemetery
Ravenscroft Cl
Oakwood Av
Cunliffe Cl
Sunny Bower Cl
Bank Hey Lane South
Rowan Cl
Whalley Old Road
Bank Hey
Sunny Bower
Cunliffe Road
Phoenix Park
Croft Head Road
Phillips Road
BB1
Lower Philips Road
Premier Business Park
Clarendon Rd East
Clarendon Rd
Lilac Rd
Laburnum Rd
A6119
Whitebirk Drive
Rishton Reservoir
Masjid-bilal Mosque
Laburnum Road
Zion Rd
Providence St
Tintern Crs
Fountains Av
Avenue
Kelsall
Furness Av
Greenhead Av
Phillips Road
Ribble Business Park
Glenfield Park Industrial Estate
Leeds and Liverpool Canal
Sidebeet Lane
Warrington St
Beardsworth St
Coniston Road
Little Harwood
Benson Street
St Stephens CE Junior School
Blakewater Rd
Challenge Way
Lancashire County Blackburn
Blackburn
A666
Cedar St
Willow St
Bay Street
Elm St
Boland St
Ryedal Rd
Whalley Robinson St
Valli Gate
Surg
PO
St Stephen's Rd
St Stephens CE Infant Sch
Glenfield Business Park
Pine St
Maple St
Plane St
Ash Street
Beech St
Mosque
Cob Wall Works
Whalley New Road
Philips Road
Blakewater Road
Dyneley Road
Whitebirk Drive
Whitebirk Drive
Green Bank Industrial Estate
Greenbank Road
Green Bank Business Park
Davies Road
Junction
Peter Street
Daisyfield Prim Sch
Bruce St
Corse St
Gladstone
Whitebirk
Works
Pool
Thorn Avenue
1 grid square represents 500 metres

Edge End
Tottleworth
RISHTON
Oakens
Clinkham Road
Delph Road
Russell Pl
Edgeside
Highfield Drive
Wordsworth
Great Harwood Prim Sch
Rushton St
Waverledge Business Park
Waverledge Rd
Shakespeare Av
BLACKBURN ROAD
Cemetery
Willow St
St Wulstans C Primary School
Lomax St
Hubert's St
Orchard St
Railway Ter
Meadow Street
Moss St
St Johns CE Prim Sch
Hope St
Queen St
Mercer Hall Leisure Centre
Segar Street Mosque
Clayton St
Back Church St
Superstore
Works
Victoria St
St Hubert's St
Albert Street
Ramsbottom
Alan
Wilpshire Road
B6535 LEE LANE
Tottleworth Rd
HARWOOD ROAD
Leeds & Liverpool Canal
Hyndburn Brook
Riverside Industrial Est
Primetime Leisure Centre
Norden High School
Bridge St
Spring St
Works
Stourton St
Livesey St
Daniell St
Cliff St
Danvers St
Commercial St
St Peter & St Pauls CE Primary Sch
Lord St
Clifton St
Brook St
Howard St
Parker Street
Oswald St
Wheatfield Street
Talbot St
Burton St
Holt St
HERMITAGE STREET
A678
Surgery
School St
Surg
HIGH STREET
PO
Fielding St
Barn Meadow Crs
Park Rd
Westwood Avenue
Cornwall Rd
Devonshire Rd
Somerset Road
Coniston Way
Copper House School
Haworth Street
Knowles Street
Edward St
Henry St
Princes St
Daisyhill Industrial Est
Rishton Methodist Primary Sch
St Charles RC Primary Sch
Eachill Gdns
Walmsley Avenue
Petre Crescent
Maple Crs
Station Close
Station Road
Rishton CC
Thornhill Avenue
St Albans Road
Woodside Av
Churchill Avenue
Cut Lane
Sussex Road
Dorset Rd
Rishton Station
Rishton Golf Club
ROAD A678
M65
Golf Course
Leeds and Liverpool Canal
Dunkenhalgh Hotel
St James Road
Cowhill Fold
Accrington & District Golf Club
Golf Course
22
34
43
72
73
74
32
31
30
29
F
G
H
J
K
1
2
3
4
5
6

34
Station Road Ind Estate
Hyndburn Road
Water St
Bridge
A
B
23
C
D
E
374
75
76
Holme
Works
Barden Cft
Mill Fld
Tarn Brigg
Av
WHALLEY ROAD
A680
Sycamore Cres
Clayton Hall Dr
Trout Beck
Cottom Cft
The Cl
Fernlea Dr
Lynwood
Fordside Av
The Sparth House Hotel
Coppice
Riverside View
Barnes St
Super St
Bell Lane
A678
BURNLEY ROAD
Bates St
Willow St
Meadowside Avenue
Street
Lodgeside
Sparth Road
Ann St
Milton St
Dryden St
Norfolk Cl
Warwick Av
Cm Av
Av
Oxford
Lancaster Dr
York Cl
Gloucester Av
Devonshire Dr
Chapel St
Bayley St
John St
Sparth Av
Queen Street
Scott St
Arthur St
Victoria St
Grange St
Oakenshaw
Rishton Road
Moor St
James St
PO
St Marys RC Prim Sch
Spring Mdw
Clayton Wy
Pilkington Dr
Hgr Firs Dr
Simmons Wy
Marthome
Moorfield Close
Moorfield Way
Moorfield Dr
Moorfield Industrial Estate
CLAYTON-LE-MOORS
Pickup St
Surgery
Surg
Church St
Albert St
Victoria St
Works
Hazel Av
Hazel Grove
Moorside
Bold Venture Farm
Brantwood
Charles Street
Collingwood
All Saints CE Primary School
Winckley Rd
Chequers
Earl St
Mount Pleasant Primary School
Gordon St
Duke St
Ml Entrance
Mill St
Canal St
Junction 7 Business Park
Petre Rd
A678
M65
Well Fld
Clayton Business Park
Clayton-Le-Moors Industrial Park
Henry St
William St
Works
Gec Business Park
BLACKBURN ROAD
St James CE Sch
Atlas St
Surgery
Whinney Hill Road
Works
Sydney St
Harrington St
Brisbane St
Tunstall Dr
Dunkenhalgh Hotel
CHURCH LA
Delamere Close
Epping Av
Beech Crs
Junction 7
First Av
Second Av
Accrington Stanley FC
Huncoat Industrial Estate
Hillock Vale
DILL HALL LANE
Cranbourne Drive
Windsor Avenue
Kingsway
Poulton Av
Cleveleys Road
WHALLEY
Livingstone Rd
Claremont Road
Haywood Road
Ribbleton Drive
Ribblesdale Avenue
Ribbleton Drive
Works
Thorneyholme Road
CHURCH
Joint Cemetery
Talbot Road
Hawksworth Rd
Marlborough Road
Moss Hall Road
DUNKENHALGH WAY
B6231
St Christophers CE High School
Moorhead County High School
PO
Cheltenham Av
Rugby Av
Clifton Av
Dill Hall
Regent St
Queensway
Queens Road West
Radnor Street
Ellerbeck Rd
Lime Road
Street
St Nicholas CE Primary School
PO
Meadoway
MANOR PLACE
Warwick Street
Worcester Av
Hereford Cl
Accrington Victoria Hosp
QUEEN'S ROAD
A6185
Grove
Norfolk Gv
Gloucester Av
Lancaster Av
Eccles St
Garden St
Haywood Road
Aitken Street
Pollard St
Peel Bank Works
Buckingham Gv
Lupin Close
St Mary Magdalens CE Prim Sch
Ramsbottom St
Prim Sch
Arago St
CEP Sch
James Road
Works
Kirk Rd
John St
Howarth Av
Buckingham Gv
Milnshaw
York St
Devonshire St
Owen Street
Church Bridge Works
Church Hall
Riding Barn St
Knowlmere St
HENRY ST
ACCRINGTON
Argyle St
A
B
C
D
E
374
75
76
44
Steiner's Lane
Albert St
Victoria St
Hyndburn Sports Centre
Hyndburn Park Primary School
Superstore
Accrington Bus Cen
A679
Inland Rev Off
EASTGATE
Arndale Shop Cen
Sydney St
Sacred Heart RC
Emma St
Princess St
Monk St
Park Rd
Tremellen
Lister St
Portland St
Frederick St
Hindle St
Walter St
Blake St
Ellison St
Surgery
King Street
Hall
Surgery
CAB
College
Eastgate
Countess
PO
1 grid square represents 500 metres
1
2
3
4
5
6
33
Works

24
F
G
H
J
K
77
78
79
Drive
Barnfield Way
Altham Lane
Burnley Way
Works
Hap
Scarth La
Leeds and Liverpool Canal
Junction 8
M65
Hapton Stn
1
32
Lyndale Road
2
31
M65
Altham Lane
Mill Hill Lane
Huncoat Station
PO
Station Rd
Edgar St
Marshall Av
Huncoat
Accrington Huncoat Primary Sch
Lynwood Rd
Lower Gate Rd
Lane
Burnley
A56
3
36
Enfield Cl
LC
Yorkshire Street
Yorkshire St
Brickworks
Whinney Hill Road
Bolton Avenue
Rd
Huncoat Business Park
Higher Ga Rd
Old Hall Dr
Vale Ct
Sutton Cl
Meadow
Woodside Road
Burnley Rd
Griffin Cl
BURNLEY
A679
4
Miste Farm
Newhouse
Windermere Av
Oakfield Avenue
Oakdene Av
Winterley Dr
Spurhouse La
Kingsway
King's Highway
Within Cv
Within Grove
Oakhurst Av
Brown Birks Road
Bolton Av
Woodside Rd
Wessex Close
Longsight Avenue
30
Accrington Crematorium
Ambleside Cl
A679
ROAD
The Triangle
Loweswater
5
Accrington Cemetery
Whitewell Road
BURNLEY
Foxwood Cha
Deer Park
Squirrels Close
Parker Street
South Street
Balmoral Rd
Heaning Av
Sawley Avenue
Peel Park Avenue
A56
Moleside Moor
6
Peel Park Primary School
Manor St
Peel Pk Cl
Alice Street
Street
Parade
Avenue
Waddington
Surrey St
Stanley
Spencer St
Bold
Clarendon
Hodder Street
Limewood Cl
Benjamin Hargreaves
Road
429
45
77
78
79
F
G
H
J
K

36
25
Hapton
Works
Simpson St
Whitefield St
PO
Wordsworth St
Manchester Rd
Water St
Cobden St
Tennyson St
M65
Hapton Stn
Carter Av
Hapton CE Methodist Primary School
St Margaret's Gardens
Ruskin Gv
Lyndale Road
Kingsway
Leigh Pk
Manchester Road
Lane Ends
Schns Fold
Andelen Cl
Hameldon Cl
Hameldon Road
Industrial Estate
35
A679
ROAD
ACCRINGTON ROAD
Junction 9
Bentley Wood Way
Bridgewater Cl
Network 65 Business Park
Brindley Close
Valley Gdns
Molly Wd La
Lower Rosegrove Lane
Swimming Pool
ACCRINGTON
Vulcan Works
Burnley Crematorium
Burnley Cemetery
Old Barn
New Barn
Burnley Way
46
A B C D E
1 2 3 4 5 6
379 80 81
32 31 30 429
1 grid square represents 500 metres

Grove
Rose Grove Station
Victoria Works Industrial Estate
Industrial Est
Moorhouses Brewery
Hargher Clough Jun Sch
Coal Clough CP Sch
Works
Sch
Burnley Manchester Road Stn
Works
Courts
Healey Wood Road Ind Est
Hollywood Park Cinema
Healey Wood Infant
Sunny Bank Prep Sch
Surgery
Myrtle Bank Infant Sch
St Hildas RC Girls High Sch
Scott Park
Rosehill House Hotel
Rose Hill
Christ the King RC Primary Sch
Rosehill County Infant School
Rosehill County Jun Sch
Industrial Estate
Trans Britannia Enterprise Est
Rossendale Road Industrial Est
A679
ROAD
ROSSENDALE ROAD
A646
ST MATTHEW ST
CLOUGH LA
MANCHESTER ROAD
A682
GLEN VIEW ROAD
Rumley's Fold
Summit Works
Burnley Golf Club
Golf Course
Crown Point Road
Woodplumpton Road
Crown Point House
Lower Micklehurst
BB11
Burnley Way
Kestrels Leisure Centre
26
38
47
F
G
H
J
K
1
2
3
4
5
6
82
83
84
429
430
431
432

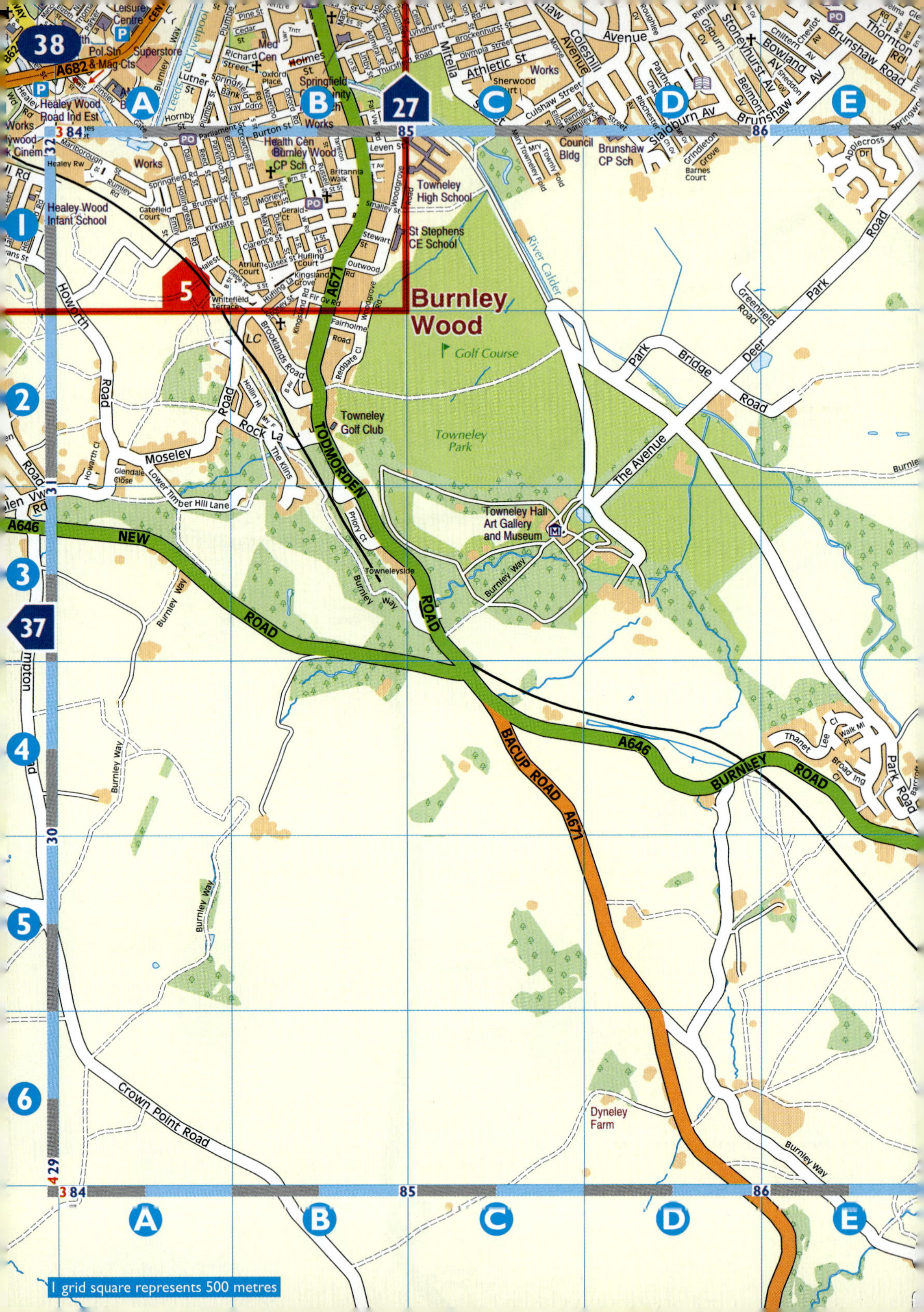
38
27
37
5
Burnley Wood
Golf Course
Towneley Golf Club
Towneley Park
Towneley Hall Art Gallery and Museum
Towneley High School
St Stephens CE School
Burnley Wood CP Sch
Health Cen
Healey Wood Infant School
Healey Wood Road Ind Est
Leisure Centre
Superstore
Pol.Stn & Mag.Cts
Works
Council Bldg
Brunshaw CP Sch
Med Cen
River Calder
Leeds & Liverpool
A682
A671
A646
TODMORDEN ROAD
NEW ROAD
BACUP ROAD
BURNLEY ROAD
The Avenue
Deer Park Road
Park Bridge Road
Greenfield Road
Howorth Road
Moseley Road
Rock La
Lower Timber Hill Lane
Crown Point Road
Burnley Way
Brooklands Road
Woodgrove Rd
Fairholme Road
Redgate Cl
Priory Ct
Towneleyside
The Kilns
Glendale Close
Howarth Cl
Kingsland Grove
Whitefield Terrace
Healey Rw
Rumley Rd
Springfield Rd
Parliament St
Burton St
Athletic St
Mitella St
Brunshaw Road
Brunshaw Av
Slaidburn Av
Bowland Av
Chiltern Av
Thornton Rd
Coleshill Avenue
Culshaw Street
Grindleton Grove
Barnes Court
Applecross Dr
Thanet Lee Cl
Broad Ing Cl
Park Road
Dyneley Farm
LC
PO
A
B
C
D
E
1
2
3
4
5
6
84
85
86
32
31
30
29
1 grid square represents 500 metres

River Brun
Hollins Farm
Wallstreams Lane
Wallhurst Cl
Raven Oak Lane
Ormerod
Saville Green
Brown Edge
28
F
G
H
J
K
87
88
89
32
31
30
29
1
2
3
4
5
6
Red Lees Av
Hill Crest Avenue
Hollins Av
Lee Gv
Richmond Av
Red Lees Road
Hurstwood Lane
Hurstwood
Burnley Way
Hurstwood Reservoir
Spenser Cl
Ormerod House
Salterford Lane
Cliviger Laithe
Foxstones Lane
PH
The Long Causeway
Mereclough
School Lane
Greencliffe Lane
Walk Mill
Mount Crs
Scholey Head Lane
Over Town
Far Pasture
BURNLEY ROAD
A646
Sunnyfield Av
Greendale
The Lees
Cliviger
Southward Bottom
Honey Holme La
Newton Drive
Grange Road
Pearsons

30
48
BB2
Westholme School
Beardwood Hospital
Beardwood School
Westholme Junior School
Wyfordby Avenue
Meins Road
Meins Croft
Heathfield Park
Carrs Wd
Carr La
Woodgates
Woodgates Rd
Billinge End Rd
Billinge End Road
Assheton Road
Bunce La
Lawley Rd
Billinge Av
B6447
Under Billinge Lane
Witton Weavers Way
Witton Park High School
Witton
Witton Park Athletics Track
Pleasington Crematorium
Pleasington Cemetery
Fenisclife
PRESTON OLD ROAD
A674
Tower Rd
Tower Road
Hillcrest Rd
Cecilia Rd
St Francis Rd
Willis Road
Feniscliffe Dr
Geddes Street
Artson Works
Cherry Tree Station
Cherry Lea
Works
Dalby Crs
Brothers
Council Building
Fielding Crs
Morley Av
Hurstwood Av
Green Lane
Rannoch Dr
Torridon Cl
Solway Av
Nook Ter
Gladstone Ter
Hunters Lodge
Old Gates Dr
Old Gates
Cherry Tree CC
St Francis CE Primary School
The Crescent
Livesey Hall Cl
Woodlands Av
Springfield
Victoria Av
Sunnyside Av
Cherry Tree La
Sandy Lane
Old Hall Lane
Old Hall La
Priory Ct
Regents Cl
Pleasington Rd
Bowden Av
Pleasington
Pleasington Station
Cherry Tree
Pleasington Golf Club
Rose Hill Road
Links Road
Feniscowles Lane
Enoch Bro
St Pauls RC Primary
A674
Kirkstone Av
Keswick Dr
Wythburn Av
Kentmere Drive
Beechwood
Witney Av
Burford Cl
Hollies Cl
Bracken Cl
The Evergreens
Pinewood
Cypress Rd
Boxwood Dr
Linden Lea
Holly Tree Wy
Banbury
Larch Cl
St Bedes RC High School
Greenside Ave
Stones Crs
BRANCH ROAD
Felden
Eclipse Rd
Fenis
Works
PO
1 grid square represents 500 metres

Revidge
Brookhouse
Corporation Park
Queen Elizabeths Grammar School
East Lancashire CC
Sacred Heart RC Prim Sch
Al-Asr Primary School
St Silas CE Prim School
Tauheedul Islam Girls High Sch
YMCA
Mosque
St Michael with St John CE Prim Sch
Brookhouse Business Centre
Brookhouse Lane
St Albans RC Prim Sch
Preston New Road
A677
A6078
Barbara Castle Way
Lark Hill
Whalley New Rd
Adult Education Cen
Blackburn Coll
Police Stn
Town Hall
Mus & Gal
Shop Cen
Mkt
Brewery
Eanam
Salford
Superstore
Cathedral
BBC Radio
Blackburn Station
Wensley Fold CE Primary School
SS Barnabas & Pauls CE Prim Sch
St Annes RC Prim Sch
Blackburn College
Thompson Street Industrial Estate
Wensley Business Park
Works
Montague St
King St
Spiritualist Temple
PO Sorting Office
Higher Audley
Lower Audley Ind Estate
Lwr Audley St
A6078
Blackburn Arena (Ice Rink)
Grimshaw Retail Pk
Townsmoor Retail Park
Superstore
Unity Trading Est
Fire Stn
Whalley Banks Trading Est
High School
Redlam
Bank Top
Whalley Banks
Griffin Park Prim Sch
Spring Lane
Stancliffe St
Windsmoor House School
Hollin Br St
Balmoral Works
Highfield Works
St Mary & Josephs RC Prim Sch
Crimshaw
A6077
Bolton Road
A666
Blackburn Royal Inf
A&E
Mill Hill Station
St Aidans CE Prim Sch
Hamilton Aqueduct Rd
The Redbrick Theatre
Longshaw Junior Sch
Higher Croft
Livesey Branch Rd
A6062
Waterloo
St. Andrews CE School
St. Bartholomews CE School
Longshaw Infant School
Our Lady of Perpetual Succour RC
Leisure Cen
Surgery
31
49
42
F G H J K
1 2 3 4 5 6
67 68 69

42
32
41
50
A
B
C
D
E
1
2
3
4
5
6
69
70
71
29
28
27
26
Junction 6
Whitebirk
Intack
Queen's Park
Shadsworth
Whinny Heights
Guide
St Stephens CE Junior School
St Stephens CE Infant Sch
Blakewater Rd
Glenfield Business Park
Green Bank Industrial Estate
Greenbank Business Park
Greenbank Road
Whitebirk Drive
Whitebirk Road
A6119
Burnley Road
A678
Daisyfield Prim Sch
Daisyfield Business Centre
Fort Street Ind Est
Science Park
Furthergate Industrial Park
Superstore
Stanley Street
Gladstone St
Gorse Street
Harwood St
Dock St
Copy Nook
Bottomgate
Furthergate
Higher Eanam
Higher Audley St
St Thomas CE Prim Sch
Accrington Rd
A679
Accrington Road
B6236
Bank Lane
Intack Primary School
Gloucester Road
Worcester Road
Leicester Road
Hereford Road
Council Building
Surgery
Mosque
Ghousia Mosque
Sports Centre
Al-Islah Private Sch
Audley Range
Queen's Park
Audley Junior & Infant School
Whitendale Cres
Kempton Rise
Queens Park Hospital
Old Bank Lane
Haslingden Road
Roman Rd
Our Lady & St John Catholic Arts Coll
St Antonys RC Primary School
Infant School
Shadsworth Close
Romney Walk
B6130
Shadsworth Road
Oban Drive
Skye Crs
Rothesay Road
Arran Avenue
Crosshill Special School
Shadsworth Junior School
Shadsworth Leisure Centre
Shadsworth Industrial Park
Sett End Rd North
Sett End Rd W
Duttons Wy
Thwaites Cl
Knuzden Brook
M65
St Ives Business Park
Oxford Drive
Kunzden St Oswalds CEVA Prim Sch
Haslingden Old Road
Garsden Av
Cambridge Dr
Rutland Av
Staffa Crescent
Lamlash Road
Brodick Road
Ballantrae Road
Fishmoor Reservoir
School Lane
B6232
Roman Leisure Cen
Surgery
Bishopstone
Haslingden New Rd
1 grid square represents 500 metres

M65
Golf Course
F
G
H
33
J
K
St James Road
72
73
74
29
Cowhill Fold
Golf Course
Accrington & District Golf Club
Devon Avenue
West End
I
Works
A679
BLACKBURN ROAD
Aspen Fold
Percy St
Tower St
Works
Ripon Rd
PO
West End Business Park
Fountains Way
Eagle St
Anglian Cl
Norman Rd
Dunster Av
Browning Av
Miller Cl
Burns Av
Buttermere Av
Emmerdale Close
Hill St
Works
Hill Street
2
Sadler
Crescent
Avenue
Road
Knuzden Hall
West End Primary School
Aspen Lane
Cranbrook Av
Dudley Av
Road
Ruskin Av
Byron Cl
Tennyson Av
28
Knuzden Brook
Stanhill
Peel Bank Road
Conway Dr
Barnard Cl
Harlech Dr
Radnor Cl
Brecon Av
Banbury Av
Stanhill Works
Harvey
STANHILL ROAD
PO
STANHILL LANE
Cardigan Av
Central Av
Thwaites
St Andrews CE Primary School
Street
Foxfield Cl
Mill Hill
3
Nab Lane
Calico Cl
Brookside
Hargreaves Road
White Ash School
White Ash Lane
Springfield St
Cross St
Holly St
Kay St
Garden St
44
Surgery
Moss Lane
OSWALDTWISTLE
New Bury Cl
UNION RD
Moor End Prim Sch
Mason St
James St
Simpson St
Bent St
Surgery
Shed St
Rhyddings Works
Stone
Lane
Brookside
Oswald St
Bury St
Hgr Peel
PO
Havelock St
Victoria St
Walter St
Robert St
John St
Merlin Drive
Heys
Surgery
4
Brookside Lane
Works
Industrial Estate
King
Brookside St
Vine St
Edward St
Church St
Stanley St
Duke St
Plant St
Trinity
Roe Greave Road
Works
Curlew Cl
Magnoll's Farm
Works
Nook Lane
Lane
Margaret St
Grove St
B6231
Beech Cl
Lime Av
Cherry Crs
Rowan Av
Street
27
Haslingden Old Road
Sough Lane
Eagle St
Green St
NEW LANE
Willow Pk
Rhoden Road
Back Rhoden Rd
5
Duckworth Hall
Works
DUCKWORTH HALL BROW
Sunnybank Dr
Duckworth Lane
DUCKWORTH HILL LANE
B6231
Red Shell Lane
6
LOTTICE LANE
Lottice Brook
Whams Brook
Four Lane Ends
Sough Lane
B6236
426
72
73
74
F
G
H
51
J
K
HASLINGDEN ROAD
Red Shell La

1 grid square represents 500 metres

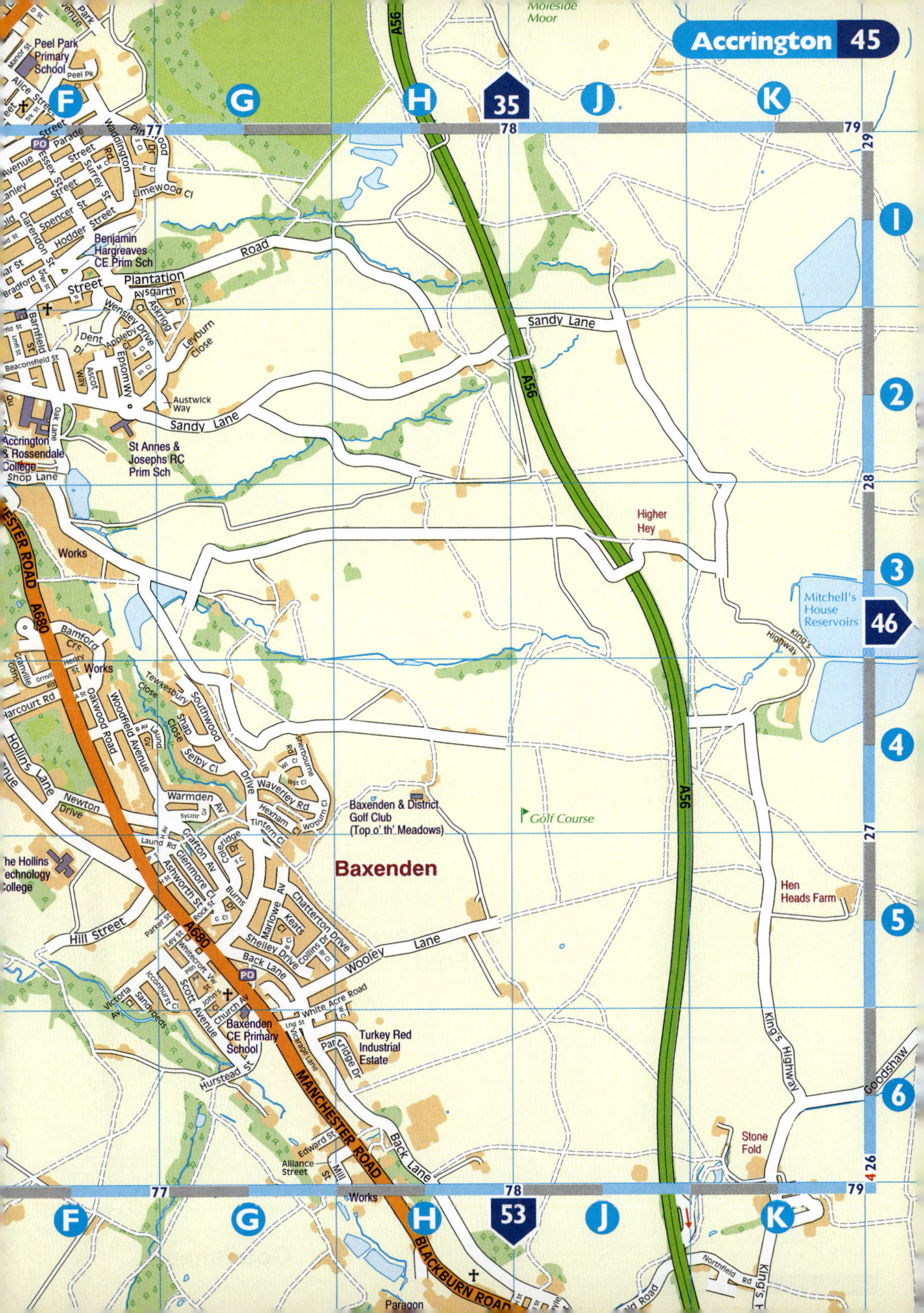
Moleside Moor
35
46
53
A56
Peel Park Primary School
Peel Pk
Benjamin Hargreaves CE Prim Sch
Plantation Road
Street
Aysgarth Dr
Askrigg
Wensley Drive
Appleby
Dent
Epsom Wy
Ascot Way
Barnfield St
Beaconsfield St
Leyburn Close
Austwick Way
Sandy Lane
St Annes & Josephs RC Prim Sch
Accrington & Rossendale College
Shop Lane
Oak Lane
Limewood Cl
Waddington Rd
Clarendon St
Spencer St
Hodder Street
Surrey St
Essex Street
Parade
Bradford St
Works
Higher Hey
Mitchell's House Reservoirs
King's Highway
Bamford Crs
Henry St
Granville
Harcourt Rd
Hollins Lane
Oakwood Road
Woodfield Avenue
Tewkesbury Close
Southwood
Shap Close
Selby Cl
Newton Drive
Warmden Av
Waverley Rd
Hexham Cl
Tintern Cl
Woburn Cl
Sherbourne
Drive
Baxenden & District Golf Club (Top o' th' Meadows)
Golf Course
Baxenden
The Hollins Technology College
Hill Street
Grafton Av
Glenmore Cl
Ashworth St
Coleridge Dr
Burns
Marlowe Av
Keats Cl
Chatterton Drive
Collins Dr
Shelley Drive
Back Lane
Wooley Lane
White Acre Road
Hen Heads Farm
MANCHESTER ROAD
A680
Parker St
Whitecroft Vw
Scott Avenue
Church Av
Baxenden CE Primary School
Victoria Av
Sandybeds
Hurstead St
Vicarage Lane
Partridge Dr
Turkey Red Industrial Estate
Edward St
Alliance Street
Mill St
Stone Fold
Goodshaw
BLACKBURN ROAD
Paragon
Northfield Rd
F
G
H
J
K
1
2
3
4
5
6
77
78
79
26
27
28
29

A
B
36
C
D
E
379
80
81
29
28
27
426
1
2
3
4
5
6
45
Burnley Way
Great Clough
Rossendale Way
Rossendale Way
Higher Withins
Farm
Lane Top Farm
Goodshaw
Lane
Silven Clod Road
Goodshaw Fold
Love Clough Road
Springbank Gardens
Goodshaw Fold Road
Goodshaw Fold Cl
Commercial Street
PO
Limy Water
Love Clough
BURNLEY ROAD
A682
Hameldon Road
Goodshaw Av
Greenfold Dr
Back Rings Row
Hamer Av
Meadows
Goodshaw Avenue
Rose Hill St
Church St
Driving Gate
Goodshaw
Stoneholme
54
1 grid square represents 500 metres

Burnley Way
37
F
G
H
J
K
82
83
84
29
1
Kestrels
Leisure Centre
Limey
Lane
ROAD
Clow Bridge
Springfield View
MANCHESTER
Clowbridge
Reservoir
2
28
Works
A682
Oak Street
Dunnockshaw
Heber St
Works
Wilkinson
Street
3
Rossendale Way
4
Meadow
Head
nshaw
27
Rossendale Way
Swallow
Shore
5
Gib Hill La
Gib Hl
La
Goodshaw
Chapel
6
26
Bank
Lane
55
Water
B6238

Pleasington
Pleasington Station
Cherry Tree
40
Pleasington Golf Club
Rose Hill Road
Links Road
Feniscowles Lane
Enoch Brow
St Pauls RC Primary School
A674 PRESTON OLD ROAD
Kirkstone Avenue
Keswick Dr
Wythburn Av
Kentmere Drive
Woodlands Av
The Crescent
Livesey Hall Cl
St Francis CE Primary School
Cherry Tree CC
Cherry Tree La
Works
Gladstone Ter
Hunters Lodge
Rannoch Dr
Torridon Cl
Solway Av
Old Gates Drive
Green Lane
Brothers
Council Building
Fielding
Hurstwood Av
Railton Av
Foxstones Crs
Greenside Av
St Bedes RC High School
Larch Cl
Pinewood
Beechwood
Witney Av
Banbury
The Evergreens
Linden Lea
Holly Tree Wy
LIVESEY BRANCH ROAD
Ernlouen Cl
Woodside Gv
Risedale Gv
Mead
Feniscowles
Feniscowles Prim Sch
Pleasington La
PO
Rosebay Av
Harebell Cl
Farm
Feilden Pl
Eclipse Rd
Langdale Cl
Eskdale Crs
Arnside Crs
Dale Crs
Dentdale Cl
Bishopdale Cl
Coverdale Dr
Littondale
LIVESEY BRANCH RD
St Michael's Close
St Michael's Cl
Horden Vw
Horden View
Horden Rake
Horden Farm
Witton Weavers Wy
A674 PRESTON OLD ROAD
Tintagell Cl
Park Pl
Moorland Av
Princess Gdns
Coronation Av
Works
Broken Stone Road
Gib Lane
Stockclough Lane
Witton Weavers Way
Stanworth Farm
M65
Witton Weavers Way
Blackburn
Lancashire County
Rock Lane
Chapels Lane
Tockholes CE Primary School
Tockholes Road
Long Lane
Tockh
Crow Trees Farms
Weasel
Higher Hill
School Lane
Abbey Village
Red Lea Farm
A B C D E
1 2 3 4 5 6
26 25 24 23
364 65 66
I grid square represents 500 metres

Waterloo
Ewood
Earcroft
Higher Croft
Meadow Head
A6062
LIVESEY BRANCH RD
ALBION RD
BOLTON ROAD
A666
BLACKBURN RD
DUCKWORTH
B6231
SANDY LANE
FORE ST
M65
Junction 4
EARCROFT WY
Blackburn Rovers FC (Ewood Park)
St. Bartholomews CE School
St. Andrews CE School
Fernhurst School
Longshaw Infant School
Our Lady of Perpetual Succour RC Prim Sch
Scotshaw Brook Industrial Estate
Riverside Industrial Est
Darwen Vale High School
Blackburn with Darwen Service Area
Travelodge
Darwen FC
St Edwards RC Prim Sch
Darwen CC
St Cuthberts CE Primary School
Darwen Golf Club
Golf Course
Avondale Prim Sch
Darwen Tennis Club
Roma Rd Leisure Cen
Surgery
Works
Bog Height Road
Tockholes Rd
Heys Lane
Meadow Head La
Jack Walker Way
Branch Rd
Higher Croft Road
Eccleshill Road
Lower Eccleshill Road
Anchor Road
Hollins Road
Greenway St
River Darwen
Sunnymere Drive
Owlet Hall Rd
41
50
58
67
68
69
F
G
H
J
K
2
3
4
5
6
23
24
25
26

50
42
49
59
A
B
C
D
E
1
2
3
4
5
6
69
70
71
Guide
Lower Darwen
Grimshaw
Chapels
Waterside
M65
Junction 5
HASLINGDEN ROAD
SCHOOL LA B6231
BLACKAMOOR ROAD
BLACKAMOOR RD
STOPES BROW B6231
RAKES BR
B6232
Haslingden New Road
Belthorn Road
Roman Road
Walker Road
Johnson Road
Goose House Road
Eccleshill Road
Newfield School
St James CE Sch
Roman Road Industrial Estate
Walker Industrial Estate
Path Industrial Estate
Shadsworth Industrial Park
Premier Travel Inn
Roman Rd Leisure Cen
Surgery
Darwen Moorland High School
St James CE Primary School
Works
Two Gates Works
Blacksnape Road
Holden Fold
Moor La
Exchange St
Aintree Drive
Chanters Way
Eccleshill Gdns
1 grid square represents 500 metres

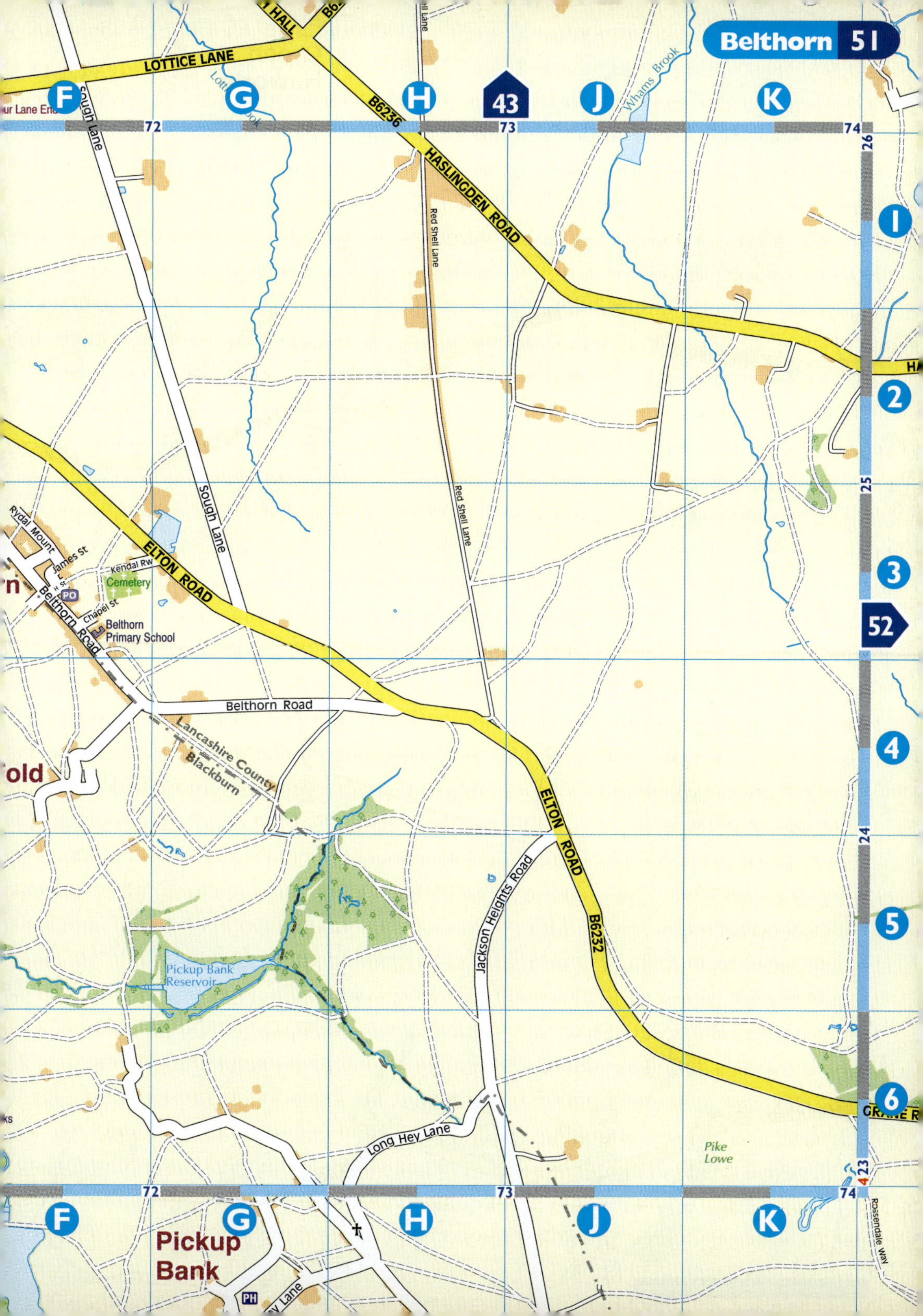

LOTTICE LANE
HALL
B6
Sough Lane
Lottice Brook
Red Shell Lane
43
Whams Brook
B6236
HASLINGDEN ROAD
F
G
H
J
K
72
73
74
26
25
24
23
1
2
3
4
5
6
52
Rydal Mount
James St
Kendal Rw
Cemetery
PO
Chapel St
Belthorn Road
Belthorn
Primary School
ELTON ROAD
Belthorn Road
Lancashire County
Blackburn
Fold
Jackson Heights Road
B6232
Pickup Bank
Reservoir
Long Hey Lane
Pike
Lowe
CRANE R
Pickup
Bank
PH
Rossendale Way

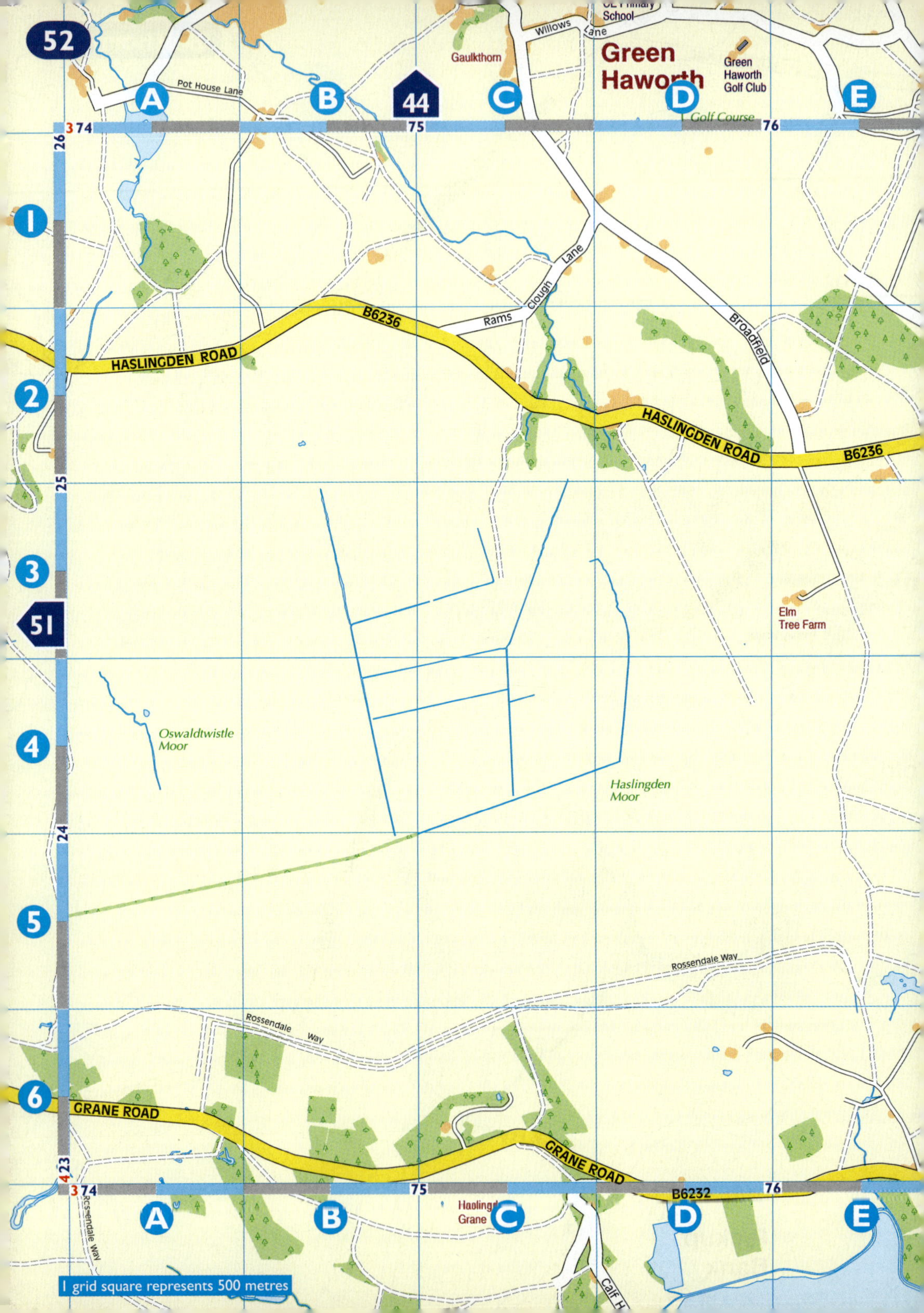

Green Haworth
Gaulkthorn
Willows Lane
School
Green Haworth Golf Club
Golf Course
Pot House Lane
44
75
74
76
A
B
C
D
E
1
2
3
4
5
6
26
25
24
23
51
Rams Clough Lane
Broadfield
B6236
HASLINGDEN ROAD
Elm Tree Farm
Oswaldtwistle Moor
Haslingden Moor
Rossendale Way
GRANE ROAD
B6232
Haslingden Grane
Calf H
1 grid square represents 500 metres

F
G
H
J
K
45
77
78
79
26
25
24
23
1
2
3
4
5
6
54
60
Hurstead St
Edward St
Alliance Street
Mill St
MANCHESTER ROAD
Back Lane
Works
Stone Fold
BLACKBURN ROAD
Paragon Works
Rising Bridge
Hoyle St
Northfield Road
Northfield Rd
Oak Vw
Roundhill Av
The Close
King's Highway
A680
PO
St Johns Stonefold CE Prim Sch
Rising Bridge Road
Lane
ROUNDHILL ROAD
Roundhill
PH
B6236
Moor Lane
Ormerod Street
Sherfin
Acre
Hud Hey Industrial Estate
HUD HEY ROAD
BROOK ST
Martin Croft Rd
Clough End Rd
Works
Rossendale Way
Hud Hey
A56
Mill Street
Cross St N
BLACKBURN ROAD
Hud Rake
Vale St
Station Rd
Booth St
West View
Porter Brewery
Higher Lane
Todd Hall Road
Commerce Street
Spring La
Lwr La
High St
HASLING
St James CE Primary School
Church Street
Cockerill St
Carrs Industrial Estate
Taylor Ct
Todd Hall Rd
Mkt Hall
Regent Street
Hargreaves St
Chapel Street
Rock Hall Road
Cob Castle Road
Underbank Road
Bentwood Rd
Carrs Industrial Est
Bank St
Clegg St
Foot
Maple Av
Birch Av
Poplar Street
Piccadilly St
Well Bank
S Shore Street
Townsend Street
Ratcliffe St
PO
Deardengate
WARNER ST
Flip Rd
Hutch Bank Rd
RANE RD
Prospect Hill
Industrial Estate
Waterside Rd
B6252
Ryefield Av
Haslingden Prim Sch
MANCHESTER
Back Lee St
Haslingden Baths
St Peter's Av
Hall St
Works
Lane Side
Meadows Ave
Crispin Way
Works
Cemetery
Hollands Rd
Hillside

46
53
61
Goodshaw
Sherfin
Cribden Side
HASLINGDEN
Height End
Laund
Stoneholme Industrial Estate
Brookside Business Park
Crawshawbooth School
Constable Lee CE School
St Marys CE School
St James the Less RC Primary School
Ski Rossendale
Rossendale Museum
Magistrates Court
Belmont School
Council Building
Valley Shopping Centre
BURNLEY ROAD
ST MARY'S WAY A682
Cribden Lane
Cribden End Lane
Pinner Lane
Haslingden Old Road
Oakenhead Wood Old Road
Laund Lane
Kirk Hill Road
Rock Hall Road
Short Clough Lane
Goodshaw Avenue
Goodshaw Lane
Stoneholme Road
Forest Bank Road
Hugh Rake
Hollin Way
Lime Tree Grove
Holland Avenue
Leebrook Road
BB4
1 grid square represents 500 metres

Chapel
F
G
H
47
J
K
82
83
84
26
Bottomley Bank Lane
Crawshawbooth
Swinshaw Moor
Bank Top
Water
Howarth's Street
Isle of Man Street
Forest Holme
Peers Clough Road
Works
BURNLEY ROAD EAST
Hargreaves Fold Lane
B6238
25
Lumb
Clough Rd
56
Pinch Clough Rd
Rock Bridge Fold
West View Road
Edge Yate Lane
Chapel Hill Lane
24
Lumb Lane
Whitewell Bottom
Brock Clough Rd
Foxhill Drive
Waingate Lane
Hurst
Hurst Crs
Saunder Height Lane
Lane
Scout Road
Works
Shaw Clough Road
Scoutbottom Industrial Estate
Marl Pits Sports Centre
Waingate Close
Newchurch Road
Marl Pits
Edge
Conway Road
Piercy Road
Ashworth Lane
Edgeside Sch
23
Ashworth Rd
62
Newchurch
Johnny Barn Cl
Patrick Crescent
Dobbin Lane
Dobbin Close
Health Centre
Lambton Gates
A681
St Peters RC School
Wall St
Rose St
Tom Lane
Crabtree Ave
Fairfield
Edgeside
Works
PO
STALL
Edg

56
Nabb Farm
Rossendale Way
Harrow Stiles
A
B
C
D
E
384
85
86
26
North Dean St
Fold
Dean Lane
Water
Brdg St
B6238
Water CP School
PO
Lwr House Green
Carr Road
Dean
Forest St
Ashworth St
Holmes St
Works
Forest Holme Close
New Gdn Fields
BURNLEY ROAD EAST
Hargreaves Fold Lane
25
Lumb
Small Shaw Height
55
Forest of Rossendale
24
Coal Pit La
Broadclough Hall
Lane
Pit Lane
Coal
Works
23
Road
Lane
The Hile
63
Fairfield
Edge
Edgeside
Maden Road
Bacup Gol
1 grid square represents 500 metres

F
G
H
J
K
87
88
89
26
25
24
23
1
2
3
4
5
6
64
WEIR
Doals
Broad Clough
Sharneyford
Greave
Wambs Farm
Higher Change
Lowers Reaps
Northern Primary School
Sharneyford County School
Thorn CP School
St Marys RC Primary School
Bacup FC
Works
OL13
Irwell Valley Way
Heald Lane
Rossendale Way
The Moorlands
Heald Cl
Heald Lane
Beaufort Road
Kateholm Road
Philips
Weir
Weir La
Lane
River Irwell
BURNLEY ROAD
A671
Bacup Old Road
Dog Pits La
Road
Old Mdw
Old Meadows Rd
Todmorden Old Road
A681
TODMORDEN ROAD
Meadows Avenue
Gordon St
Farm Av
Russel St
Cooper Street
Cowtoot Lane
Coniston Wy
Pendle Av
Greenshook Lane
Blackthorn Crs
Clover St
YORKSHIRE STREET
Albion St
Beech Industrial Est
Vale St
Zion Street
Clough Road
Rosendale Crs
Warcock Lane
Greave Clough Drive
Oakenclough Rd
Oaken Close
Hazel Grove
Greave Coal Pit La
Moorside Crs
Rosemount
Greens Lane
Carlton Street
Grove Street
Earnshaw Road
Ash Street
Dale St
Albert Ter
Birch St
Hammerton St
South St
Tong
Lane
Bank
Hawthorn Road
Alma St
Inkerman St
Crimea St
Gladstone Street
Pendle Close
Industrial St
Thorn St
Bath St
King St
Lee St
Unn St
ST JAMES
MARKET STREET
Henrietta St
Henrietta St Ind Est
St Marys RC Primary School
Tong
Works
PO

1 grid square represents 500 metres

Waterside
Chapels
Darwen Moorland High School
Works
50
F
G
H
J
K
70
71
Pot House La
Ivinson Road
Hazel Avenue
Exchange St
Blacksnape Road
Coniston Drive
Thirlmere Drive
Hawthorn Av
Ambleside Dr
Lilac Gv
Holden Fold
Moor La
Chapels
Knowle La
St James CE Primary School
Olive La
Ash Gv
Two Gates Works
Century Works
Anyon St
Darwen Stn
Railway Road Industrial Est
Robin Bank Road
Richmond Ter
Darwen Mkt
Council Building
Holy Trinity VC School
Surg
Burns Wk
Ellison Fold Terrace
Sudell Prim Sch
Sudell Cl
Avallon Way
Lisbon Drive
Marsham Grove
Marsh House Lane
Marsh House Industrial Estate
Hoddlesden Road
Harwood's Lane
Glencoe Avenue
Gleneagles Av
Carus Av
Chapman Rd
Johnson New Road
I
2
3
4
5
6
22
21
20
23
Earls Dr
Dukes Dr
Cloister Drive
Priory Grange
Abbey Crescent
Minster Crs
Chapter Road
Pole Lane
Moor Close
Thorncliffe Dr
Rudyard Drive
India Mill Business Centre
St Peters CE Prim School
Rosehill
Blacksnape
BB3
Cross St
Junction Street
The Sidings
Spring Meadows
Pickup Fold Rd
Huntington Drive
Astley St
A666
Grimshaw St
Hampden
Spring Vale Road
Springvale Business Park
Clough Street
Watery Lane Ind Est
Sch
Bury Fold
Whitehall
Ashleigh Prim Sch
Cranberry Lane
Kirkdale Close
St Barnabas CE Primary School
Works
BOLTON ROAD
Darwen Cemetery
Key View Drive
Jacks Key
Eastern Cemetery
Whitehall Road
Queen's Rd
Willow Bank

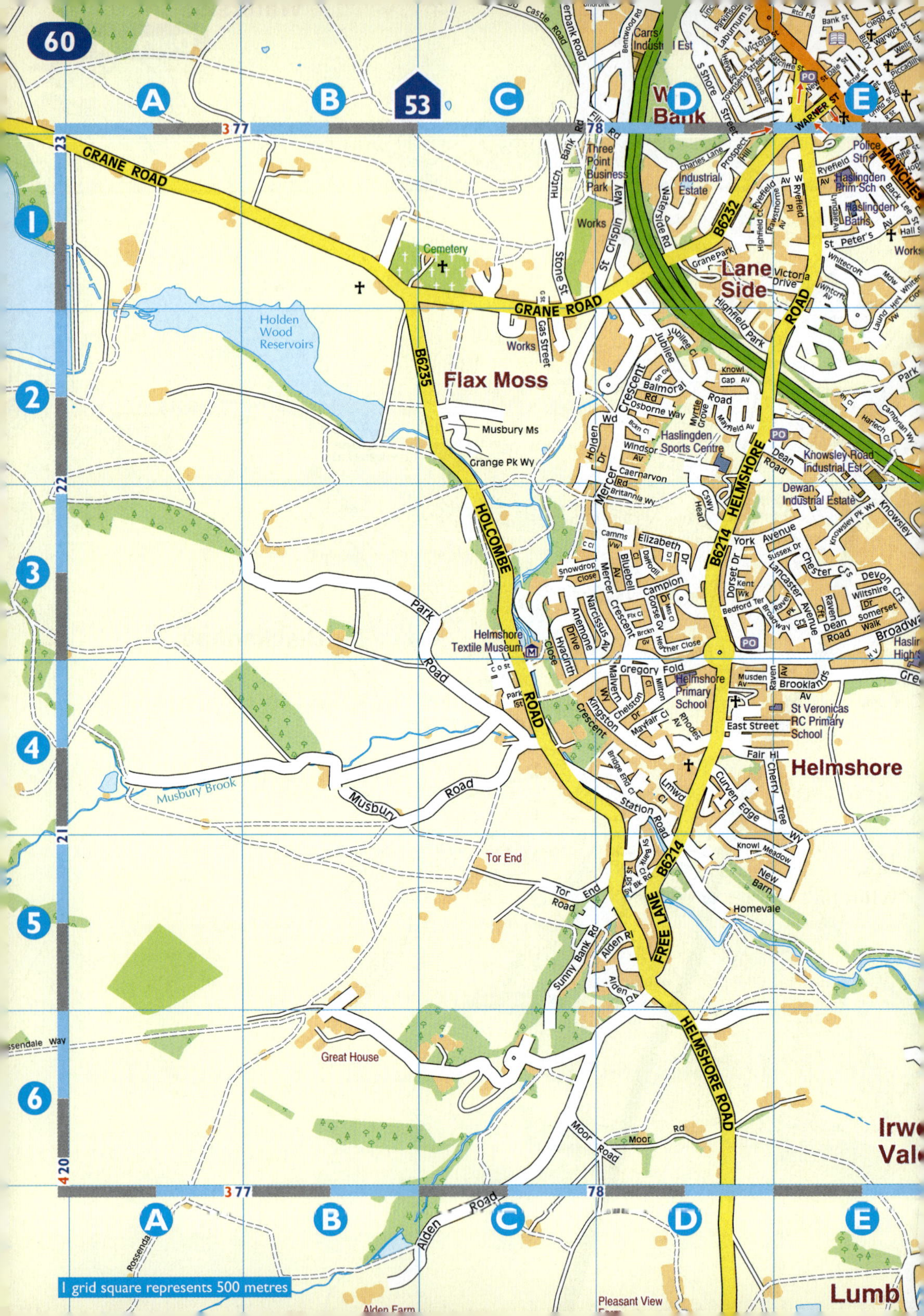

1 grid square represents 500 metres

Helmshore 61
54
62
Height End
New Hall Hey
Townsend Fold
Balladen
Bent Gate
ood Bridge
F
G
H
J
K
80
81
1
2
3
4
5
6
Haslingden Road
A681
A682
A680
A56
B6527
Bocholt Way
Manchester Road
Blackburn Road
St Mary's Way
Oakenhead Wood Old Road
Haslingden Old Road
Ski Rossendale
St James the Less RC Primary School
Valley Shopping Centre
Barnes Avenue
Schofield Road
Hargreaves Dr
Oakley Road
Magistrates Court
Rossendale Museum Whitaker Park
Belmont School
Oaklands Drive
Cedar Av
Willow Tree Avenue
Union Road
General Hospital
All Saints RC High Sch Language Col
Cribden House Comm School
Rawtenstall Station
Accrington & Rossendale College
Superstore
Hall Carr Road
Hardmans Business Cen
New Hall Hey Business Park
Andrew Av
Bury Road
Holme La
Irwell Valley Way
East Lancashire Railway
Lwr Clowes Road
Clayton Av
Duckworth Lane
Cherry Crescent
Redwood Dr
Balladen Community School
New Barn La
Lomas Lane
Dearden Nook
Dearden Moor
Fish Rake Lane
Sand Beds La
Haslingden CC
Bentgate School
Grasmere Rd
Rydal Road
Rossendale Golf Club
Golf Course
River Irwell
Works
Irwell Vale Road
Irwell Vale Station
Hardsough Lane
Aitken Street
Louis St
Burnley Road
Edenfield CE Primary School
East St
Church Lane
Alderwood
St Marys RC Primary School
Moorland Rise
Yarmouth Av
Richmond Avenue
Kirkhill Av
Hillside
Police Stn
Council Building
County Court
Town Hall
Bacup Road
Fire Stn

62
55
61
A
B
C
D
E
1
2
3
4
5
6
382
383
423
422
421
420
Hurst Crs
Green St
Newchurch Road
Marl Pits
Marl Pits Sports Centre
Grange Rd
Greenbank Pk
Council County Building Court
Health Centre
Police Stn
Rawtenstall CC
Plantation St
Greenbank St
Rose V St
A681
Lever St
Lambton Gates
Works
Fallbarn Road
Victoria St
East Wood St
Newchurch Road
Patrick Crescent
Dobbin Lane
Dobbin Close
Conway Road
Johnny Barn Cl
Peel St
Cloughfold CP School
Heys St
Heys Cl
Hope Street
Cloughfold
Hill End Lane
Irwell Valley Wy
Highfield Rd
Bacup Road
Lench Road
River Irwell
Lane
Saunder Height Lane
Edgeside Sch
Harehome Lane
Lea Bank
Brow Edge
Staghills Road
Weber Street
Brookland St
Gilbert Street
Woodside Crs
Top Barn Lane
Rectory Close
Newchurch
St Peters RC School
Newchurch Road
Heightside Av
Hillside Dr
Church St
North St
South St
Windsor Av
Dark Lane
Church Lane
Queensway
Newchurch CE School
Rossendale United FC
Waterfoot
Springfield Dr
Holt Mill Rd
Fern Lea St
West St
St James' St
Works
Horse & Bamboo Theatre
Hugh Mill
Rake Head
Waterfoot Health Centre
Scout Road
Works
Shaw Clough Rd
Scoutbottom Industrial Estate
Piercy Road
Ashworth Lane
Ashworth Rd
St Annes CE Prim Sch
Fairfield
PO
Wall St
Rose St
Bridleway
Tom Lane
Crabtree Avenue
Taylor Avenue
Waterfoot Business Centre
New Rd
Turnpike
Old Street
Thistlemount Avenue
Burnley Road East
Bridge St
Todd Carr Rd
Clough St
Gresham St
Prospect St
Wales
Staghills Rd
Thornfield Av
Booth
Sch
Wood Road
Millar Barn Lane
Glen Rd
Lench St
Stone St
Ashworth St
Works
Carr Lane
Lumb Holes Lane
Cowpe Road
Hardman Drive
Hardman Cl
Cowpe
Higher Lench
Rossendale Way
Sand Beds Lane
Rossendale Way
1 grid square represents 500 metres

Stacksteads
Huttock Top
Nun Hills
Boarsgreave
dgeside
Brandwood Moor
Cowpe Reservoir
Golf Course
Bacup Golf Club
Maden Road
Highfield
Meadow Way
Acorn St
Fern St
Goose Hill Street
Dale St
Ash Street
Birch St
Albert
Newchurch Old Road
Bankside Lane
Lodge
Plan Mill Esta
Wesley Place
Rockcliffe Av
Fullers Ter
Park Rd
A681
NEWCHURCH ROAD
Works
Stubbylee Park
Glen St
Flag St
Lee Road
Cemetery
Toll Bar Business Park
Line St
Irwell Valley Way
Works
Cutler Crs
Cutler Lane
Unsworth St
Greens Lane
Acre Avenue
Acre View
Springhill Av
Mill Road
Brunswick Ter
Farnolme Lane
Holme St
Surgery
Stuart Av
Miles Av
Toll Bar Business Park
Hammond Av
Fernhill
Fernhill Drive
Fernhill Way
Fernhill Pk
Fernhill Crs
Terrace
Osborne
Hl Crest
Sow Clough Road
St Josephs School
Huttock End Lane
Holy Trinity Stacksteads CE Prim Sch
Bnkfld St
Haworth Dr
Tunstead Rd
Tunstead Crs
Lord Av
Glenborough Avenue
Church St
Union Street
Plantation St
Heath Hill Dr
Heathbourne Rd
Western Rd
Booth Road
Rook Hill Road
School St
Four Lanes End Road
Lane
Tunstead
Fearns Moss
Fearns High School
Belvedere Av
Kirk View
Crescent
Road
Lane
nstall
Taylor Holme Ind Est
Glen Crs
Brandwood Road
Brandwood Park
Rakehead Lane
Atherton Way
Atherton Holme Works
Baldwin St
Mark St
Railway Street
Hugh Bus Park
PO
Blackwood Road
Road
oyds
Rooley Moor Road
The Hill
F
G
H
J
K
I
2
3
4
5
6
56
64
85
86
23
22
21
420

BACUP
Rockcliffe
Britannia
Belgrave
Higher Hogs
Trough G
Shawfo
Millgate
Lowers Reaps
Yorkshire Street
Market Street
St James
Newchurch Road
Rochdale Road
New Line
A681
A671
A6066
Earnshaw Road
Ash Street
Dale St
Fern St
Tong Lane
Pennine Road
Thorn Bank
Thorn Drive
Hawthorn
Gladstone Street
Pendle Close
Industrial St
Inkerman St
Alma St
Crimea St
Bath St
Thom St
Lee St
Henrietta St
Henrietta St Ind Est
Empire Theatre
St Marys RC Primary School
Sandfield Road
Crabtree Av
Ronaldsway Close
Peel Dr
Onchan Drive
Douglas Road
Ramsey Av
Churchtown Crs
Walton Cl
Avenue
Hoghton
Rockcliffe Rd
Heys St
Hemp Street
River Street
Crafton Villas
Plantation Mill Ind Estate
Lodge Lane
Park Road Industrial Estate
Park Rd
Fullers Ter
Wesley Place
Works
Stubbylee Park
Stubbylee Lane
Height Barn La
The Sidings
New Line Industrial Estate
Stack Lane
Railgate
Lee's St
Ernest St
K St
Britannia Community Primary School
Warren Dr
Edge La
Deansgreave Road
Prince Street
Beech Industrial
Vale St
Albion St
Clover St
Greave Clough Drive
Oaken Close
Warcock Lane
Goose Hill Street
Twr St
Unn St
King St
Lord St
Meadow Way
Bacup Golf Club
Oak St
Oak Cl
Oak Vw
Heatherlands
Valley View
Spring Side
Market Street
South St
School
57
63
A B C D E
1 2 3 4 5 6
387 88
423 22 21 420
I grid square represents 500 metres

Gate
Works
F
G
H
J
K
90
91
Gorpley Reservoir
23
I
Lancashire County
Calderdale
Inchfield Moor
Reaps Moss
Rossendale Way
d
2
Calderdale
Lancashire County
22
3
Clough
Road
Foul Clough
Rossendale Way
Ramsden Clough Res
4
Works
STREET
21
Calderdale
Rochdale
Freeholds
Road
5
Percy St
Jane St
Knowsley
Rossendale Way
Knott Hill Street
Quarry Street
Crs
St John with St Michael Primary School
Moss Side Street
Land Gate
Land Gate
Lancashire County
Rochdale
6
20
4
90
91
F
G
H
J
K

Accrington 44 C1
Altham 24 A5
Bacup 64 B1
Balladen 61 K4
Bank Fold 50 E4
Bank Hey 32 B4
Barrowford 8 B3
Baxenden 45 G5
Beardwood 30 D6
Belgrave 64 A4
Belthorn 50 E3
Bent Gate 61 F3
Billington 13 G6
Blackburn 3 F6
Blackburn 31 J5
Blacksnape 59 J3
Boarsgreave 63 F6
Brierfield 18 D4
Britannia 64 D3
Broad Clough 57 G4
Broadfield 44 B4
Brockhall Village 12 C3
Brookhouse 2 E1
Brownhill 31 J2
Brownside 28 B5
Brunshaw 27 H5
Burnley 5 F7
Burnley Lane 26 E2
Burnley Wood 5 K7
Chapels 50 B6
Cherry Tree 40 B6
Church 34 B5
Church Clough 10 A4
Clayton Le Dale 20 B4
Clayton-le-Moors 34 C2
Cliffe 22 C5
Clitheroe 6 C2
Cliviger 39 G6
Cloughfold 62 B2
Clow Bridge 47 F2
Cockden 28 B1
Colne 9 J1
Constable Lee 54 E5
Copster Green 20 C3
Cowpe 62 E5
Crawshawbooth 55 F2
Cribden Side 54 A3
Darwen 58 E2
Dean 56 C1
Dill Hall 34 C6
Dunnockshaw 47 F3
Earcroft 49 H3
Edge End 22 B6
Edgeside 63 F1
Ewood 49 H1
Ewood Bridge 60 E5
Fence 17 H1
Feniscliffe 40 D5
Feniscowles 48 A1
Flax Moss 60 C2
Forest Holme 55 K2
Four Lane Ends 31 H5
Goodshaw 54 D1
Goodshaw Chapel 47 F6
Goodshaw Fold 46 C5
Great Harwood 22 B5
Greave 57 H6
Green Haworth 44 D6
Grimshaw 50 C4
Guide 50 D1
Habergham 25 J4
Haggate 19 G6
Hapton 25 F6
Harle Syke 18 E6
Haslingden 53 K5
Height End 54 B6
Helmshore 60 E4
Higham 16 D4
Higher Audley 3 J5
Higher Croft 41 J6
Higherford 8 D1
Higher Hogshead 64 E2
Hillock Vale 34 E5
Hindle Fold 22 D5
Hollin Hall 10 E6
Hud Hey 53 J4
Hugh Mill 62 C3
Huncoat 35 H3
Hurstwood 39 J1
Huttock Top 63 J2
Intack 42 C2
Irwell Vale 60 E6
Knuzden Brook 43 F3
Lammack 31 F5
Lane Bottom 19 G5
Lane Ends 36 A2
Lane Side 60 D1
Langho 21 H3
Laund 54 D5
Little Harwood 32 A6
Little Marsden 18 E2
Little Moor 6 E5
Little Moor End 44 A5
Lomeshaye 18 B1
Love Clough 46 D4
Lower Darwen 50 B2
Lowerford 8 B3
Lowerhouse 25 J5
Low Moor 6 B3
Lumb 55 K3
Marsden Height 18 E4
Mellor 30 C2
Mellor Brook 30 A2
Mereclough 39 H4
Mill Hill 40 E6
Milnshaw 34 C6
Nelson 19 F2
Nethertown 13 G3
Newbridge 8 C5
Newchurch 62 D1
New Hall Hey 61 H2
Nun Hills 63 H4
Oakenshaw 33 K2
Old Langho 12 C5
Osbaldeston 30 B1
Oswaldtwistle 43 G4
Over Town 39 H5
Padiham 25 G3
Pike Hill 27 K5
Pimlico 6 E1
Pleasington 40 A6
Pleckgate 31 H4
Queen's Park 42 B3
Rake Head 62 D3
Rawtenstall 54 E6
Read 24 A1
Reedley 18 B5
Reeds Holme 54 E3
Revidge 31 G6
Rishton 33 F4
Rising Bridge 53 H1
Rockcliffe 64 A2
Roe Lee 31 J4
Rose Grove 26 A6
Rose Hill 4 E7
Rosehill 59 H3
Roughlee 8 A2
Sabden 15 H2
Salesbury 20 C5
Scaitcliffe 44 B2
Shadsworth 42 C4
Sharneyford 57 J4
Shawforth 64
Sherfin 53
Simonstone 24
Spring Hill 44
Stacksteads 63
Stanhill 43
Stoneyholme 26
Sunny Bower 32
Sunnyhurst 58
Tockholes 48
Tottleworth 33
Townsend Fold 61
Trawden 11
Trough Gate 64
Walk Mill 39
Water 55
Waterfoot 62
Waterloo 49
Waterside 50
Weir 57
Well Bank 53
West End 43
Whalley 13
Whinny Heights 42
Whitebirk 42
Whitehall 59
Whitewell Bottom 55
Wilpshire 21
Winewall 10
Wiswell 14
Woodnook 44
Worsthorne 28
Worston 7
Wycoller 11
York 21

USING THE STREET INDEX

Street names are listed alphabetically. Each street name is followed by its postal town or area locality, the Postcode District, the page number, and the reference to the square in which the name is found.

Standard index entries are shown as follows:

Abbey Crs *DWN* BB3 **59** H3

Street names and selected addresses not shown on the map due to scale restrictions are shown in the index with an asterisk:

Berkeley Cl *NLSN* BB9 * **18** E2

GENERAL ABBREVIATIONS

ACC	ACCESS
ALY	ALLEY
AP	APPROACH
AR	ARCADE
ASS	ASSOCIATION
AV	AVENUE
BCH	BEACH
BLDS	BUILDINGS
BND	BEND
BNK	BANK
BR	BRIDGE
BRK	BROOK
BTM	BOTTOM
BUS	BUSINESS
BVD	BOULEVARD
BY	BYPASS
CATH	CATHEDRAL
CEM	CEMETERY
CEN	CENTRE
CFT	CROFT
CH	CHURCH
CHA	CHASE
CHYD	CHURCHYARD
CIR	CIRCLE
CIRC	CIRCUS
CL	CLOSE
CLFS	CLIFFS
CMP	CAMP
CNR	CORNER
CO	COUNTY
COLL	COLLEGE
COM	COMMON
COMM	COMMISSION
CON	CONVENT
COT	COTTAGE
COTS	COTTAGES
CP	CAPE
CPS	COPSE
CR	CREEK
CREM	CREMATORIUM
CRS	CRESCENT
CSWY	CAUSEWAY
CT	COURT
CTRL	CENTRAL
CTS	COURTS
CTYD	COURTYARD
CUTT	CUTTINGS
CV	COVE
CYN	CANYON
DEPT	DEPARTMENT
DL	DALE
DM	DAM
DR	DRIVE
DRO	DROVE
DRY	DRIVEWAY
DWGS	DWELLINGS
E	EAST
EMB	EMBANKMENT
EMBY	EMBASSY
ESP	ESPLANADE
EST	ESTATE
EX	EXCHANGE
EXPY	EXPRESSWAY
EXT	EXTENSION
F/O	FLYOVER
FC	FOOTBALL CLUB
FK	FORK
FLD	FIELD
FLDS	FIELDS
FLS	FALLS
FLS	FLATS
FM	FARM
FT	FORT
FWY	FREEWAY
FY	FERRY
GA	GATE
GAL	GALLERY
GDN	GARDEN
GDNS	GARDENS
GLD	GLADE
GLN	GLEN
GN	GREEN
GND	GROUND
GRA	GRANGE
GRG	GARAGE
GT	GREAT
GTWY	GATEWAY
GV	GROVE
HGR	HIGHER
HL	HILL
HLS	HILLS
HO	HOUSE
HOL	HOLLOW
HOSP	HOSPITAL
HRB	HARBOUR
HTH	HEATH
HTS	HEIGHTS
HVN	HAVEN
HWY	HIGHWAY
IMP	IMPERIAL
IN	INLET
IND EST	INDUSTRIAL ESTATE
INF	INFIRMARY
INFO	INFORMATION
INT	INTERCHANGE
IS	ISLAND
JCT	JUNCTION
JTY	JETTY
KG	KING
KNL	KNOLL
L	LAKE
LA	LANE
LDG	LODGE
LGT	LIGHT
LK	LOCK
LKS	LAKES
LNDG	LANDING
LTL	LITTLE
LWR	LOWER
MAG	MAGISTRATE
MAN	MANSIONS
MD	MEAD
MDW	MEADOWS
MEM	MEMORIAL
MKT	MARKET
MKTS	MARKETS
ML	MALL
ML	MILL
MNR	MANOR
MS	MEWS
MSN	MISSION
MT	MOUNT
MTN	MOUNTAIN
MTS	MOUNTAINS
MUS	MUSEUM
MWY	MOTORWAY
N	NORTH
NE	NORTH EAST
NW	NORTH WEST
O/P	OVERPASS
OFF	OFFICE
ORCH	ORCHARD
OV	OVAL
PAL	PALACE
PAS	PASSAGE
PAV	PAVILION
PDE	PARADE
PH	PUBLIC HOUSE
PK	PARK
PKWY	PARKWAY
PL	PLACE
PLN	PLAIN
PLNS	PLAINS
PLZ	PLAZA
POL	POLICE STATION
PR	PRINCE
PREC	PRECINCT
PREP	PREPARATORY
PRIM	PRIMARY
PROM	PROMENADE
PRS	PRINCESS
PRT	PORT
PT	POINT
PTH	PATH
PZ	PIAZZA
QD	QUADRANT
QU	QUEEN
QY	QUAY
R	RIVER
RBT	ROUNDABOUT
RD	ROAD
RDG	RIDGE
REP	REPUBLIC
RES	RESERVOIR
RFC	RUGBY FOOTBALL CLUB
RI	RISE
RP	RAMP
RW	ROW
S	SOUTH
SCH	SCHOOL
SE	SOUTH EA
SER	SERVICE ARE
SH	SHO
SHOP	SHOPPIN
SKWY	SKYWA
SMT	SUMM
SOC	SOCIET
SP	SPU
SPR	SPRIN
SQ	SQUAR
ST	STRE
STN	STATIO
STR	STREA
STRD	STRAN
SW	SOUTH WES
TDG	TRADIN
TER	TERRAC
THWY	THROUGHWA
TNL	TUNN
TOLL	TOLLWA
TPK	TURNPIK
TR	TRAC
TRL	TRA
TWR	TOWE
U/P	UNDERPAS
UNI	UNIVERSIT
UPR	UPPE
V	VA
VA	VALLE
VIAD	VIADUC
VIL	VIL
VIS	VIST
VLG	VILLAG
VLS	VILLA
VW	VIE
W	WES
WD	WOO
WHF	WHAR
WK	WAL
WKS	WALK
WLS	WEL
WY	WA
YD	YAR
YHA	YOUTH HOST

POSTCODE TOWNS AND AREA ABBREVIATIONS

ACC	Accrington
BBN	Blackburn
BBNW	Blackburn west
BCUP	Bacup
BIRK/DRI	Birkenshaw/Drighlington
BLY	Burnley
CHLYE	Chorley east/Adlington/Whittle-le-Woods
CLI	Clitheroe
COL	Colne
DWN	Darwen
GAR/LONG	Garstang/Longridge
GTH/LHO	Great Harwood/Langho
HBR	Hebden Bridge
IDLE	Idle
LM/WK	Low Moor/Wyke
NLSN	Nelson
RAMS	Ramsbottom
RAW/HAS	Rawtensta Haslingde
TOD	Todmord
TOT/BURYW	Tottington/Bury we
WHIT	Whitwor

A

Abbey Crs *DWN* BB3 **59** H3
Abbey Flds *CLI* BB7 **13** H4
Abbey Rd *CLI* BB7 **13** J4
Abbey St *ACC* BB5 **44** E2
Abbots Cl *RAW/HAS* BB4 **54** E5
Abbots Cft *CLI* BB7 **13** J4
Abbotsford Av *BBNW* BB2 **41** H6
Abbott Brow *BBNW* BB2 **30** B1
Abbott Clough Av *BBN* BB1 **42** E3
Abbott Clough Cl *BBN* BB1 **42** E3
Abbot Wk *CLI* BB7 **7** F3
Abel St *BRFD/BLYE* BB10 **27** F3
Aberdare Cl *BBN* BB1 **31** J6
Aberdeen Dr *BBN* BB1 **3** J5
Abingdon Rd *PDHM/BLYW* BB12 **25** G4
Abinger St *BRFD/BLYE* BB10 **27** H2
Abraham Altham Ct
BRFD/BLYE BB10 * **18** B4
Abraham St *ACC* BB5 **44** D2
BBNW BB2 **41** J5
Accrington Rd *BBN* BB1 **42**
BLY BB11 **4**
BLY BB11 **25**
BLY BB11 **36**
CLI BB7 **13**
CLI BB7 **23**

corn Av ACC BB5 44 B4
corn St BBN BB1 42 B3
BCUP OL13 63 K1
cre Av BCUP OL13 63 J3
crefield BBNW BB2 30 E6
PDHM/BLYW BB12 25 F2
cre Mill Rd BCUP OL13 63 J4
cresbrook Rd
PDHM/BLYW BB12 16 D4
cresfield COL BB8 * 10 C2
cre St BRFD/BLYE BB10 27 G2
cre Vw BCUP OL13 63 J3
ctive Wy BLY BB11 5 G2
damson St
PDHM/BLYW BB12 25 F2
PDHM/BLYW BB12 26 B5
da St BBNW BB2 2 B3
BRFD/BLYE BB10 27 G2
NLSN BB9 18 E3
ddington St BBN BB1 3 K5
ddison Cl BBNW BB2 2 B4
ddison St ACC BB5 34 E6
BBNW BB2 2 B4
delaide St ACC BB5 34 C4
ACC BB5 44 E2
BLY BB11 * 4 A3
BLY BB11 * 26 B6
RAW/HAS BB4 54 E2
delaide Ter BBNW BB2 2 B3
delphi St BLY BB11 5 G1
dlington St BLY BB11 5 H2
dmiral St BRFD/BLYE BB10 5 K4
gate St BBN BB1 31 K4
gnes St BBNW BB2 * 41 G4
isa Rd BBN BB1 42 D4
insdale Av BRFD/BLYE BB10 18 C5
insdale Dr DWN BB3 59 G6
inslie Cl GTH/LHO BB6 * 22 C6
nslie St PDHM/BLYW BB12 * 26 B5
nsworth Ml BBN BB1 3 F4
insworth St BBN BB1 3 F4
intree Dr DWN BB3 50 A2
irdrie Crs BLY BB11 4 B7
rey St ACC BB5 45 F4
irton Garth NLSN BB9 8 C4
itken St ACC BB5 34 E6
RAW/HAS BB4 61 F6
an Ramsbottam Wy
GTH/LHO BB6 33 K1
aska St BBNW BB2 41 J5
bany Dr BBN BB1 20 B3
bany Rd BBNW BB2 41 F1
bemarle St CLI BB7 6 C3
lberta Cl BBNW BB2 31 F5
lbert Pl DWN BB3 49 K2
lbert Rd COL BB8 9 J3
RAW/HAS BB4 54 E1
bert St ACC BB5 34 B3
ACC BB5 44 A1
ACC BB5 44 A5
ACC BB5 44 E2
BBN BB1 33 H4
BBNW BB2 41 G5
BLY BB11 5 J3
DWN BB3 59 G6
GTH/LHO BB6 33 K1
NLSN BB9 18 B4
NLSN BB9 18 D1
PDHM/BLYW BB12 25 F3
RAW/HAS BB4 55 J4
bert Ter BCUP OL13 57 F6
bion Ct BLY BB11 4 C6
CLI BB7 * 6 E2
bion Rd BBNW BB2 41 H6
bion St ACC BB5 * 44 D1
BBNW BB2 41 G6
BCUP OL13 57 G6
BLY BB11 4 D5
CLI BB7 6 E3
NLSN BB9 18 B4
NLSN BB9 18 D1
PDHM/BLYW BB12 25 G4
bion Ter BLY BB11 4 E5
den Cl RAW/HAS BB4 60 D5
den Ri RAW/HAS BB4 60 D5
der Av RAW/HAS BB4 62 A1
der Bank BBNW BB2 41 F3
RAW/HAS BB4 55 F6
derford Cl CLI BB7 6 B4
der Gv ACC BB5 35 G3
derney Cl BBNW BB2 41 F6
der St BBN BB1 32 A6
BCUP OL13 57 F6
PDHM/BLYW BB12 26 B5
RAW/HAS BB4 55 F6
exander Gv
PDHM/BLYW BB12 26 A5
exander St NLSN BB9 9 G5
exandra Pl GTH/LHO BB6 22 E5
exandra Rd BBNW BB2 2 A1
DWN BB3 58 E1
exandra St ACC BB5 34 A1
exandria St RAW/HAS BB4 54 D5
fred St DWN BB3 * 59 G5
gar St NLSN BB9 9 F5
ice St ACC BB5 35 F6
ACC BB5 44 A4
DWN BB3 59 F3
kincoats Rd COL BB8 9 J2
lan St BCUP OL13 64 A2
len Ct BRFD/BLYE BB10 27 F3
lendale Gv BRFD/BLYE BB10 39 F1
lendale St COL BB8 10 B2
PDHM/BLYW BB12 26 A5
len St BRFD/BLYE BB10 27 F3
lerton Cl DWN BB3 59 F1
lerton Dr PDHM/BLYW BB12 4 B2
leys Gn CLI BB7 6 D2
leytroyds ACC BB5 44 A2
liance St ACC BB5 45 G6
lison Gv COL BB8 10 A1
l Saint's Cl ACC BB5 43 H3
PDHM/BLYW BB12 25 J4
RAW/HAS BB4 46 E6
lsprings Cl GTH/LHO BB6 22 E5
Allsprings Dr GTH/LHO BB6 22 E4
Alma Pl CLI BB7 6 C4
Alma Rd COL BB8 11 F1
Alma St ACC BB5 34 B2
BBNW BB2 2 D3
BCUP OL13 64 B1
PDHM/BLYW BB12 25 F3
Almond Crs RAW/HAS BB4 61 J2
Almond St DWN BB3 59 F3
Alnwick Cl PDHM/BLYW BB12 26 D4
Alpha St DWN BB3 59 G3
NLSN BB9 9 F5
Alpine Cl DWN BB3 59 K2
Alpine Gv BBNW BB2 49 F1
Alston Cl CLI BB7 15 H2
Altham Br ACC BB5 24 B4
Altham La ACC BB5 24 B5
Altham St BRFD/BLYE BB10 27 F3
PDHM/BLYW BB12 25 G3
Altom St BBN BB1 2 E2
Alwin St BLY BB11 * 4 C5
Amber Av BBN BB1 31 K3
Amberley St BBNW BB2 41 G5
Amberwood Dr BBNW BB2 40 E6
Ambleside Av RAW/HAS BB4 61 H1
Ambleside Cl ACC BB5 35 G5
BBN BB1 3 J2
Ambleside Dr DWN BB3 50 C6
Amelia St BBN BB1 42 B1
Amethyst St BBN BB1 31 J3
Anchor Av DWN BB3 49 J5
Anchor Gv DWN BB3 49 J5
Anchor House BBN BB1 * 3 G6
Anchor Rd DWN BB3 49 J5
Andelen Cl BLY BB11 36 A2
Anderson Rd BBN BB1 21 F4
Anderton Cl RAW/HAS BB4 62 E4
Anderton Rd
PDHM/BLYW BB12 16 D4
Andrew Av RAW/HAS BB4 61 J2
Andrew Cl BBNW BB2 49 F1
Andrew Rd NLSN BB9 9 H6
Anemone Dr RAW/HAS BB4 60 C3
Angela St BBNW BB2 41 F6
Anglesey St BBNW BB2 49 F1
Angle St BRFD/BLYE BB10 27 F3
Anglian Cl ACC BB5 43 J2
Annarly Fold BRFD/BLYE BB10 28 B6
Anne Cl BRFD/BLYE BB10 5 K4
Anne St BLY BB11 * 5 J4
Annie St ACC BB5 34 E6
RAW/HAS BB4 61 K1
Ann St ACC BB5 34 B2
NLSN BB9 8 D4
NLSN BB9 18 B3
Ansdell Ter BBNW BB2 41 J6
Antigua Dr DWN BB3 49 K3
Anvil St BCUP OL13 63 K3
Anyon St DWN BB3 59 G1
Appleby Cl ACC BB5 45 F2
Appleby Dr NLSN BB9 8 D3
Appleby St BBN BB1 3 J3
NLSN BB9 18 D1
Apple Cl BBNW BB2 2 A5
Apple Ct BBNW BB2 2 A5
Applecross Dr
BRFD/BLYE BB10 38 E1
Applegarth NLSN BB9 8 B6
Apple St BBNW BB2 2 A5
Apple Tree Wy ACC BB5 44 A2
Approach Wy BLY BB11 37 J3
Aqueduct Rd BBNW BB2 41 H6
Arago St ACC BB5 34 E6
Arbories Av PDHM/BLYW BB12 24 E3
Arbory Dr PDHM/BLYW BB12 24 E2
Arbour Dr DWN BB3 49 H3
Arboury St PDHM/BLYW BB12 24 E3
Arch St BLY BB11 * 5 F2
Ardwick St BRFD/BLYE BB10 27 F3
Argyle St ACC BB5 44 D1
COL BB8 9 K2
DWN BB3 49 K6
Arkwright Fold BBNW BB2 49 G1
Arkwright St
PDHM/BLYW BB12 26 B4
Arley Gdns PDHM/BLYW BB12 26 E4
Arley Ri BBNW BB2 30 C3
Arlington Rd DWN BB3 58 E3
Arncliffe Av ACC BB5 44 B3
Arncliffe Gv NLSN BB9 8 C4
Arncliffe Rd BRFD/BLYE BB10 27 K6
Arnold Cl BBNW BB2 42 A6
BLY BB11 37 J3
Arnold St ACC BB5 34 E6
Arnside Cl ACC BB5 34 A3
Arnside Crs BBNW BB2 48 C2
Arran Av BBN BB1 42 D5
Arran St BLY BB11 4 B4
Arthur St ACC BB5 34 B2
BBNW BB2 2 A5
BCUP OL13 57 H6
BLY BB11 4 D3
GTH/LHO BB6 22 E5
NLSN BB9 8 E6
NLSN BB9 18 B4
Arthur Wy BBNW BB2 2 B5
Artillery St ACC BB5 44 B2
Ascot Wy ACC BB5 45 F2
Ash Av RAW/HAS BB4 54 A6
Ashburnham Rd COL BB8 9 G5
Ash Cl BBN BB1 33 H5
Ash Ct BBN BB1 * 32 A6
Ashendean Vw
PDHM/BLYW BB12 25 G2
Ashfield Cl NLSN BB9 8 C6
Ashfield Rd BLY BB11 4 E2
Ashford St NLSN BB9 18 E1
Ash Gv CLI BB7 * 11 G1
DWN BB3 59 G1
RAW/HAS BB4 56 A1
Ash La GTH/LHO BB6 22 C5
Ashleigh St DWN BB3 59 G5
Ashley St PDHM/BLYW BB12 26 E4
Ash St ACC BB5 43 K3
BBN BB1 32 A6
BCUP OL13 57 F6
BLY BB11 5 J4
COL BB8 10 E5
GTH/LHO BB6 22 D5
NLSN BB9 19 F1
Ashton Dr NLSN BB9 18 E3
Ashton La DWN BB3 59 F3
Ashton Rd DWN BB3 59 G3
Ash Tree Wk NLSN BB9 8 D5
Ashville Ter BBNW BB2 49 H1
Ashwood Av DWN BB3 49 H3
Ashworth Cl BBNW BB2 2 B4
Ashworth La RAW/HAS BB4 55 K6
Ashworth Rd RAW/HAS BB4 62 E1
Ashworth St ACC BB5 45 G5
BBN BB1 * 33 H4
BCUP OL13 57 G6
BCUP OL13 63 J3
RAW/HAS BB4 56 A2
RAW/HAS BB4 62 E3
Ashworth Ter DWN BB3 59 F3
Askrigg Cl ACC BB5 45 F1
Aspen Dr BRFD/BLYE BB10 27 H4
Aspen Fold ACC BB5 43 H2
Aspen La ACC BB5 43 H3
Aspinall Fold BBN BB1 31 J5
Assheton Rd BBNW BB2 40 E2
Aster Cha DWN BB3 50 A2
Astley Ga BBNW BB2 2 E4
Astley Hts DWN BB3 59 F4
Astley St DWN BB3 59 F4
Athens Vw BRFD/BLYE BB10 * 27 H6
Atherton St BCUP OL13 * 63 G3
Atherton Wy BCUP OL13 63 G3
Athletic St BRFD/BLYE BB10 27 H6
Athol St NLSN BB9 19 F1
Athol St North BLY BB11 4 B4
Athol St South BLY BB11 4 B5
Atkinson St BRFD/BLYE BB10 * 19 F6
COL BB8 9 K3
Atlas Rd DWN BB3 59 G2
Atlas St ACC BB5 34 C4
Atrium Ct BLY BB11 5 J7
Auckland St DWN BB3 59 G4
Audley Cl NLSN BB9 * 18 E1
Audley La BBN BB1 3 J4
Audley Range BBN BB1 3 H6
Audley St BBN BB1 3 J4
Augusta St ACC BB5 44 E3
Austin St BCUP OL13 64 A1
BLY BB11 * 4 D4
Austwick Wy ACC BB5 45 G2
Avallon Wy DWN BB3 59 H2
Avalon Cl PDHM/BLYW BB12 * 25 J4
Avebury Cl BBNW BB2 50 A1
Avenue Pde ACC BB5 45 F1
The Avenue BLY BB11 38 D3
GTH/LHO BB6 * 12 C4
Aviemore Cl BBN BB1 * 3 K5
Avon Ct PDHM/BLYW BB12 26 C4
Avondale Av BBN BB1 42 E2
PDHM/BLYW BB12 26 B4
Avondale Cl DWN BB3 58 D1
Avondale Ms DWN BB3 49 J6
Avondale Rd DWN BB3 58 D1
NLSN BB9 18 D2
Avondale St COL BB8 10 C2
Avonwood Cl DWN BB3 58 D1
Aylesbury Wk
BRFD/BLYE BB10 18 D6
Ayr Gv BLY BB11 37 H2
Ayr Rd BBN BB1 42 D4
Ayrton St COL BB8 10 A2
Aysgarth Dr ACC BB5 45 F1
DWN BB3 58 D1
Azalea Rd BBNW BB2 41 F1

B

Back Albert Rd COL BB8 * 9 K3
Back Albert St
PDHM/BLYW BB12 25 F3
Back Altham St
PDHM/BLYW BB12 25 G3
Back Arthur St ACC BB5 34 B2
Back Atkinson St COL BB8 9 J3
Back Bond St COL BB8 9 K2
Back Boundary St COL BB8 * 9 K3
Back Brown St COL BB8 * 9 J3
Back Burnley Rd ACC BB5 * 44 E1
Back Cambridge St COL BB8 9 K3
Back Carr Mill St
RAW/HAS BB4 * 53 K4
Back Chapel St COL BB8 9 K3
Back Church St GTH/LHO BB6 22 D6
NLSN BB9 8 D4
PDHM/BLYW BB12 * 36 A1
RAW/HAS BB4 62 D1
Back Clayton St NLSN BB9 8 D6
Back Commercial St NLSN BB9 18 B3
Back Commons CLI BB7 6 C2
Back Duckworth St DWN BB3 59 F2
Back Duke St COL BB8 9 K3
Back Earl St COL BB8 9 K3
Back East Bank NLSN BB9 * 8 D3
Back Hall St COL BB8 9 K3
Back Harry St NLSN BB9 8 D4
Back Heys ACC BB5 * 44 A4
Back Hill St RAW/HAS BB4 54 E2
Back Hope St BCUP OL13 57 F5
Backhouse St ACC BB5 44 A3
Back La ACC BB5 45 G5
CLI BB7 14 B2
COL BB8 10 D5
PDHM/BLYW BB12 14 C6
PDHM/BLYW BB12 16 C3
RAW/HAS BB4 54 E6
Back Leach St COL BB8 * 9 J3
Back Lee St RAW/HAS BB4 60 E1
Back Lord St RAW/HAS BB4 54 E2
Back Lune St COL BB8 * 10 A3
Back Owen St ACC BB5 34 E6
Back Peter St NLSN BB9 8 D3
Back Queen St GTH/LHO BB6 22 D6
Back Rhoden Rd ACC BB5 43 K5
Back Rings Rw RAW/HAS BB4 46 E5
Back Rushton St BCUP OL13 * 63 K3
Back St John St BCUP OL13 * 57 F6
Back Scotland Rd NLSN BB9 18 D1
Back Shuttleworth St
PDHM/BLYW BB12 25 F3
Back Spencer St RAW/HAS BB4 54 E1
Back Water St ACC BB5 * 44 E1
Back Wellington St ACC BB5 44 E2
Back Willow St
PDHM/BLYW BB12 * 4 D2
Back York St CLI BB7 * 6 D3
RAW/HAS BB4 54 E2
Back Zion St COL BB8 * 9 K3
Bacon St NLSN BB9 18 E1
Bacup Rd BLY BB11 38 C4
RAW/HAS BB4 61 K1
Baden Ter BBNW BB2 41 G6
Badge Brow ACC BB5 44 A2
Bailey St BLY BB11 4 C4
Baker St BBN BB1 42 B3
BCUP OL13 57 F6
BLY BB11 4 D5
NLSN BB9 8 E6
Balaclava St BBN BB1 2 E1
Bala Cl BBN BB1 2 E1
Balderstone Cl
BRFD/BLYE BB10 27 J1
Balderstone La
BRFD/BLYE BB10 27 K2
Baldwin Hl CLI BB7 6 C3
Baldwin Rd CLI BB7 6 C3
Baldwin St BBNW BB2 * 2 B7
BCUP OL13 63 G3
Balfour Cl NLSN BB9 18 D4
Balfour St BBNW BB2 2 A6
GTH/LHO BB6 22 E6
Ballam St BLY BB11 * 5 H7
Ballantrae Rd BBN BB1 42 D4
Ballater St BLY BB11 37 H2
Balle St DWN BB3 59 F3
Ball Grove Dr COL BB8 10 D2
Balliol Cl PDHM/BLYW BB12 25 G5
Ball St NLSN BB9 * 8 D6
Balmoral Av BBN BB1 32 A1
CLI BB7 6 B5
Balmoral Crs BBN BB1 43 F3
Balmoral Rd ACC BB5 35 F6
DWN BB3 59 G5
RAW/HAS BB4 60 D2
Baltic Buildings
RAW/HAS BB4 * 62 D3
Baltic Rd RAW/HAS BB4 62 D3
Bamburgh Dr
PDHM/BLYW BB12 26 D4
Bamford Crs ACC BB5 45 F3
Bamford St BLY BB11 * 5 G2
NLSN BB9 19 G1
Banastre St ACC BB5 34 C4
Banbury Av ACC BB5 43 J3
Banbury Cl BBNW BB2 48 D1
Bancroft Rd BRFD/BLYE BB10 27 H3
Bancroft St BBN BB1 3 H4
Bangor St BBN BB1 31 K6
Bank Bottom DWN BB3 59 F2
Bankcroft Cl
PDHM/BLYW BB12 25 H3
Bankfield BLY BB11 5 G3
Bankfield St BCUP OL13 63 H3
COL BB8 9 H3
COL BB8 10 D3
Bank Fold NLSN BB9 8 E3
Bankhall Ter BRFD/BLYE BB10 27 F4
Bank Hey La North BBN BB1 31 K2
Bank Hey La South BBN BB1 32 A4
Bank House La BCUP OL13 64 A1
Bankhouse Rd NLSN BB9 8 E6
Bankhouse St BLY BB11 5 G2
Bank House St NLSN BB9 8 E3
Bank La BBN BB1 42 D3
Bank Pde BLY BB11 5 G3
Bankside BBNW BB2 41 J5
Bankside Cl BCUP OL13 63 K2
Bankside La BCUP OL13 63 K2
Banks St BRFD/BLYE BB10 19 H6
Bank St ACC BB5 44 A1
ACC BB5 44 E2
BCUP OL13 64 A1
COL BB8 10 E6
DWN BB3 59 F2
NLSN BB9 8 E6
NLSN BB9 18 B3
PDHM/BLYW BB12 25 F2
RAW/HAS BB4 53 K6
RAW/HAS BB4 61 K1
Bank Top BBNW BB2 2 B7
BLY BB11 5 G1
Bannister Cl COL BB8 10 D4
Bannister Ct NLSN BB9 * 18 E2
Barbara Castle Wy BBN BB1 2 E3
Barbon St BRFD/BLYE BB10 27 H1
Barclay Av BLY BB11 37 G1
Barcroft Gn BRFD/BLYE BB10 38 E4
Barcroft St COL BB8 9 J2
Barden Cft ACC BB5 34 B1
Barden La PDHM/BLYW BB12 17 K6
Barden Rd ACC BB5 44 B3
Barden St BRFD/BLYE BB10 27 G3
Bargee Cl BBN BB1 3 G7
Barkerfield Cl
PDHM/BLYW BB12 16 C4
Barkerhouse Rd NLSN BB9 19 F1
Barker La BBNW BB2 31 F3
Barley Bank St DWN BB3 58 E1
Barley Cl BBNW BB2 2 C4
Barleydale Rd NLSN BB9 8 E2
Barley Gv BRFD/BLYE BB10 27 H5
Barley Holme Rd
RAW/HAS BB4 54 E1
Barley La BBNW BB2 2 C4
Barley St PDHM/BLYW BB12 25 F4
Barley Wy BBNW BB2 2 C4
Barlow St ACC BB5 44 C1
RAW/HAS BB4 54 E6
Barmouth Crs BBN BB1 31 H4
Barnard Cl ACC BB5 43 J3
Barnes Av RAW/HAS BB4 61 J1
Barnes Ct BRFD/BLYE BB10 38 D1
Barnes Sq ACC BB5 34 B2
Barnes St ACC BB5 34 B2
ACC BB5 44 E1
BLY BB11 5 G2
RAW/HAS BB4 53 K5
Barnfield Av BRFD/BLYE BB10 28 A5
Barn Field Cl COL BB8 10 C2
Barnfield St ACC BB5 45 F2
Barnfield Wy ACC BB5 24 B6
Barn Gill Cl BBN BB1 41 K4
Barn Meadow Crs BBN BB1 33 J4
Barnmeadow La GTH/LHO BB6 22 D6
Barons Cl DWN BB3 50 A2
Baron St DWN BB3 58 D1
RAW/HAS BB4 62 C2
Barons Wy DWN BB3 50 A3
Barracks Rd BLY BB11 4 B3
Barrett St BRFD/BLYE BB10 27 F3
Barrington Ct ACC BB5 34 B6
Barritt Rd RAW/HAS BB4 61 J1
Barrowford Rd COL BB8 9 G2
PDHM/BLYW BB12 8 B6
PDHM/BLYW BB12 16 B6
Barry St PDHM/BLYW BB12 26 A5
Bar St BRFD/BLYE BB10 27 G3
Bartle St BLY BB11 26 B6
Barton St BBNW BB2 2 E4
Basil St COL BB8 9 K3
Basnett St BRFD/BLYE BB10 27 H2
Bastwell Rd BBN BB1 31 K6
Bates St ACC BB5 34 A2
Bath St ACC BB5 44 D3
BBNW BB2 2 A6
BCUP OL13 64 B1
COL BB8 10 A2
NLSN BB9 19 F1
Bathurst St BBNW BB2 2 D3
Bawdlands CLI BB7 6 C3
Bayard St PDHM/BLYW BB12 * 25 K5
Bayley Fold CLI BB7 6 D3
Bayley St ACC BB5 34 A2
Bay St BBN BB1 32 A6
Baywood St BBN BB1 31 K6
Beachley Sq
PDHM/BLYW BB12 26 D4
Beacon Cl COL BB8 9 J4
Beaconsfield St ACC BB5 45 F2
GTH/LHO BB6 22 C5
RAW/HAS BB4 53 K6
Beale Cl BBN BB1 42 B6
Beale Rd NLSN BB9 18 B1
Beamish Av BBNW BB2 49 H1
Beardsworth St BBN BB1 32 A5
Beardwood BBNW BB2 30 E6
Beardwood Brow BBNW BB2 30 E6
Beardwood Meadow
BBNW BB2 30 E6
Beardwood Pk BBNW BB2 31 F6
Bear St PDHM/BLYW BB12 25 H5
Beatie St NLSN BB9 * 18 B3
Beatrice Av PDHM/BLYW BB12 26 B4
Beatrice Pl BBNW BB2 50 A1
Beaufort Cl PDHM/BLYW BB12 24 B1
Beaufort Rd BCUP OL13 57 G2
Beaufort St NLSN BB9 18 D2
Beauley Av PDHM/BLYW BB12 24 B1
Beaumaris Av BBNW BB2 40 E6
Beaumont Wy DWN BB3 59 J3
Beaver Cl BBN BB1 20 E6
Beaver Ter BCUP OL13 57 G6
Beckenham Ct
BRFD/BLYE BB10 18 D6
Beckside COL BB8 10 D4
Beddington St NLSN BB9 * 8 D6
Bedford Cl ACC BB5 43 J3
Bedford Ms DWN BB3 49 K5
Bedford Pl PDHM/BLYW BB12 25 G4
Bedfordshire Av
PDHM/BLYW BB12 26 A4
Bedford St BBNW BB2 41 G5
DWN BB3 49 K5
NLSN BB9 8 C6
Bedford Ter RAW/HAS BB4 60 D3
Beech Av DWN BB3 59 G1
Beech Cl ACC BB5 43 J5
BBN BB1 20 D5
BBN BB1 33 H5
BCUP OL13 57 G6
CLI BB7 6 C3
Beech Crs ACC BB5 34 C4
Beech Dr CLI BB7 13 G2
RAW/HAS BB4 61 F1
Beech Gv ACC BB5 44 C3
BRFD/BLYE BB10 18 C5
DWN BB3 49 H3
Beech Mt BBN BB1 31 K2
Beech St ACC BB5 * 34 B4
ACC BB5 44 E2
BBN BB1 32 A6
BCUP OL13 57 G6
CLI BB7 6 C3
GTH/LHO BB6 22 D5
NLSN BB9 8 E6
PDHM/BLYW BB12 25 G4
RAW/HAS BB4 54 D6
Beech Tree Cl NLSN BB9 18 E2
Beechwood Av ACC BB5 45 F4
BLY BB11 37 J2
CLI BB7 6 D5
Beechwood Dr BBNW BB2 48 C1
Beechwood Ms BBNW BB2 50 A1
Beechwood Rd BBN BB1 32 A6
Beetham Ct ACC BB5 34 A2
Begonia St DWN BB3 59 G2
Begonia Vw DWN BB3 50 A2
Belfield Rd ACC BB5 44 D2
Belford St PDHM/BLYW BB12 26 E4
Belfry Man GTH/LHO BB6 * 12 C3
The Belfry DWN BB3 * 59 H3

Belgarth Rd ACC BB5 34 E6
Belgrave Rd COL BB8 9 K1
DWN BB3 58 E3
Belgrave Sq DWN BB3 * 59 F2
Belgrave St ACC BB5 53 J1
NLSN BB9 18 A3
NLSN BB9 19 F1
PDHM/BLYW BB12 26 E4
Belle Vue Pl BLY BB11 * 4 D3
Belle Vue St BBNW BB2 2 A4
BLY BB11 * 4 D3
Bell La ACC BB5 34 D1
Bell's Ar BRFD/BLYE BB10 27 F3
Bell St RAW/HAS BB4 53 K6
Belmont Gv BRFD/BLYE BB10 27 J6
Belmont Rd GTH/LHO BB6 22 C6
Belper St BBN BB1 3 J1
Belthorn Rd BBN BB1 50 E2
Belvedere Av RAW/HAS BB4 63 F2
Belvedere Rd BBN BB1 32 A2
BRFD/BLYE BB10 5 J3
Bence St COL BB8 10 A2
Bennett St NLSN BB9 9 F5
Bennington St BBN BB1 41 K4
Benson St BBN BB1 32 B6
Bent Gap La BBNW BB2 2 A5
Bentham Av BRFD/BLYE BB10 18 B6
Bentham Cl BBNW BB2 41 F6
Bentham Rd BBNW BB2 41 F6
Bent La COL BB8 10 D1
Bentley St BBN BB1 42 C2
BCUP OL13 57 G6
DWN BB3 59 G4
NLSN BB9 18 D2
Bentley Wood Wy BLY BB11 36 D1
Bents COL BB8 * 10 D1
Bent St ACC BB5 43 K4
BBNW BB2 2 D5
RAW/HAS BB4 61 G3
Bentwood Rd RAW/HAS BB4 53 J6
Beresford Rd BBN BB1 31 H6
Beresford St BLY BB11 4 A4
Bergen St BLY BB11 26 A6
Berkeley Cl NLSN BB9 * 18 E2
Berkeley Crs
PDHM/BLYW BB12 25 F2
Berkeley Dr PDHM/BLYW BB12 24 A1
Berkeley St NLSN BB9 18 A4
NLSN BB9 18 E3
Berkshire Av
PDHM/BLYW BB12 26 A4
Berkshire Cl BBN BB1 20 E5
Berridge Av PDHM/BLYW BB12 25 K5
Berriedale Rd NLSN BB9 9 G6
Berrys La CLI BB7 22 D1
Berry St BLY BB11 5 F7
NLSN BB9 * 18 B4
Bertha St ACC BB5 45 F1
Berwick Dr PDHM/BLYW BB12 26 D4
Beryl Av BBN BB1 31 K3
Besant Cl BBN BB1 42 B6
Bethel Rd BBN BB1 32 A6
Bethesda Cl BBNW BB2 41 H4
Bethesda St BLY BB11 5 F3
Bevan Pl NLSN BB9 9 F5
Beverley Dr CLI BB7 6 C5
Beverley St BBNW BB2 41 F6
BLY BB11 4 C5
Bevington Cl BLY BB11 4 D4
Bicknell St BBN BB1 2 E2
Billinge Av BBNW BB2 40 E2
Billinge Cl BBNW BB2 41 F2
Billinge St BBN BB1 3 K5
Billington Av RAW/HAS BB4 54 E4
Billington Gdns CLI BB7 13 G5
Billington Rd BLY BB11 36 E2
Binns St RAW/HAS BB4 54 E2
Birch Av RAW/HAS BB4 54 A6
Birchbank Gdns BBN BB1 32 A6
Birch Cl ACC BB5 35 G3
Birch Crs ACC BB5 44 B4
Birchenlee La COL BB8 9 K4
Birch Gv CLI BB7 13 K1
Birch Hall Av DWN BB3 49 J5
Birch St ACC BB5 * 44 D1
BCUP OL13 57 F6
Birch Wk BBN BB1 42 B3
Bird St NLSN BB9 18 B4
Birkbeck Wy BRFD/BLYE BB10 27 F2
Birkett Rd ACC BB5 34 E6
Birley Pl BRFD/BLYE BB10 27 F3
Birley St BBN BB1 3 H3
Birtwhistle Cl NLSN BB9 * 18 B4
Birtwistle Av COL BB8 9 J1
Birtwistle Cl COL BB8 10 A2
Birtwistle Hyde Pk COL BB8 * 9 K2
Birtwistle St ACC BB5 44 E2
GTH/LHO BB6 22 C6
Bisham Cl DWN BB3 59 H3
Bishopdale Cl BBNW BB2 48 B2
Bishopstone Cl BBNW BB2 50 A1
Bishop St ACC BB5 * 44 E2
BRFD/BLYE BB10 27 G2
NLSN BB9 18 D1
Bispham Rd NLSN BB9 18 E3
Bivel St PDHM/BLYW BB12 4 B2
Black Abbey St ACC BB5 44 E2
Blackamoor Rd BBN BB1 50 C1
Blackburn Old Rd BBN BB1 32 C3
GTH/LHO BB6 21 K6
Blackburn Rd ACC BB5 33 K4
ACC BB5 43 F2
ACC BB5 44 C1
ACC BB5 45 G5
ACC BB5 53 H1
BBN BB1 32 E6
DWN BB3 49 J5
GTH/LHO BB6 33 J1
PDHM/BLYW BB12 24 D4
RAW/HAS BB4 61 G5
Blackburn St BBN BB1 3 F1
BLY BB11 5 F2
Blacker St BRFD/BLYE BB10 27 F1
Black House La
BRFD/BLYE BB10 19 K6
Blacklane Cft CLI BB7 6 D2
Blacko Bar Rd NLSN BB9 8 B1
Blackpool St ACC BB5 44 A2
DWN BB3 59 G5
Blacksnape Rd DWN BB3 59 H1
Blackthorn Crs BCUP OL13 57 F6
Blackwood Rd BCUP OL13 63 G4
Blake St ACC BB5 44 D1
Blakewater Rd BBN BB1 32 C6
Blakey Moor BBNW BB2 2 E4
Blakey St BLY BB11 5 J3
Blannel St BLY BB11 4 C3
Blea Cl PDHM/BLYW BB12 26 B3
Bleasdale Av CLI BB7 6 B4
Blenheim Cl BBN BB1 31 J4
Blenheim St COL BB8 10 C2
Blind La PDHM/BLYW BB12 16 E3
Blossom Av ACC BB5 44 A2
Blucher St COL BB8 10 A3
Bluebell Av RAW/HAS BB4 60 D3
Bluebell Gv BLY BB11 25 K6
Board St BRFD/BLYE BB10 27 F2
Boarsgreave La RAW/HAS BB4 62 E5
Bobbin Cl ACC BB5 * 44 C2
Bocholt Wy RAW/HAS BB4 61 K1
Bog Height Rd DWN BB3 49 G3
Boland St BBN BB1 32 A6
Bold St ACC BB5 45 F1
BBN BB1 2 E2
BCUP OL13 64 A2
COL BB8 10 A3
Bold Venture Wy ACC BB5 34 C3
Bolland Prospect CLI BB7 6 E3
Bolton Av ACC BB5 35 G5
Bolton Gv NLSN BB9 8 D4
Bolton Rd BBNW BB2 41 H6
DWN BB3 59 G6
Bolton's Ct BBN BB1 * 2 E3
Bolton St COL BB8 9 H3
RAW/HAS BB4 62 D2
Bombay St BBNW BB2 41 G4
Bonchurch St BBN BB1 * 42 C3
Bond St BRFD/BLYE BB10 27 F3
COL BB8 9 K2
DWN BB3 50 A6
NLSN BB9 * 18 D2
Bonfire Hill Cl RAW/HAS BB4 54 E2
Bonfire Hill Rd RAW/HAS BB4 54 E2
Bonsall St BBNW BB2 41 F5
Booth Ct BRFD/BLYE BB10 27 F3
Booth Crs RAW/HAS BB4 62 E2
Boothman Pl NLSN BB9 8 E5
Boothman St BBNW BB2 * 41 H5
Booth Rd RAW/HAS BB4 62 E2
Booth St ACC BB5 44 E2
BCUP OL13 64 B1
NLSN BB9 18 D1
RAW/HAS BB4 53 J5
RAW/HAS BB4 62 D3
Boot Wy BLY BB11 5 G4
Borough Rd DWN BB3 58 E3
Borrowdale Av BBN BB1 42 C4
Borrowdale Cl ACC BB5 35 F4
BRFD/BLYE BB10 18 C6
Borrowdale Dr
BRFD/BLYE BB10 18 C5
Bosburn Dr BBNW BB2 30 A3
Bosley Cl DWN BB3 59 J3
Boston Rd BCUP OL13 57 F6
Bostons GTH/LHO BB6 22 C6
Boston St NLSN BB9 19 F3
Bott House La NLSN BB9 9 G5
Bottomgate BBN BB1 3 K4
Bottomley Bank La
RAW/HAS BB4 55 F1
Bottomley St NLSN BB9 18 E1
Bottomley Yd NLSN BB9 * 18 E1
Boulder St RAW/HAS BB4 54 E2
Bouldsworth Rd
BRFD/BLYE BB10 27 K6
Boulsworth Crs NLSN BB9 9 H6
Boulsworth Dr COL BB8 10 E6
Boulsworth Gv COL BB8 10 C2
Boulview Ter COL BB8 10 C2
Boundary Rd ACC BB5 34 E6
Boundary St BRFD/BLYE BB10 27 H1
COL BB8 9 K3
Bowden Av BBNW BB2 40 A6
Bowen St BBNW BB2 41 F5
Bower Cl BBNW BB2 41 F5
Bower St BBNW BB2 41 F5
Bowland Av BRFD/BLYE BB10 27 K6
Bowland Ct CLI BB7 6 D3
Bowland Vw NLSN BB9 18 D5
Bowling Green Cl DWN BB3 59 G4
Bowman Ct BBN BB1 3 H2
Bowness Av NLSN BB9 18 E3
Bowness Cl BBN BB1 3 J2
Bowness Rd
PDHM/BLYW BB12 25 F1
Boxwood Dr BBNW BB2 48 D1
Boxwood St BBN BB1 31 K5
Boyle St BBN BB1 3 G2
Bracewell Cl NLSN BB9 * 18 E1
Bracewell St BRFD/BLYE BB10 27 G2
NLSN BB9 19 F1
Bracken Cl BBNW BB2 48 D1
Bracken Gv RAW/HAS BB4 60 D3
Bracken Hey CLI BB7 7 F3
Bradda Rd BBNW BB2 41 J6
Bradford St ACC BB5 45 F1
Bradley Fold NLSN BB9 * 8 E6
Bradley Gdns
PDHM/BLYW BB12 26 A6
Bradley Hall Rd NLSN BB9 9 F6
Bradley Rd NLSN BB9 8 E6
Bradley Rd East NLSN BB9 8 E6
Bradley St COL BB8 10 B2
Bradley Vw NLSN BB9 * 8 E6
Bradshaw Cl BBN BB1 31 J5
NLSN BB9 18 E2
Bradshaw Rw ACC BB5 44 B1
Bradshaw St ACC BB5 * 44 B1
NLSN BB9 18 D2
Bradshaw St East ACC BB5 * 44 E1
Bradshaw St West ACC BB5 * 44 B1
Bradyll Ct GTH/LHO BB6 12 C3
Braeside BBNW BB2 2 A1
The Brambles BBNW BB2 30 E5
Bramble St BRFD/BLYE BB10 27 F2
Bramley Av PDHM/BLYW BB12 26 B3
Bramley Cl ACC BB5 44 B2
Bramley St ACC BB5 44 D1
Branch Rd BLY BB11 5 H6
DWN BB3 49 J2
Branch St BCUP OL13 63 J3
NLSN BB9 18 E1
Brandwood RAW/HAS BB4 * 62 D2
Brandwood Gv
BRFD/BLYE BB10 27 H5
Brandwood Pk BCUP OL13 63 F3
Brandwood Rd BCUP OL13 63 G3
Brandwood St DWN BB3 59 G2
Brandy House Brow
BBNW BB2 41 K5
Brantfell Dr PDHM/BLYW BB12 26 A3
Brantfell Rd BBN BB1 31 H6
GTH/LHO BB6 22 D5
Brantwood ACC BB5 34 A3
Brantwood Av BBN BB1 42 E2
Brassey St PDHM/BLYW BB12 26 B4
Bread St PDHM/BLYW BB12 * 4 A2
Brearley St BCUP OL13 63 J3
Brecon Av ACC BB5 43 J3
Brecon Rd BBN BB1 42 C2
Brennand St BRFD/BLYE BB10 27 G2
CLI BB7 6 D2
Brent St BRFD/BLYE BB10 18 C6
Brentwood Av BLY BB11 37 J2
Brentwood Rd NLSN BB9 9 G6
Brett Cl CLI BB7 7 F4
Brewery St BBNW BB2 2 C4
Briarcroft DWN BB3 50 A3
Briar Hill Cl BBN BB1 3 J5
Briar Rd BBN BB1 31 K5
Briar St BCUP OL13 64 B2
Bridge Cft ACC BB5 34 B1
Bridge End Cl RAW/HAS BB4 60 D4
Bridgefield St
PDHM/BLYW BB12 36 A1
Bridgemill Rd BBN BB1 3 G5
Bridge Mill Rd NLSN BB9 18 C1
Bridge St ACC BB5 44 A1
ACC BB5 44 E1
BBN BB1 3 F5
BBN BB1 33 H3
BLY BB11 * 5 G3
COL BB8 9 J3
GTH/LHO BB6 22 D6
NLSN BB9 18 B3
PDHM/BLYW BB12 24 E3
RAW/HAS BB4 56 A1
RAW/HAS BB4 62 E2
Bridgewater Cl BLY BB11 36 D1
Bridleway RAW/HAS BB4 62 E1
Brief St BRFD/BLYE BB10 27 F3
Briercliffe Av COL BB8 9 H5
Briercliffe Rd BRFD/BLYE BB10 27 G3
Briercliffe St COL BB8 9 H4
Brier Crs NLSN BB9 18 D3
Brier Heights Cl NLSN BB9 18 D4
Brigg Fld ACC BB5 34 B1
Brighton Rd BRFD/BLYE BB10 18 C6
Brighton Ter BBNW BB2 41 F1
DWN BB3 58 D1
Bright St ACC BB5 43 K4
BBN BB1 42 B1
BRFD/BLYE BB10 27 F2
CLI BB7 6 E3
COL BB8 9 K2
COL BB8 10 D2
DWN BB3 58 E1
RAW/HAS BB4 54 E6
Bright Ter COL BB8 10 D5
Brigsteer Cl ACC BB5 34 A3
Brindle St BBNW BB2 41 F6
Brindley Cl BLY BB11 36 D1
Brisbane St ACC BB5 34 C4
Bristol Cl BBN BB1 3 J5
Bristol St BLY BB11 4 B7
COL BB8 10 A2
Britannia Av BCUP OL13 64 B1
Britannia St GTH/LHO BB6 22 D6
Britannia Wk BLY BB11 5 J6
Britannia Wy RAW/HAS BB4 60 D3
Britten Cl BBNW BB2 42 A5
Britten St DWN BB3 58 E1
Britwell Cl BBNW BB2 50 A1
Broadfield ACC BB5 44 C6
Broadfield Rd ACC BB5 44 C4
Broadfield St ACC BB5 44 B4
Broadfold Av BBN BB1 32 A6
Broad Ga DWN BB3 59 G1
Broadhurst Wy
BRFD/BLYE BB10 18 C5
Broad Ing Cl
BRFD/BLYE BB10 38 E4
Broad La CLI BB7 13 H4
Broadley St RAW/HAS BB4 54 E6
Broadness Dr NLSN BB9 18 E3
Broad Oak Rd ACC BB5 44 E2
Broad St NLSN BB9 18 D1
Broadtree Cl BBNW BB2 30 A2
Broadway ACC BB5 44 E1
BBN BB1 31 J3
NLSN BB9 18 D1
RAW/HAS BB4 60 E3
Broadway Crs RAW/HAS BB4 60 D3
Broadway Pl NLSN BB9 8 D4
NLSN BB9 9 G6
Broadway St BBNW BB2 41 F6
Brock Clough Rd
RAW/HAS BB4 55 K5
Brockenhurst St
BRFD/BLYE BB10 27 H6
Brocklehurst Av ACC BB5 44 D4
Brodick Rd BBN BB1 42 D4
Broken Banks COL BB8 10 A3
Broken Stone Rd BBNW BB2 48 D3
Bromley St BBNW BB2 2 A3
Bromsgrove Rd
BRFD/BLYE BB10 27 G3
Bronte Av BRFD/BLYE BB10 27 J5
Bronte Wy BRFD/BLYE BB10 28 E3
COL BB8 11 H3
PDHM/BLYW BB12 25 J3
Brooden Dr BRFD/BLYE BB10 18 C5
Brooke Cl ACC BB5 45 G5
Brookes St BCUP OL13 63 J3
Brookfield BBNW BB2 30 C3
Brookfield St BBN BB1 3 F1
Brookford Cl
PDHM/BLYW BB12 26 C3
Brookhouse Cl BBN BB1 3 G1
Brookhouse Gdns BBN BB1 * 3 G1
Brookhouse La BBN BB1 3 G2
Brookland Cl ACC BB5 34 A1
Brooklands Av BLY BB11 38 B2
RAW/HAS BB4 60 E4
Brooklands Rd BLY BB11 38 B2
Brooklands Ter BBN BB1 * 32 A6
Brookland St RAW/HAS BB4 62 C2
Brooklyn Rd BBN BB1 20 D6
Brookside GTH/LHO BB6 12 C4
Brookside Cl CLI BB7 13 J4
Brookside La ACC BB5 43 F4
Brookside St ACC BB5 43 J4
Brookside Vw ACC BB5 43 H3
Brook St ACC BB5 44 A4
BBN BB1 33 H4
BBNW BB2 41 F5
CLI BB7 6 E2
COL BB8 9 K2
NLSN BB9 18 E1
RAW/HAS BB4 53 K4
Brookway BBNW BB2 49 F1
Broomfield Pl BBNW BB2 41 F4
Brothers St BBNW BB2 40 E6
Brotherston Dr BBNW BB2 49 G1
Brotherton Mdw CLI BB7 6 E3
Brougham St
PDHM/BLYW BB12 26 E4
Broughton Cl BBNW BB2 42 A6
Broughton St DWN BB3 58 E1
PDHM/BLYW BB12 4 A2
Broughtons Yd ACC BB5 * 44 E1
Brow Ct RAW/HAS BB4 53 K5
Brow Edge RAW/HAS BB4 62 C2
Browhead Rd
BRFD/BLYE BB10 27 G3
Brown Birks Rd ACC BB5 35 G5
Brownhill Av BRFD/BLYE BB10 27 H5
Brownhill Dr BBN BB1 31 K3
Brownhill Rd BBN BB1 31 K2
Browning Av ACC BB5 43 J2
Browning Cl COL BB8 9 K1
Brownlow St BBN BB1 42 D3
CLI BB7 6 D4
Brownside Rd
BRFD/BLYE BB10 27 K6
Brown Sq BLY BB11 5 H2
Brown St ACC BB5 44 D2
BBN BB1 3 F3
BCUP OL13 57 F5
BLY BB11 5 F2
CLI BB7 6 C4
Brown St East COL BB8 9 K2
Brown St West COL BB8 * 9 J3
Browsholme Av
BRFD/BLYE BB10 27 H5
Brow Vw BRFD/BLYE BB10 * 27 G3
Bruce St BBN BB1 42 B1
BLY BB11 4 A4
Brundhurst Fold BBNW BB2 30 B3
Brunel Dr BBN BB1 3 H5
Brunel St PDHM/BLYW BB12 26 B4
Brunel Wk BBN BB1 3 H5
Brungerley Av CLI BB7 6 D2
Brungerley Br CLI BB7 6 C1
Brunshaw Av BRFD/BLYE BB10 27 J6
Brunshaw Rd
BRFD/BLYE BB10 27 H6
Brun St BLY BB11 5 F2
Brunswick Dr COL BB8 9 G4
Brunswick St BBNW BB2 2 C6
BLY BB11 5 H6
DWN BB3 59 G3
NLSN BB9 18 E2
Brunswick Ter ACC BB5 44 D1
BCUP OL13 63 J3
Brush St BLY BB11 26 B6
Brussels Rd DWN BB3 59 H2
Bryan St BBNW BB2 41 J5
Bryer's Cft BBN BB1 20 E5
Buccleuch Av CLI BB7 6 C3
Buccleuch Cl CLI BB7 6 C3
Buccleuch St BLY BB11 4 C4
Buckden Ga NLSN BB9 * 8 C4
Buckden Rd ACC BB5 44 B3
Buckingham Cl RAW/HAS BB4 60 D2
Buckingham Dr
PDHM/BLYW BB12 24 A1
Buckingham Gv ACC BB5 34 C6
Buck St BLY BB11 4 B4
COL BB8 10 A2
Buff St DWN BB3 58 E3
Bulcock St BRFD/BLYE BB10 27 G2
Buller St RAW/HAS BB4 61 K1
Bullough Cl ACC BB5 44 C2
Bull St BLY BB11 5 G3
Buncer La BBNW BB2 40 E3
Bunkers Hill Cl BBNW BB2 49 F1
Burdett St BLY BB11 4 A4
Burford Cl BBNW BB2 48 C1
Burgess St BBN BB1 42 C2
Burleigh St PDHM/BLYW BB12 26 E3
Burlington St BBNW BB2 2 A3
NLSN BB9 18 C2
Burnham Cl BLY BB11 4 C4
Burnham Ga BLY BB11 4 C4
Burnley Cl BBN BB1 42 B2
Burnley La ACC BB5 35 H3
Burnley Rd ACC BB5 24 B5
ACC BB5 34 D2
ACC BB5 35 F5
ACC BB5 * 44 E
BBN BB1 42 C
BLY BB11 38 D
BRFD/BLYE BB10 18 E
BRFD/BLYE BB10 19 F
COL BB8 9 C
PDHM/BLYW BB12 25 H
RAMS BL0 61 C
Burnley Rd East RAW/HAS BB4 55 K
Burnley St BBN BB1 42 D
Burnley Wy BLY BB11 35 K
BLY BB11 36 E
BRFD/BLYE BB10 27 C
BRFD/BLYE BB10 28 E
BRFD/BLYE BB10 39 K
PDHM/BLYW BB12 25 H
Burnsall Cl BRFD/BLYE BB10 18 E
Burnsall Pl NLSN BB9 8 C
Burnsall Rd ACC BB5 44 E
Burns Av ACC BB5 43
Burns Dr ACC BB5 45 C
Burns St NLSN BB9 8 D
PDHM/BLYW BB12 25 C
PDHM/BLYW BB12 26 E
PDHM/BLYW BB12 * 36 A
Burns Wk DWN BB3 59 H
Burns Wy GTH/LHO BB6 33 H
Burrell Av COL BB8 9 K
Burton Gdns NLSN BB9 18 E
Burton St BBN BB1 33
BLY BB11 5
Burwen Cl BLY BB11 37 H
Bury Fold La DWN BB3 59 F
Bury Rd RAW/HAS BB4 53 K
RAW/HAS BB4 61 C
Bury St ACC BB5 43 K
DWN BB3 59 F
Bushburn Dr GTH/LHO BB6 21 H
Bush St BRFD/BLYE BB10 27 F
Bute Rd BBN BB1 42 D
Bute St BLY BB11 37 H
Butler St BBN BB1 33
BRFD/BLYE BB10 * 27 F
Buttercross Cl BLY BB11 37 H
Buttermere Av ACC BB5 43 K
COL BB8 10 E
Buttermere Cl BBN BB1 3 H
Buttermere Rd
BRFD/BLYE BB10 27 K
Butts GTH/LHO BB6 22 C
Butts Gv CLI BB7 6 D
Butts Mt GTH/LHO BB6 22 D
Buxton St ACC BB5 44 C
Byland Cl PDHM/BLYW BB12 24 A
Byrom St BBNW BB2 2 D
Byron Cl ACC BB5 43
ACC BB5 45 C
Byron Rd COL BB8 10 C
Byron Sq GTH/LHO BB6 * 33 H
Byron St PDHM/BLYW BB12 25

C

Cadogan St NLSN BB9 8 D
Cadshaw Cl BBN BB1 31
Caernarvon Av
PDHM/BLYW BB12 25 K
Caernarvon Rd RAW/HAS BB4 60 D
Cairns Cl NLSN BB9 8 C
Cairo St PDHM/BLYW BB12 4 E
Calcott St BLY BB11 37
Caldbeck Cl NLSN BB9 18 E
Calder Av DWN BB3 49 H
Calder Bank BBN BB1 31
Calder Banks BBN BB1 31
Calderbrook Av BLY BB11 37
Calderbrook Pl BLY BB11 37
Calder Cl NLSN BB9 8 D
Calder Ct ACC BB5 24 E
Calder Pl GTH/LHO BB6 23 F
Calder Rd RAW/HAS BB4 54 E
Calderstones Dr CLI BB7 13 C
Calder St BBN BB1 31 K
BLY BB11 5 F
COL BB8 9
NLSN BB9 8 D
PDHM/BLYW BB12 25 F
Calder V CLI BB7 13
NLSN BB9 8 D
Calder Vale Rd BLY BB11 4 E
Caleb St NLSN BB9 8 E
Calf Hey ACC BB5 34 E
Calgary Av BBNW BB2 31 F
Calico Cl ACC BB5 43 H
Calico St BBNW BB2 41 H
Caltha Dr DWN BB3 50 A
Calva Cl PDHM/BLYW BB12 26 A
Cambrian Cl BBN BB1 31 K
Cambrian Wy RAW/HAS BB4 60 E
Cambridge Cl BBN BB1 3 H
PDHM/BLYW BB12 25 C
Cambridge Dr BBN BB1 42 E
PDHM/BLYW BB12 25 C
Cambridge St ACC BB5 * 34 E
BBN BB1 3 H
BLY BB11 * 4 A
COL BB8 * 9 K
DWN BB3 59 H
GTH/LHO BB6 22 E
NLSN BB9 * 18 E
NLSN BB9 * 18 D
Camden St NLSN BB9 * 8 D
NLSN BB9 18 D
Cameron St BRFD/BLYE BB10 27 F
Camms Vw RAW/HAS BB4 60
Campbell St BBN BB1 31
PDHM/BLYW BB12 24 A
Campion Dr RAW/HAS BB4 60 D
Camp St BRFD/BLYE BB10 18 E
Canalside BBN BB1 3 H
Canal Side NLSN BB9 8 D
Canal St ACC BB5 34 E

ACC BB5 ....44 A1
BBNW BB2 ....41 F6
BLY BB11 ....4 E4
ındlemakers Ct CLI BB7 ....6 D3
nning St PDHM/BLYW BB12 ....5 F1
PDHM/BLYW BB12 * 25 C4
nnon St ACC BB5 ....44 D2
NLSN BB9 ....9 F6
ınterbury St BBNW BB2 ....2 D6
pe St RAW/HAS BB4 ....61 K1
ptain St BCUP OL13 ....57 G2
rdigan Av ACC BB5 ....43 J3
CLI BB7 ....6 D3
PDHM/BLYW BB12 ....25 K4
rdigan Cl CLI BB7 ....6 C3
rdinal St BRFD/BLYE BB10 ....27 G2
rdwell Pl BBNW BB2 ....2 E4
rdwell St PDHM/BLYW BB12 ....25 H4
rham Rd BBN BB1 ....31 J5
rholme Av BRFD/BLYE BB10 ....27 H5
rleton Av PDHM/BLYW BB12 ....24 B1
rleton Rd COL BB8 ....9 G4
rleton St NLSN BB9 ....18 E2
rley St DWN BB3 ....58 D1
rlinghurst Rd BBNW BB2 ....2 C5
rlisle Rd ACC BB5 * 35 F5
rlisle St BBN BB1 ....3 G6
rlton Gdns BBN BB1 ....2 E1
rlton Pl CLI BB7 ....6 D4
rlton Rd BBN BB1 ....2 D1
BLY BB11 ....4 D5
rlton St BCUP OL13 ....57 G6
NLSN BB9 ....18 B4
rluke St BBN BB1 ....42 C2
rnarvon Rd BBNW BB2 ....41 F3
rnforth Cl BBNW BB2 ....42 A6
rradice Cl NLSN BB9 ....18 D2
rr Hall Dr NLSN BB9 ....8 B6
rr Hall Gdns NLSN BB9 ....8 B6
rr Hall Rd NLSN BB9 ....8 B5
rr Hall St RAW/HAS BB4 ....53 J4
rrier's Rw COL BB8 ....11 G1
rr La BBNW BB2 ....40 D1
RAW/HAS BB4 ....61 K2
RAW/HAS BB4 ....62 D4
rr Rd BLY BB11 ....37 J2
COL BB8 ....10 A1
DWN BB3 ....59 G3
NLSN BB9 ....8 C6
RAW/HAS BB4 ....56 B1
RAW/HAS BB4 ....61 J2
rr St BBN BB1 ....3 F2
rrs Wd BBNW BB2 ....40 D1
rrwood Gn
PDHM/BLYW BB12 ....25 F3
rry La COL BB8 ....10 A2
rter Av BLY BB11 ....36 A1
rter Fold BBNW BB2 ....30 C3
rter Pl NLSN BB9 * 19 F1
rter St ACC BB5 ....44 D3
PDHM/BLYW BB12 ....26 B4
rtmel Av ACC BB5 ....44 C4
rtmel Dr PDHM/BLYW BB12 ....26 A3
rtmel Rd BBNW BB2 ....40 E4
rus Av DWN BB3 ....59 K3
sserley Rd COL BB8 ....10 B1
stercliffe Rd NLSN BB9 ....19 H1
sterton Av BRFD/BLYE BB10 ....18 B6
stle Cl COL BB8 ....10 A1
stlerigg Dr
PDHM/BLYW BB12 ....26 A3
stle Rd COL BB8 ....10 A1
stle St BBN BB1 ....42 B2
CLI BB7 ....6 D3
NLSN BB9 * 18 B3
NLSN BB9 ....19 F1
PDHM/BLYW BB12 ....26 E4
PDHM/BLYW BB12 ....36 A1
stletown Dr BCUP OL13 ....64 C3
stle Vw CLI BB7 ....6 D3
thedral Cl BBN BB1 ....3 F5
tlow Hall St ACC BB5 ....44 A4
tterall St BBNW BB2 ....49 G1
ttle St GTH/LHO BB6 ....22 D6
useway GTH/LHO BB6 ....22 C6
useway Cft CLI BB7 ....6 E4
useway End RAW/HAS BB4 * 60 D4
useway Head RAW/HAS BB4 ....60 D3
usey Foot NLSN BB9 ....18 D2
valry Wy PDHM/BLYW BB12 ....4 A3
vell Cl BBN BB1 ....42 B6
vendish Pl BBNW BB2 ....41 F4
vendish St DWN BB3 ....49 K6
ve St BBNW BB2 ....41 F6
vour St PDHM/BLYW BB12 ....4 E1
cilia Rd BBNW BB2 ....40 D5
cil St ACC BB5 ....44 A3
BBN BB1 ....33 J4
dar Av RAW/HAS BB4 ....54 A6
RAW/HAS BB4 ....61 H1
dar Cl BBN BB1 ....33 H5
dar St ACC BB5 ....45 F1
BBN BB1 ....31 K6
BLY BB11 ....5 J4
lia St BRFD/BLYE BB10 ....27 H6
emetery La BLY BB11 ....36 E1
ntenary Wy BLY BB11 ....5 G5
ntral Av ACC BB5 ....43 J3
CLI BB7 ....6 C4
ntral Vw BCUP OL13 ....64 B1
nturian Wy BBN BB1 ....50 B3
nturion Cl BBN BB1 ....50 B2
nturion Ct BBN BB1 ....50 B3
ad St NLSN BB9 * 9 G5
adwick St BBNW BB2 ....41 H5
allenge Wy BBN BB1 ....32 C6
ancel Pl DWN BB3 ....59 H2
ancel Wy DWN BB3 ....59 H3
ange Cl BCUP OL13 ....57 H5
anters Wy DWN BB3 ....50 A4
apel Cl CLI BB7 ....6 A3
apel Fold CLI BB7 ....14 B2
COL BB8 * 9 K3
apel Hill La RAW/HAS BB4 ....55 F5
apel House Rd NLSN BB9 ....18 D3
Chapel La GTH/LHO BB6 ....21 G1
Chapel Ri CLI BB7 ....13 H5
Chapels DWN BB3 ....50 A6
Chapels Brow DWN BB3 ....50 A6
Chapels La DWN BB3 ....48 D6
Chapel St ACC BB5 ....34 A2
ACC BB5 ....44 A3
ACC BB5 ....44 E2
BBN BB1 ....33 J4
BBN BB1 ....51 F3
BBNW BB2 ....2 D6
BCUP OL13 ....63 H3
BLY BB11 ....5 H3
BRFD/BLYE BB10 ....28 B6
COL BB8 ....9 K3
DWN BB3 ....59 F3
NLSN BB9 ....18 B3
NLSN BB9 ....18 E1
PDHM/BLYW BB12 ....16 D4
RAW/HAS BB4 ....53 K6
RAW/HAS BB4 ....54 E1
RAW/HAS BB4 ....62 D2
Chapel Vls BCUP OL13 * 57 H5
Chapel Wk PDHM/BLYW BB12 ....25 F2
Chapter Rd DWN BB3 ....59 H3
Charles La RAW/HAS BB4 ....60 D1
Charles St ACC BB5 ....34 A2
ACC BB5 ....44 A4
BBNW BB2 ....41 H5
COL BB8 ....10 A2
DWN BB3 ....58 E1
GTH/LHO BB6 ....33 J1
NLSN BB9 ....8 E6
RAW/HAS BB4 ....62 E1
Charlotte St BBN BB1 ....2 E1
BLY BB11 * 4 E4
Charnley St BBNW BB2 ....41 G5
Charnwood Cl BBNW BB2 ....30 E5
Charter Brook GTH/LHO BB6 * 22 E6
Charterhouse Pl BBNW BB2 ....41 F4
Charter St ACC BB5 ....44 B2
The Chase PDHM/BLYW BB12 ....26 C3
Chatburn Av BRFD/BLYE BB10 ....27 J6
CLI BB7 ....6 E2
Chatburn Cl GTH/LHO BB6 ....23 F6
RAW/HAS BB4 ....54 E5
Chatburn Park Dr CLI BB7 ....6 E1
NLSN BB9 ....18 A3
Chatburn Rd CLI BB7 ....6 E2
Chatburn St BBNW BB2 ....2 A4
Chatham Crs COL BB8 ....10 A1
Chatham St COL BB8 ....10 A1
NLSN BB9 ....8 D6
Chatsworth Cl NLSN BB9 ....8 B6
Chatterton Dr ACC BB5 ....45 G5
Chaucer Gdns GTH/LHO BB6 ....33 H1
Cheetham St BBNW BB2 ....2 A4
Chelburn Gv BRFD/BLYE BB10 ....27 H5
Chelston Dr RAW/HAS BB4 ....60 D4
Cheltenham Av ACC BB5 ....34 E6
Cheltenham Rd BBNW BB2 ....2 A3
Chequers ACC BB5 ....34 B3
Cherry Cl BBN BB1 ....42 B2
Cherryclough Wy BBNW BB2 ....48 E1
Cherry Crs ACC BB5 ....43 K5
RAW/HAS BB4 ....61 J3
Cherry Dr GTH/LHO BB6 ....12 C3
Cherry Lea BBNW BB2 ....40 D6
Cherry St BBN BB1 ....42 B2
Cherry Tree La BBNW BB2 ....48 C1
RAW/HAS BB4 ....61 J2
Cherry Tree Ms BLY BB11 ....37 H2
Cherry Tree Wy RAW/HAS BB4 ....60 D4
Chester Av CLI BB7 ....6 D2
Chester Cl BBN BB1 ....3 J7
Chester Crs RAW/HAS BB4 ....60 E3
Chester St ACC BB5 ....44 C2
BBN BB1 ....3 J5
Chestnut Dr CLI BB7 ....13 G2
RAW/HAS BB4 ....61 J3
Chestnut Gv ACC BB5 ....34 C1
ACC BB5 ....44 C3
DWN BB3 ....59 F6
Chestnut Ri BLY BB11 ....4 E5
Chevassut Cl NLSN BB9 ....8 C6
Cheviot Av BRFD/BLYE BB10 ....27 K6
Chichester Cl BRFD/BLYE BB10 ....5 K3
Chicken St BBNW BB2 ....2 B6
Chiltern Av BRFD/BLYE BB10 ....27 K6
China St ACC BB5 ....44 B1
Chingford Bank
BRFD/BLYE BB10 ....18 D6
Chipping Gv BRFD/BLYE BB10 ....38 D1
Chipping St PDHM/BLYW BB12 ....25 G2
Chislehurst Gv
BRFD/BLYE BB10 ....18 D5
Chorlton Cl BRFD/BLYE BB10 ....27 J1
Chorlton St BBN BB1 ....31 K6
Christ Church Sq ACC BB5 * 44 E2
Christ Church St ACC BB5 * 44 E2
BCUP OL13 ....57 G6
Christleton Cl
BRFD/BLYE BB10 ....19 F6
Church Aly ACC BB5 * 34 B3
Church Av ACC BB5 ....45 G6
Church Bank ACC BB5 ....34 A6
Church Bank St DWN BB3 * 59 F2
Church Br ACC BB5 * 44 B1
Church Brow CLI BB7 ....6 D2
Church Brow Gdns CLI BB7 ....6 E2
Church Cl BBNW BB2 ....30 C3
CLI BB7 ....6 D2
PDHM/BLYW BB12 ....23 K1
Church Dr CLI BB7 ....13 G2
Church Hall ACC BB5 ....44 B1
Church Hill Rd BBN BB1 ....32 A6
Churchill Av BBN BB1 ....33 G5
Churchill Rd NLSN BB9 ....8 D6
Churchill Wy NLSN BB9 ....18 B2
Church La ACC BB5 ....34 C4
BBNW BB2 ....30 C3
CLI BB7 ....13 J4
GTH/LHO BB6 ....22 D5
RAW/HAS BB4 ....62 D2
Church Mdw COL BB8 ....9 K2
Church Srteet
PDHM/BLYW BB12 ....36 A1
Church St ACC BB5 ....34 B3
ACC BB5 ....43 K4
ACC BB5 ....44 A1
ACC BB5 ....44 E2
BBN BB1 ....3 F4
BBN BB1 ....33 G4
BCUP OL13 ....63 H3
BLY BB11 ....5 H2
BRFD/BLYE BB10 ....28 A1
CLI BB7 ....6 D3
COL BB8 ....9 K2
COL BB8 ....10 E5
DWN BB3 ....59 F2
GTH/LHO BB6 ....22 D6
NLSN BB9 ....8 D3
NLSN BB9 ....18 B4
PDHM/BLYW BB12 ....24 A2
PDHM/BLYW BB12 ....24 E3
RAW/HAS BB4 ....53 K6
RAW/HAS BB4 ....54 E1
RAW/HAS BB4 ....62 D3
Church Ter DWN BB3 * 59 F2
Churchtown Crs BCUP OL13 ....64 B2
Church Wk BBN BB1 ....31 K2
Church Wy NLSN BB9 ....18 D3
Cicely La BBN BB1 ....3 G4
Cicely St BBN BB1 ....3 G5
Clare Av COL BB8 ....9 G5
Claremont Av CLI BB7 ....6 E4
Claremont Dr CLI BB7 ....6 E4
Claremont Rd ACC BB5 ....34 D5
Claremont St NLSN BB9 ....18 A3
PDHM/BLYW BB12 ....4 A2
Claremont Ter NLSN BB9 ....18 D2
Clarence Pk BBNW BB2 ....31 F6
Clarence Rd ACC BB5 ....44 C3
Clarence St BBN BB1 ....2 D2
BLY BB11 ....5 J7
COL BB8 ....10 C2
COL BB8 ....10 E5
DWN BB3 ....49 K6
RAW/HAS BB4 ....54 E2
Clarendon Rd BBN BB1 ....31 K5
Clarendon Rd East BBN BB1 ....32 A5
Clarendon St ACC BB5 ....45 F1
COL BB8 ....10 D2
Clare St BLY BB11 ....4 C3
Claret St ACC BB5 ....44 C2
Clarke Holme St
RAW/HAS BB4 * 62 E1
Clarke St BBN BB1 ....33 H4
Clarke Wood Cl CLI BB7 ....14 B1
Claughton St BRFD/BLYE BB10 ....27 G2
Claybank PDHM/BLYW BB12 ....25 F2
Clay St BLY BB11 ....26 B6
Clayton Av RAW/HAS BB4 ....61 H3
Clayton Cl NLSN BB9 ....8 D6
Clayton Gv BBN BB1 ....20 C5
Clayton Hall Dr ACC BB5 ....34 B1
Clayton Rw GTH/LHO BB6 ....21 J2
Clayton St BBNW BB2 ....2 E5
COL BB8 ....10 A3
GTH/LHO BB6 ....22 D6
NLSN BB9 ....8 D6
Clayton Wy ACC BB5 ....34 C2
BBNW BB2 ....49 H2
Cleaver St BBN BB1 ....3 H3
BRFD/BLYE BB10 ....27 G3
Clegg St BRFD/BLYE BB10 ....27 F3
BRFD/BLYE BB10 ....28 B6
NLSN BB9 ....18 B4
RAW/HAS BB4 ....53 K6
Clegg St East
BRFD/BLYE BB10 * 27 F3
Clematis St BBNW BB2 ....41 F2
Clements Dr BRFD/BLYE BB10 ....18 C5
Clement St ACC BB5 ....44 E2
DWN BB3 ....59 F3
Clerkhill St BBN BB1 ....42 B2
Clevelands Gv BLY BB11 ....4 D6
Clevelands Mt BLY BB11 ....4 D6
Clevelands Rd BLY BB11 ....4 D6
Cleveland St COL BB8 ....10 B1
Cleveleys Rd ACC BB5 ....34 C5
BBNW BB2 ....41 J6
Cliffe La GTH/LHO BB6 ....22 C4
Cliffe St NLSN BB9 ....8 E6
Clifford St COL BB8 ....10 A2
Cliff St BBN BB1 ....33 H3
COL BB8 ....9 H4
PDHM/BLYW BB12 ....25 G2
Clifton Av ACC BB5 ....34 E6
Clifton Dr GTH/LHO BB6 ....22 D5
Clifton Rd NLSN BB9 ....18 C5
PDHM/BLYW BB12 ....26 B4
Clifton St ACC BB5 ....44 C3
BBN BB1 ....33 H4
COL BB8 ....9 K2
COL BB8 ....10 D5
DWN BB3 ....49 J5
PDHM/BLYW BB12 ....4 D2
Clinkham Rd GTH/LHO BB6 ....22 B6
Clinton St BBN BB1 ....3 K1
Clippers Quay BBN BB1 * 3 G6
Clitheroe Rd CLI BB7 ....13 J2
NLSN BB9 ....18 A4
PDHM/BLYW BB12 ....17 K4
Clitheroe St PDHM/BLYW BB12 ....25 F3
Clive St PDHM/BLYW BB12 ....26 E3
Clockhouse Av
BRFD/BLYE BB10 ....18 D6
Clockhouse Ct
BRFD/BLYE BB10 ....18 D6
Clockhouse Gv
BRFD/BLYE BB10 ....18 D6
Clod La RAW/HAS BB4 ....61 F4
Cloister Dr DWN BB3 ....59 H2
The Cloisters CLI BB7 ....13 K4
RAW/HAS BB4 ....62 D3
The Close ACC BB5 ....34 B1
ACC BB5 ....53 J1
Clough End Rd RAW/HAS BB4 ....53 K4
Clough La PDHM/BLYW BB12 ....24 C1
Clough Rd BCUP OL13 ....57 G6
NLSN BB9 ....19 G1
Clough St BCUP OL13 ....63 J3
BLY BB11 ....4 A4
DWN BB3 ....59 H5
RAW/HAS BB4 ....62 E2
Clover Crs PDHM/BLYW BB12 ....26 C3
Cloverfields BBN BB1 ....3 J1
Clover Hl BCUP OL13 * 57 G6
Clover Hill Rd NLSN BB9 ....19 F2
Clover St BCUP OL13 ....57 G6
Clover Ter DWN BB3 ....50 A6
Clyde St BBNW BB2 * 41 F4
Coach Rd ACC BB5 ....44 A2
Coal Clough La BLY BB11 ....4 C4
Coal Pit La ACC BB5 ....44 B3
BCUP OL13 ....57 H6
COL BB8 ....10 B3
DWN BB3 ....48 B3
RAW/HAS BB4 ....56 B5
Coal St BLY BB11 ....5 F3
Cob Castle Rd RAW/HAS BB4 ....53 H6
Cobden Ct BBN BB1 ....3 F4
Cobden St BCUP OL13 ....64 C3
BRFD/BLYE BB10 ....19 F6
BRFD/BLYE BB10 ....27 G3
DWN BB3 ....59 F3
NLSN BB9 ....18 D2
PDHM/BLYW BB12 ....25 G2
PDHM/BLYW BB12 ....36 A1
Cobham Rd ACC BB5 ....44 E2
Cobourg Cl BBNW BB2 ....41 K5
Cob Wall BBN BB1 ....32 A6
Cochran St DWN BB3 * 59 F3
Cock Br GTH/LHO BB6 ....23 G2
Cockerill St RAW/HAS BB4 ....53 K5
Cockermouth Cl DWN BB3 ....49 K2
Cockridge Cl BBNW BB2 ....49 F2
Coddington St BBN BB1 * 42 B2
Cog La BLY BB11 ....26 B6
BLY BB11 ....37 H2
Cog St BLY BB11 ....4 A4
Colbran St BRFD/BLYE BB10 ....27 G2
NLSN BB9 ....9 F5
Coldstream Pl BBNW BB2 ....41 J5
Coldweather Av NLSN BB9 ....19 F4
Coleman St NLSN BB9 ....19 F1
Colenso Rd BBN BB1 ....31 H6
Coleridge Cl COL BB8 ....9 K1
Coleridge Dr ACC BB5 ....45 G5
Coleridge Pl GTH/LHO BB6 ....33 H1
Coleridge St BBNW BB2 ....2 A7
Coleshill Av BRFD/BLYE BB10 ....27 H6
Colin St BLY BB11 ....4 B5
College Cl PDHM/BLYW BB12 ....25 G5
College St ACC BB5 ....44 C1
Colliers St ACC BB5 ....44 A2
Collier St ACC BB5 * 44 B2
Collinge Fold La RAW/HAS BB4 ....54 D5
Collinge St PDHM/BLYW BB12 ....25 F4
Collingwood ACC BB5 ....34 A3
Collingwood St COL BB8 ....9 H3
Collins Dr ACC BB5 ....45 G5
Colne La COL BB8 ....10 A3
Colne Rd BLY BB11 ....5 G1
BRFD/BLYE BB10 ....18 B6
BRFD/BLYE BB10 ....27 G3
COL BB8 ....10 C5
NLSN BB9 ....8 E3
NLSN BB9 ....18 B4
Colthurst Dr CLI BB7 ....7 F1
Columbia Wy BBNW BB2 ....31 F5
Colville Rd DWN BB3 ....49 J5
Colville St BRFD/BLYE BB10 ....27 F3
Comet St BCUP OL13 ....57 F2
Commerce St BCUP OL13 ....64 A1
RAW/HAS BB4 ....53 J5
Commercial Rd GTH/LHO BB6 ....22 D6
NLSN BB9 ....18 E1
Commercial St ACC BB5 ....43 K4
BBN BB1 ....33 H3
BCUP OL13 ....63 J3
RAW/HAS BB4 ....46 E4
Como Av BLY BB11 ....37 G1
Company St BBN BB1 * 33 H4
Compston Av RAW/HAS BB4 ....46 E6
Comrie Crs BLY BB11 ....37 H2
Conduit St NLSN BB9 ....8 D6
Coniston Av ACC BB5 ....44 B3
PDHM/BLYW BB12 ....25 F1
Coniston Dr DWN BB3 ....59 H1
Coniston Gv COL BB8 ....10 B1
Coniston Rd BBN BB1 ....32 A6
Coniston St PDHM/BLYW BB12 ....26 B5
Coniston Wy BBN BB1 ....33 F4
BCUP OL13 ....57 G5
Constable Av BLY BB11 ....37 K2
Constable Lee Crs
RAW/HAS BB4 ....54 E5
Conway Av BBN BB1 ....31 J6
CLI BB7 ....6 B4
Conway Cl RAW/HAS BB4 ....60 E2
Conway Dr ACC BB5 ....43 J3
Conway Gv BRFD/BLYE BB10 ....18 C6
Conway Rd RAW/HAS BB4 ....55 G6
Cook Gdns BBN BB1 ....3 K5
Cook House Rd COL BB8 ....10 A1
The Cooperage ACC BB5 ....43 K4
Co-operation St BCUP OL13 * 64 B1
RAW/HAS BB4 ....54 E2
RAW/HAS BB4 ....62 A1
RAW/HAS BB4 * 62 E1
Co-operative St RAW/HAS BB4 ....60 C4
Coopers Cl ACC BB5 * 43 K4
Cooper St BCUP OL13 ....57 F6
BLY BB11 ....5 G5
NLSN BB9 ....8 E6
Copper Beeches BBNW BB2 * 41 F2
Copperfield Cl
BRFD/BLYE BB10 ....28 A5
Copperfield St BBN BB1 ....3 H7
Coppice Av ACC BB5 ....35 F6
Coppice Cl NLSN BB9 * 9 G5
The Coppice ACC BB5 ....34 B1
BBNW BB2 ....30 E6
The Copse ACC BB5 ....44 B2
Copster Hill Cl BBN BB1 ....42 D6
Copthurst Av
PDHM/BLYW BB12 ....16 D3
Copthurst St
PDHM/BLYW BB12 * 25 F2
Copy Nook BBN BB1 ....3 J4
Corlass St NLSN BB9 ....8 D4
Cornel Gv BLY BB11 ....37 G1
Cornelian St BBN BB1 ....31 K3
Cornfield Gv
PDHM/BLYW BB12 ....25 K2
Cornfield St DWN BB3 ....59 F1
Cornholme BRFD/BLYE BB10 ....27 K1
Corn Mill Yd ACC BB5 * 34 B3
Cornwall Av BBN BB1 ....42 E3
Cornwall Pl ACC BB5 * 34 B6
Cornwall Rd BBN BB1 ....33 G4
Coronation Av BBNW BB2 ....48 A2
PDHM/BLYW BB12 ....25 F5
Coronation Gv RAW/HAS BB4 ....62 D2
Coronation Pl NLSN BB9 ....8 D4
Coronation Rd
BRFD/BLYE BB10 ....18 C4
Coronation St GTH/LHO BB6 ....22 E5
Corporation St ACC BB5 ....44 C2
BBNW BB2 ....2 E4
CLI BB7 ....6 C3
COL BB8 ....9 G4
Corwen Cl BBN BB1 ....2 E1
Cotswold Ms BBN BB1 * 50 B1
Cottam Cl CLI BB7 ....13 J4
Cottesloe Pl NLSN BB9 ....8 C4
Cottom Cft ACC BB5 ....34 B1
Cotton Ct COL BB8 ....9 J4
Cotton Hall St DWN BB3 ....59 F1
Cotton Rw BLY BB11 * 47 H2
Cotton St ACC BB5 ....44 D2
PDHM/BLYW BB12 ....4 B2
PDHM/BLYW BB12 ....25 F4
Cotton Tree La COL BB8 ....10 C2
Coultate St PDHM/BLYW BB12 ....26 B5
Coulton Rd NLSN BB9 ....18 B2
Countess Rd DWN BB3 ....49 K2
Countess St ACC BB5 ....44 B1
Country Ms BBNW BB2 ....30 D5
Court Gv BBN BB1 ....20 D5
The Courtyard BCUP OL13 ....57 G6
Coverdale Dr BBNW BB2 ....48 B2
Coverdale Wy
PDHM/BLWY BB12 ....4 B1
Cowan Brae BBN BB1 ....2 C1
Cowell Wy BBNW BB2 ....2 B4
Cow La BLY BB11 ....5 F3
Cowley Crs PDHM/BLYW BB12 ....25 H4
Cowm St WHIT OL12 ....65 F6
Cowper Av CLI BB7 ....6 D2
Cowpe Rd RAW/HAS BB4 ....62 D4
Cowper St BBN BB1 ....31 K6
BLY BB11 ....26 B6
Cowtoot La BCUP OL13 ....57 G5
Crabtree Av BCUP OL13 ....64 B2
RAW/HAS BB4 ....62 E1
Crabtree St BBN BB1 ....42 B2
COL BB8 ....9 J3
NLSN BB9 ....18 B4
RAW/HAS BB4 ....55 K5
Cracoe Gill NLSN BB9 * 8 C4
Craddock Rd COL BB8 ....10 A2
Cragg St COL BB8 ....9 J2
Crambe Hts DWN BB3 ....50 A2
Cranberry Cl DWN BB3 ....59 J5
Cranberry La DWN BB3 ....59 J5
Cranberry Ri RAW/HAS BB4 ....46 E6
Cranborne Ter BBNW BB2 * 2 A2
Cranbourne Dr ACC BB5 ....34 C5
Cranbourne St COL BB8 ....10 A1
Cranbrook Av ACC BB5 ....43 J3
Cranbrook St BBNW BB2 ....41 H5
Cranfield Vw DWN BB3 ....59 J5
Crankshaw St RAW/HAS BB4 ....54 E6
Cranmer St BLY BB11 ....4 C3
Cranshaw Dr BBN BB1 ....31 J5
Cranwell Cl BBN BB1 ....3 H5
Cravendale Av NLSN BB9 ....8 E4
Craven's Av BBNW BB2 ....49 J3
Cravens Hollow DWN BB3 ....49 J3
Craven St ACC BB5 ....44 C2
BLY BB11 ....5 H4
CLI BB7 ....6 D4
COL BB8 ....10 C2
NLSN BB9 ....18 B4
RAW/HAS BB4 ....61 J1
Crawford St NLSN BB9 ....8 E6
Crawshaw Dr RAW/HAS BB4 ....54 E3
Crawshaw Gra RAW/HAS BB4 ....54 E3
Crawshaw La BRFD/BLYE BB10 ....19 K3
Crawshaw St ACC BB5 ....44 D1
Crediton Cl BBNW BB2 * 49 G1
The Crescent BBNW BB2 ....40 C6
BRFD/BLYE BB10 ....18 B5
BRFD/BLYE BB10 ....28 B6
CLI BB7 ....6 C4
CLI BB7 ....13 G3
COL BB8 ....9 K1
Creswick Av BLY BB11 ....37 K3
Creswick Cl BLY BB11 ....37 K2
Crewdson St DWN BB3 ....58 E1
Cribden End La RAW/HAS BB4 ....54 A5
Cribden La RAW/HAS BB4 ....54 C4
Cribden St RAW/HAS BB4 ....54 D5
Criccieth Cl RAW/HAS BB4 * 60 E2
Crimea St BCUP OL13 ....64 B1
Cringle Wy CLI BB7 ....7 F1
Croasdale Av BRFD/BLYE BB10 ....27 J1
Croasdale Dr CLI BB7 ....6 E4
Croasdale Sq BBN BB1 ....3 J7
Crocus Cl RAW/HAS BB4 ....60 C3
Croft Cl RAW/HAS BB4 ....54 E4
Croft Head Rd BBN BB1 ....32 B4
Croft La PDHM/BLYW BB12 ....16 D3
Croft St ACC BB5 * 44 D1
BCUP OL13 ....57 F6
BLY BB11 ....5 G4
CLI BB7 ....6 D4

DWN BB3 * 59 F2
GTH/LHO BB6 33 J1
The Croft BBN BB1 31 H6
Cromer Av BRFD/BLYE BB10 27 H2
Cromer Gv BRFD/BLYE BB10 27 H2
Cromer Pl BBN BB1 31 J6
Crompton Pl BBNW BB2 2 A4
Cromwell St ACC BB5 34 D5
BBN BB1 3 J6
PDHM/BLYW BB12 26 E4
Cronkshaw St
PDHM/BLYW BB12 27 F4
Cronshaw Dr GTH/LHO BB6 21 H2
Crooked Shore BCUP OL13 57 F6
Crookhalgh Av
BRFD/BLYE BB10 28 A5
Croos St ACC BB5 44 E2
Crosby Cl DWN BB3 59 G5
Crosby Rd BBNW BB2 41 J6
Crosley Cl ACC BB5 44 D4
Cross Barn Gv DWN BB3 59 G3
Crossfield St BBNW BB2 41 K4
Cross Hagg St COL BB8 * 9 J3
Cross Helliwell St COL BB8 * 9 K3
Crosshill Rd BBNW BB2 41 F2
Crossland St ACC BB5 44 C2
Crossley Fold BLY BB11 4 B7
Cross School St COL BB8 * 9 K3
Cross Skelton St COL BB8 10 A2
Cross St ACC BB5 43 K3
BRFD/BLYE BB10 28 A1
BRFD/BLYE BB10 * 28 C5
CLI BB7 * 6 C3
DWN BB3 49 K2
DWN BB3 59 G4
GTH/LHO BB6 22 E6
NLSN BB9 18 B4
NLSN BB9 18 D1
PDHM/BLYW BB12 16 D4
RAW/HAS BB4 54 E2
Cross St North RAW/HAS BB4 53 K5
Cross St West COL BB8 9 H3
Croston St BBN BB1 * 42 C2
Crown Point Rd BLY BB11 37 J4
Crown St ACC BB5 44 C2
DWN BB3 59 F3
Crown Wy COL BB8 9 J3
Crowther St ACC BB5 34 A2
BLY BB11 5 J5
Crow Tree Av BCUP OL13 * 63 G3
Crowtrees Rd CLI BB7 15 H1
Crow Wood Av
PDHM/BLYW BB12 4 B1
Crow Wood Ct
PDHM/BLYW BB12 * 26 D4
Croydon St BBNW BB2 2 A3
Cuba St NLSN BB9 * 18 D1
Cuckoo Brow BBN BB1 31 G5
Cuckstool La
PDHM/BLYW BB12 17 J2
Cuerdale St BRFD/BLYE BB10 18 E6
Cuerden St COL BB8 9 H4
Culshaw St BBN BB1 3 J4
BRFD/BLYE BB10 27 H6
Cumberland Av ACC BB5 34 C2
PDHM/BLYW BB12 25 K4
Cumberland Cl DWN BB3 59 H5
Cumberland St BBN BB1 3 K5
NLSN BB9 * 8 E6
Cumbrian Wy
PDHM/BLYW BB12 26 A3
Cumpstey St BBNW BB2 * 41 J4
Cunliffe Cl BBN BB1 32 B4
Cunliffe La CLI BB7 14 B1
Cunliffe Rd BBN BB1 32 C4
Cunningham Gv
PDHM/BLYW BB12 26 A5
Curate St GTH/LHO BB6 22 D6
Curlew Cl ACC BB5 43 K4
BBN BB1 31 J4
Curlew Gdns BLY BB11 26 A6
Curtis St RAW/HAS BB4 54 E6
Curven Edge RAW/HAS BB4 60 D4
Curve St BCUP OL13 64 A2
Curzon Pl BBNW BB2 * 2 A7
Curzon St BLY BB11 5 F3
BRFD/BLYE BB10 19 G6
CLI BB7 6 C4
Cut La BBN BB1 33 F5
Cutler Cl BBNW BB2 2 B4
Cutler Crs BCUP OL13 63 J4
Cutler La BCUP OL13 63 J4
Cypress Rdg BBNW BB2 48 D1
Cyprus St DWN BB3 59 G5

D

Daffodil Cl RAW/HAS BB4 60 D3
Daisy Bank BCUP OL13 * 57 F6
Daisy Bank Crs
BRFD/BLYE BB10 27 K6
Daisyfield St DWN BB3 49 J4
Daisy Hl RAW/HAS BB4 54 E6
Daisy La BBN BB1 3 H1
Daisy St BBN BB1 3 J2
COL BB8 9 K3
Dalby Crs BBNW BB2 40 E6
Dalby Lea BBNW BB2 40 D6
Dale Cl PDHM/BLYW BB12 4 B2
Dale Crs BBNW BB2 48 C2
Dalesford RAW/HAS BB4 60 E2
The Dales GTH/LHO BB6 21 F3
Dale St ACC BB5 44 C2
BBNW BB2 * 2 C6
BCUP OL13 57 H6
COL BB8 9 J2
NLSN BB9 18 A4
NLSN BB9 18 C1
PDHM/BLYW BB12 * 4 B2
RAW/HAS BB4 53 K6
Dalesway NLSN BB9 8 C4
Dale Vw CLI BB7 13 H5
DWN BB3 49 J3
Dalglish Dr BBNW BB2 49 H2
Dalkeith Rd NLSN BB9 * 18 C1
Dall St BLY BB11 5 H6
Dalton Cl BBN BB1 3 K4
Dalton St BLY BB11 37 H2
NLSN BB9 8 E6
Dame Fold
PDHM/BLYW BB12 16 D3
PDHM/BLYW BB12 * 24 E3
Dam Side COL BB8 9 K3
Damson Cl GTH/LHO BB6 12 C3
Daneshouse Rd
BRFD/BLYE BB10 27 F3
Dane St PDHM/BLYW BB12 27 F4
Daniell St BBN BB1 33 G3
Daniel St ACC BB5 34 A2
Danvers St BBN BB1 33 H3
Dark La RAW/HAS BB4 62 D2
Darnley St BRFD/BLYE BB10 27 H6
Dartford Cl BBN BB1 3 H5
Darwen St BBNW BB2 3 F5
PDHM/BLYW BB12 * 25 F3
Darwin St BRFD/BLYE BB10 27 F1
Davenham Rd DWN BB3 49 J6
David St BCUP OL13 63 J3
BLY BB11 5 F7
NLSN BB9 8 D3
Davies Rd BBN BB1 42 D1
Davy Field Rd DWN BB3 50 A3
Dawlish Cl BBNW BB2 49 G1
Dawson Av PDHM/BLYW BB12 24 B1
Dawson Sq BLY BB11 * 5 H1
Day St NLSN BB9 18 E2
Deal St BBN BB1 31 K6
Deanfield CLI BB7 7 G1
Dean Fold RAW/HAS BB4 56 A1
Dean La GTH/LHO BB6 22 C4
RAW/HAS BB4 56 A1
Dean Meadow CLI BB7 6 C4
Dean Rd RAW/HAS BB4 60 E3
Deansgreave Rd BCUP OL13 64 C4
Dean St BLY BB11 4 C3
COL BB8 10 D5
DWN BB3 49 K5
PDHM/BLYW BB12 25 G2
Dearden Nook RAW/HAS BB4 61 K2
Deepdale Ct NLSN BB9 8 C4
Deepdale Dr BRFD/BLYE BB10 18 C5
Deepdale Gn NLSN BB9 8 C4
Deer Chace PDHM/BLYW BB12 17 H1
Deer Pk ACC BB5 35 G5
Deer Park Rd BRFD/BLYE BB10 38 D2
Deerplay Cl BRFD/BLYE BB10 27 K1
Deerstone Av
BRFD/BLYE BB10 27 H5
Deerstone Rd NLSN BB9 19 H1
Deganwy Av BBN BB1 31 J6
De Lacy St CLI BB7 6 C3
Delamere Cl ACC BB5 34 D4
BBNW BB2 2 B7
Delamere Rd BRFD/BLYE BB10 19 F6
Delius Cl BBNW BB2 42 A6
The Dell DWN BB3 49 H3
Delma Rd BRFD/BLYE BB10 27 K6
Delph Ap BBN BB1 42 C3
Delph Cl BBN BB1 42 C3
Delph Ct GTH/LHO BB6 22 D6
Delphinium Wy DWN BB3 50 A2
Delph La BBN BB1 * 42 C4
Delph Mt GTH/LHO BB6 22 C5
Delph Rd GTH/LHO BB6 22 C6
Delph St DWN BB3 * 50 B6
Delves La BRFD/BLYE BB10 19 J2
Denbigh Dr CLI BB7 6 E1
Dene Bank Rd ACC BB5 44 A4
The Dene BBNW BB2 30 E5
Dent Dl ACC BB5 45 F2
Dentdale Cl BBNW BB2 48 B2
Dent Rw BLY BB11 4 E5
Dent St COL BB8 9 H4
Denville Rd BBNW BB2 2 C3
Derby Cl DWN BB3 59 G6
Derby St ACC BB5 44 E1
BBN BB1 3 J1
BBN BB1 33 J4
BLY BB11 4 E4
CLI BB7 6 E3
COL BB8 9 K2
NLSN BB9 8 A4
Derby Ter RAW/HAS BB4 61 K1
Derham St BBNW BB2 41 J4
Derwent Av BRFD/BLYE BB10 27 F1
PDHM/BLYW BB12 25 F1
Derwent Cl BBN BB1 33 F4
COL BB8 10 C1
DWN BB3 59 H3
RAW/HAS BB4 53 K5
Derwent Crs CLI BB7 6 B4
Derwent St DWN BB3 * 58 E1
Devon Av ACC BB5 43 H2
Devon Crs RAW/HAS BB4 60 E3
Devon Gv PDHM/BLYW BB12 25 K4
Devon Pl ACC BB5 * 44 A2
Devonport Ct BBNW BB2 2 B4
Devonport Rd BBNW BB2 2 B4
Devon Rd BBN BB1 42 D2
Devonshire Dr ACC BB5 35 G4
Devonshire Rd BBN BB1 33 G4
BRFD/BLYE BB10 27 F4
Devonshire St ACC BB5 34 D6
Devon St DWN BB3 59 G5
Dewhurst Cl DWN BB3 59 H5
Dewhurst Rd GTH/LHO BB6 20 E2
Dewhurst St BBN BB1 3 K6
COL BB8 9 K4
DWN BB3 59 G5
Dickens St BBN BB1 3 H7
Dickinson Cl BBNW BB2 2 B7
Dickinson St BBNW BB2 2 C7
Dickson St COL BB8 10 A2
PDHM/BLYW BB12 26 B5
Didsbury St BBN BB1 42 C2
Dill Hall La ACC BB5 34 C5
Dinckley Sq BBNW BB2 41 F1
Dinely St ACC BB5 44 B1
Disraeli St BRFD/BLYE BB10 27 G1
Dixon St BBNW BB2 2 A6
NLSN BB9 8 C4
Doals Ga BCUP OL13 57 G1
Dobbin Cl RAW/HAS BB4 62 B1
Dobbin La RAW/HAS BB4 62 B1
Dobson St DWN BB3 58 E1
Dockray St COL BB8 10 A2
Dock St BBN BB1 3 J4
Dog Pits La BCUP OL13 57 F3
Dombey St BBN BB1 3 K6
Dominica Av DWN BB3 49 K3
Dominion Rd BBNW BB2 31 G5
Donshort Ms NLSN BB9 * 8 C6
Dorchester Av ACC BB5 43 J3
Dorchester Cl BBN BB1 42 B4
Doris St BLY BB11 * 5 K1
Dorothy St BBNW BB2 * 49 G1
Dorritt St BBN BB1 * 3 J7
Dorset Av DWN BB3 * 49 K6
PDHM/BLYW BB12 25 G4
Dorset Dr BBN BB1 42 E3
CLI BB7 6 E1
RAW/HAS BB4 60 D3
Dorset Rd BBN BB1 33 G4
Dorset St PDHM/BLYW BB12 25 K5
Double Rw PDHM/BLYW BB12 24 E3
Doughty St COL BB8 9 K3
Douglas Cl BBNW BB2 49 H2
Douglas Gv DWN BB3 49 H5
Douglas Pl BBN BB1 31 K4
Douglas Rd BCUP OL13 64 B2
BRFD/BLYE BB10 19 G6
Douglas St COL BB8 10 A1
Dovedale Cl BRFD/BLYE BB10 18 C5
PDHM/BLYW BB12 26 B3
Dovedale Dr PDHM/BLYW BB12 26 B3
Dove La DWN BB3 58 E1
Dover Cl BBN BB1 42 C3
Dover St ACC BB5 44 C3
DWN BB3 49 K2
NLSN BB9 8 E6
Downham Av GTH/LHO BB6 23 F5
RAW/HAS BB4 54 E5
Downham Dr ACC BB5 44 C4
Downham Gv BRFD/BLYE BB10 27 J6
Downham St BBNW BB2 41 F3
Dowry St ACC BB5 44 E1
Drammen Av BLY BB11 26 A6
Drew St BLY BB11 26 A6
Driver St RAW/HAS BB4 54 E2
The Drive BCUP OL13 64 A1
GTH/LHO BB6 12 C4
Driving Ga RAW/HAS BB4 46 E6
Dryden Gv GTH/LHO BB6 * 33 H1
Dryden St ACC BB5 34 B2
PDHM/BLYW BB12 25 H4
Duchess St DWN BB3 49 K2
Duckett St BLY BB11 4 C3
Duckshaw Rd DWN BB3 58 E6
Duck St CLI BB7 6 E3
Duckworth Hall Brow ACC BB5 43 G5
Duckworth Hill La ACC BB5 43 H6
Duckworth La ACC BB5 43 J5
RAW/HAS BB4 61 H3
Duckworth St ACC BB5 44 A1
BBNW BB2 2 C7
DWN BB3 58 E1
NLSN BB9 8 D5
Duddon Av DWN BB3 49 H6
Dudley Av ACC BB5 43 J3
Dudley St COL BB8 10 B2
NLSN BB9 * 18 C4
Duerden St NLSN BB9 18 D1
Dugdale Rd PDHM/BLYW BB12 26 A4
Dugdale St BLY BB11 5 G4
Duke of Sussex St BBNW BB2 * 49 F1
Dukes Ct BBNW BB2 41 F1
Dukes Dr DWN BB3 59 K2
Duke St ACC BB5 34 C3
ACC BB5 43 J4
BBNW BB2 2 D4
BLY BB11 5 J6
BRFD/BLYE BB10 19 F6
COL BB8 9 K3
GTH/LHO BB6 22 C6
RAW/HAS BB4 62 D3
Duncan Cl BRFD/BLYE BB10 28 A6
Duncan St PDHM/BLYW BB12 25 K6
Duncroft Cl CLI BB7 6 D1
Dundas St COL BB8 9 J3
Dundee Dr BBN BB1 3 J5
Dunderdale Av NLSN BB9 18 C2
Dundonnell Rd NLSN BB9 9 G6
Dunkenhalgh Wy ACC BB5 34 A5
Dunny Shop Av ACC BB5 44 C3
Dunoon Dr BBN BB1 42 D4
Dunoon St BLY BB11 4 A5
Dunsop St BBN BB1 3 G1
Dunster Av ACC BB5 43 J2
Dunster Gv CLI BB7 6 B5
Durban Gv BLY BB11 4 C7
Durham Av PDHM/BLYW BB12 26 A4
Durham Cl BBN BB1 3 H6
Durham Dr ACC BB5 44 B4
BBN BB1 20 E5
Durham Rd BBN BB1 20 E4
DWN BB3 58 D1
Durham St ACC BB5 35 F6
Dutton St ACC BB5 44 E1
Duttons Wy BBN BB1 42 D6
Duxbury St DWN BB3 59 G5
Dyke Nook CLI BB7 6 E5
Dyneley Av BRFD/BLYE BB10 39 F1
Dyneley Rd BBN BB1 32 C6
Dyson St BBNW BB2 41 H5

E

Eachill Gdns BBN BB1 33 H5
Eachill Rd BBN BB1 33 H4
Eagle St ACC BB5 43 J5
ACC BB5 44 D2
BBN BB1 42 C3
NLSN BB9 9 F6
Eagley Rd BRFD/BLYE BB10 18 C5
Eanam BBN BB1 3 H4
Eanam Old Rd BBN BB1 3 G4
Eanam Whf BBN BB1 3 H4
Earcroft Wy DWN BB3 49 J4
Earls Dr DWN BB3 59 K2
Earl St ACC BB5 34 B3
BBN BB1 31 J6
BRFD/BLYE BB10 27 F3
COL BB8 9 K3
GTH/LHO BB6 22 C6
NLSN BB9 9 F6
Earnsdale Av DWN BB3 58 C1
Earnsdale Cl DWN BB3 58 D1
Earnsdale Rd DWN BB3 49 J6
Earnshaw Rd BCUP OL13 57 F6
Earnshaw Rw BCUP OL13 57 F6
Easedale Cl PDHM/BLYW BB12 26 A3
East Bank NLSN BB9 8 D3
East Bank Av RAW/HAS BB4 * 60 E1
Eastcott Cl BBNW BB2 50 A1
East Crs ACC BB5 34 D5
East End St COL BB8 9 J3
Eastern Av BRFD/BLYE BB10 27 H2
Eastgate ACC BB5 44 E1
Eastham Pl BLY BB11 5 J3
Eastham St BRFD/BLYE BB10 5 K4
CLI BB7 6 D2
East Lancashire Rd BBN BB1 31 K2
East Lodge Pl
BRFD/BLYE BB10 * 38 E4
Eastmoor Dr CLI BB7 6 E4
East Pde RAW/HAS BB4 54 E6
East Park Av BBN BB1 31 H6
DWN BB3 58 E3
East Park Rd BBN BB1 2 C1
East St BBNW BB2 2 A7
BBNW BB2 48 B1
NLSN BB9 8 D6
NLSN BB9 18 C4
PDHM/BLYW BB12 25 F2
PDHM/BLYW BB12 36 A1
RAW/HAS BB4 54 D4
RAW/HAS BB4 60 D4
East Vw BCUP OL13 64 A1
COL BB8 10 E5
PDHM/BLYW BB12 24 A1
Eastwood Crs RAW/HAS BB4 62 B1
Eastwood St BBN BB1 3 K1
RAW/HAS BB4 62 B1
Eaves Av BLY BB11 37 H3
Ebony St BBN BB1 32 A6
Ebor St BRFD/BLYE BB10 27 G1
Eccleshill Gdns DWN BB3 50 C5
Eccleshill Rd DWN BB3 49 K3
Eccleshill St PDHM/BLYW BB12 25 F3
Eccles St ACC BB5 34 D6
BBNW BB2 41 J5
Eckersley Cl BBNW BB2 49 H1
Eclipse Rd BBNW BB2 48 B1
Ecroyd St NLSN BB9 18 B1
Edale Av RAW/HAS BB4 61 F1
Eden Cl NLSN BB9 8 D3
Eden Pk BBNW BB2 30 E5
Edensor Ter DWN BB3 58 E1
Eden St ACC BB5 44 C2
BBN BB1 3 J3
Edgar St ACC BB5 35 G3
ACC BB5 44 D1
NLSN BB9 * 9 F5
Edge End GTH/LHO BB6 22 C6
Edge End Av NLSN BB9 18 D4
Edge End La GTH/LHO BB6 22 C6
NLSN BB9 18 D3
Edge End Rd GTH/LHO BB6 22 C6
Edge La BCUP OL13 64 D3
RAW/HAS BB4 62 C1
Edgeley Ct PDHM/BLYW BB12 26 C4
Edgeside GTH/LHO BB6 22 C6
Edgeside La RAW/HAS BB4 62 E1
Edgeware Rd BBNW BB2 2 A1
Edgeworth Gv
BRFD/BLYE BB10 27 H5
Edge Yate La RAW/HAS BB4 55 F5
Edinburgh Dr ACC BB5 44 B4
Edisford Rd CLI BB7 6 A4
Edison St DWN BB3 58 E2
Edith St BBN BB1 3 K6
NLSN BB9 19 F1
Edleston St ACC BB5 44 B2
Edmonton Dr BBNW BB2 30 E5
Edmundson St ACC BB5 44 A1
BBNW BB2 2 B4
Edmund St ACC BB5 44 E3
BBNW BB2 49 H2
BRFD/BLYE BB10 27 G2
DWN BB3 59 G2
Edward Ct ACC BB5 * 44 A1
Edward St ACC BB5 44 A1
ACC BB5 45 G6
BBN BB1 33 H4
BCUP OL13 57 G6
BLY BB11 5 G3
DWN BB3 59 F1
GTH/LHO BB6 22 D6
NLSN BB9 9 F5
RAW/HAS BB4 53 K3
RAW/HAS BB4 54 E1
Eight Acre Av CLI BB7 * 15 H1
Elder St NLSN BB9 9 F5
Eldwick St BRFD/BLYE BB10 27 H2
Eleanor St BBN BB1 3 H4
NLSN BB9 8 E6
Electricity St ACC BB5 34 D6
Elgar Cl BBNW BB2 42 A6
Elgin Crs BLY BB11 4 A6
Elizabeth Dr RAW/HAS BB4 60 D3
Elizabeth St ACC BB5 44 B2
BBN BB1 3 H4
BLY BB11 5 G4
NLSN BB9 8 D6
PDHM/BLYW BB12 25 F
RAW/HAS BB4 55 K
Eliza St BRFD/BLYE BB10 5 K
Elker La CLI BB7 12 E
Elker Ms CLI BB7 * 13 F
Elland Rd NLSN BB9 18 C
Ellenshaw Cl DWN BB3 59 G
Ellen St DWN BB3 59 F
NLSN BB9 18 D
Ellerbeck Cl BRFD/BLYE BB10 27 K
Ellerbeck Rd ACC BB5 34 D
Ellerbrook Rd DWN BB3 59 G
Ellesmere Av COL BB8 10 B
Ellesmere Rd DWN BB3 49 J
Elliott Av DWN BB3 59 G
Elliott St BRFD/BLYE BB10 27 H
Ellison Fold ACC BB5 * 34 A
Ellison Fold Ter DWN BB3 59 H
Ellison St ACC BB5 44 D
DWN BB3 59 F
Ellis St BLY BB11 4 C
Elm Cl BBN BB1 33 H
RAW/HAS BB4 53 K
Elmfield St ACC BB5 34 B
Elm Gv DWN BB3 50 B
Elm St BBN BB1 32 A
BCUP OL13 57 G
BRFD/BLYE BB10 27 F
COL BB8 10 A
GTH/LHO BB6 33 J
NLSN BB9 8 E
RAW/HAS BB4 54 D
Elm Tree Gv GTH/LHO BB6 12 C
Elmwood Cl ACC BB5 45 F
Elmwood St BLY BB11 4 B
Elswick Gdns BBNW BB2 30 B
Elswick Ldg BBNW BB2 30 C
Elswick St DWN BB3 59 G
Elton Rd BBN BB1 51 F
Ely Cl BBN BB1 20 E
DWN BB3 59 H
Emerald Av BBN BB1 31 K
Emerald St BBN BB1 31 K
Emily St BBN BB1 3 J
BLY BB11 5 H
Emma St ACC BB5 44 B
Emmerdale Cl ACC BB5 43 K
Emmott Ct COL BB8 11 G
Empire St GTH/LHO BB6 22 E
Empress St ACC BB5 44 B
COL BB8 10 A
DWN BB3 * 49 K
End St COL BB8 9 H
Enfield Cl ACC BB5 35 F
Enfield Rd ACC BB5 35 F
England Av BBNW BB2 49 H
Ennerdale Av BBN BB1 42 C
Ennerdale Cl CLI BB7 6 B
Ennerdale Rd
BRFD/BLYE BB10 27 K
CLI BB7 6 B
Ennismore St BRFD/BLYE BB10 27 H
Enoch Brow BBNW BB2 48 A
Enterprise Wy COL BB8 9 F
Entwisle Rd ACC BB5 34 D
Entwistle St DWN BB3 59 F
Epping Av ACC BB5 34 D
Epsom Wy ACC BB5 45 F
Epworth St DWN BB3 59 G
Equity St DWN BB3 59 F
Ermine Cl BBNW BB2 50 A
Ernest St ACC BB5 44 A
BCUP OL13 64 D
Ernlouen Cl BBNW BB2 48 E
Escar St BLY BB11 * 4 E
Escott Gdns
BRFD/BLYE BB10 * 27 F
Eshton Ter CLI BB7 6 C
Eskdale Cl BRFD/BLYE BB10 18 B
Eskdale Crs BBNW BB2 48 C
The Esplanade BBN BB1 33 G
Essex Av PDHM/BLYW BB12 26 A
Essex Cl BBNW BB2 41 H
Essex Rd BBN BB1 33 G
Essex St ACC BB5 45 F
COL BB8 10 A
DWN BB3 59 H
NLSN BB9 8 E
Esther St BBN BB1 42 C
Ethersall Rd NLSN BB9 18 E
Eton Av ACC BB5 34 E
Eton Cl PDHM/BLYW BB12 25 H
Evans St BLY BB11 5 F
Evelyn Rd DWN BB3 49 J
Evelyn St BRFD/BLYE BB10 27 F
The Evergreens BBNW BB2 48 D
Eversholt Cl
PDHM/BLYW BB12 17 H
Everton St DWN BB3 * 58 E
Every St BLY BB11 4 D
NLSN BB9 8 D
Ewood BBNW BB2 41 H
Ewood La RAW/HAS BB4 61 F
Exchange St ACC BB5 44 B
BBN BB1 2 E
COL BB8 9 K
DWN BB3 59 F
Exeter St BBNW BB2 41 G
Exmouth St BLY BB11 5 G
Exton St NLSN BB9 18 A
Extwistle Rd BRFD/BLYE BB10 28 C
Extwistle Sq BRFD/BLYE BB10 27 J
Extwistle St
BRFD/BLYE BB10 * 27 F
NLSN BB9 18 D

F

Factory La PDHM/BLYW BB12 25 F
Fairbairn Av
PDHM/BLYW BB12 26 B
Fairbank Wk RAW/HAS BB4 46 E

Fairclough Rd *ACC* BB5 44 C4
Fairfield Av *RAW/HAS* BB4 62 E1
Fairfield Cl *CLI* BB7 6 B4
Fairfield Dr *BRFD/BLYE* BB10 18 B6
CLI BB7 6 B4
Fairfield Rd *NLSN* BB9 19 H1
Fairfields Dr *DWN* BB3 49 K3
Fairfield St *ACC* BB5 44 B3
Fairhaven Rd *BBNW* BB2 41 K6
Fair Hl *RAW/HAS* BB4 60 D4
Fairholme Rd *BLY* BB11 38 B2
Fair Hope Ct *BBNW* BB2 2 A2
Fairview *RAW/HAS* BB4 54 D4
Fair View Crs *BCUP* OL13 64 C1
Fair View Rd *BLY* BB11 5 K5
Fairways Ct *BBN* BB1 20 E6
Fairways Dr *BLY* BB11 37 J3
Falcon Av *DWN* BB3 49 J6
Falcon Cl *BBN* BB1 31 H5
Fallbarn Crs *RAW/HAS* BB4 61 K2
Fall Barn Rd *RAW/HAS* BB4 62 A1
Fallbarn Rd *RAW/HAS* BB4 62 A1
Fallowfield Dr
PDHM/BLYW BB12 26 C3
Falmouth Av *RAW/HAS* BB4 61 F1
Faraday Av *CLI* BB7 6 C3
Faraday St *PDHM/BLYW* BB12 26 B4
Farholme La *BCUP* OL13 63 J3
Farm Av *BCUP* OL13 57 F5
Farmer's Rw *BBNW* BB2 49 F2
Farm House Cl *BBN* BB1 * 42 C3
Faroes Cl *BBNW* BB2 41 K6
Farrer St *NLSN* BB9 18 C1
Farrington Cl *BBNW* BB2 41 G6
BLY BB11 37 G2
Farrington Ct *BLY* BB11 37 F2
Farrington Pl *BLY* BB11 37 G2
Farrington Rd *BLY* BB11 37 F2
Favordale Rd *COL* BB8 10 C1
Fawcett Cl *BBNW* BB2 2 C7
Fearns Moss *BCUP* OL13 63 F2
Fecitt Brow *BBN* BB1 42 D3
Fecitt Rd *BBNW* BB2 41 F1
Feilden Pl *BBNW* BB2 48 B1
Feilden St *BBNW* BB2 2 D5
Felix St *BLY* BB11 5 J1
Fell Vw *BCUP* OL13 57 G1
BRFD/BLYE BB10 18 D6
Feniscliffe Dr *BBNW* BB2 40 D5
Fenwick St *BLY* BB11 37 G2
Ferguson St *BBNW* BB2 49 H2
Fern Av *ACC* BB5 44 B4
Fern Bank *NLSN* BB9 18 E2
Ferndale *BBN* BB1 3 J1
Ferndale St *BRFD/BLYE* BB10 27 H3
Fern Gore Av *ACC* BB5 44 C4
Fernhill Av *BCUP* OL13 63 K3
Fernhill Cl *BCUP* OL13 63 K3
Fernhill Crs *BCUP* OL13 63 K3
Fernhill Dr *BCUP* OL13 63 J3
Fernhill Gv *BCUP* OL13 63 K2
Fernhill Pk *BCUP* OL13 63 K3
Fernhill Wy *BCUP* OL13 63 K3
Fernhurst St *BBNW* BB2 49 H1
Fernlea Av *ACC* BB5 44 C4
Fernlea Cl *BBNW* BB2 49 F1
Fernlea Dr *ACC* BB5 34 A1
Fern Lea St *RAW/HAS* BB4 62 C3
Fern Rd *BLY* BB11 4 B7
The Ferns *BCUP* OL13 64 B2
Fern St *BCUP* OL13 64 A1
COL BB8 10 B1
RAW/HAS BB4 62 E2
Fern Ter *RAW/HAS* BB4 * 53 J6
Fielden St *BLY* BB11 4 A4
Fielding Crs *BBNW* BB2 40 E6
Fielding La *ACC* BB5 44 A4
GTH/LHO BB6 22 C6
Fielding St *BBN* BB1 33 J4
Fields End *GTH/LHO* BB6 21 H3
Fields Rd *RAW/HAS* BB4 60 E2
Field St *BBNW* BB2 41 F5
Fife St *ACC* BB5 44 C3
NLSN BB9 8 C6
Fifth Av *BRFD/BLYE* BB10 18 B6
Finch Cl *BBN* BB1 3 F2
Finch St *DWN* BB3 * 58 E1
Finsbury Pl *BBNW* BB2 49 H2
Finsley Ga *BLY* BB11 5 G5
Finsley St *BRFD/BLYE* BB10 * 18 E6
Fir Grove Rd *BLY* BB11 5 J7
First Av *ACC* BB5 34 C5
Fir St *BBN* BB1 31 K6
BRFD/BLYE BB10 5 K4
NLSN BB9 19 F1
RAW/HAS BB4 54 A6
Firtrees Dr *BBNW* BB2 48 D1
Fir Trees Gv *PDHM/BLYW* BB12 16 C4
Fir Trees La *PDHM/BLYW* BB12 16 C4
Fishmoor Dr *BBNW* BB2 49 K1
Fish Rake La *RAW/HAS* BB4 61 H5
Flag St *BCUP* OL13 63 K3
Flax Cl *RAW/HAS* BB4 60 D3
Fleet St *NLSN* BB9 8 E6
Fleet Wk *BLY* BB11 5 G3
Fleetwood Cl *BBNW* BB2 * 41 K6
Fleetwood Rd
BRFD/BLYE BB10 27 H1
PDHM/BLYW BB12 25 G3
Fleming Sq *BBNW* BB2 2 E5
Fletcher Rd *BBN* BB1 * 33 G4
Fletcher St *NLSN* BB9 19 F2
Flimby Cl *BBNW* BB2 49 K1
Flip Rd *RAW/HAS* BB4 53 H6
Florence Av *BLY* BB11 37 G1
Florence Pl *BBN* BB1 3 J1
Florence St *ACC* BB5 44 A1
BBN BB1 3 J1
BLY BB11 26 B6
Folds St *PDHM/BLYW* BB12 26 E4
Fordside Av *ACC* BB5 34 A1
Ford St *BRFD/BLYE* BB10 27 G2
NLSN BB9 8 E3
Foreside *NLSN* BB9 8 E2
Forest Bank Rd *RAW/HAS* BB4 54 E2
Forester Dr *PDHM/BLYW* BB12 17 H1
Forest Holme Cl *RAW/HAS* BB4 56 A2
Forest La *NLSN* BB9 8 B5
Fore St *DWN* BB3 49 K2
Forest St *BLY* BB11 5 H2
NLSN BB9 8 D6
RAW/HAS BB4 56 A2
Forfar Gv *BLY* BB11 37 H2
Forfar St *BLY* BB11 37 H2
Forge St *BCUP* OL13 64 A1
Formby Cl *BBNW* BB2 49 K1
Forrestside *BBNW* BB2 49 H2
Forrest St *BBN* BB1 3 J3
Fort St *ACC* BB5 34 B2
ACC BB5 * 44 D1
BBN BB1 3 J3
CLI BB7 6 C4
PDHM/BLYW BB12 24 A1
Fosse Cl *BBNW* BB2 3 F6
Foster St *ACC* BB5 34 E6
Fothergill St *COL* BB8 9 J2
Foul Clough Rd *TOD* OL14 65 K4
Foulds Cl *COL* BB8 9 J3
Foulds Rd *COL* BB8 10 D4
Foundry St *BBNW* BB2 2 B6
BCUP OL13 64 A1
BLY BB11 * 5 F2
RAW/HAS BB4 61 J2
Fountains Av *BBN* BB1 32 B5
PDHM/BLYW BB12 24 A2
Fountain Sq *NLSN* BB9 8 D4
Fountain St *ACC* BB5 44 C3
COL BB8 9 K3
DWN BB3 * 59 F3
NLSN BB9 8 E6
Fountains Wy *ACC* BB5 43 H2
Fouracre *BBNW* BB2 30 C3
Four Lanes End Rd *BCUP* OL13 63 G3
Fowler Height Cl *BBNW* BB2 49 F2
Foxcroft *PDHM/BLYW* BB12 26 C3
Foxdale Cl *BCUP* OL13 64 B2
Foxen Dole La
PDHM/BLYW BB12 16 E4
Foxfield Cl *ACC* BB5 43 K3
Foxhill Bank Brow *ACC* BB5 44 A2
Foxhill Dr *RAW/HAS* BB4 55 K5
Foxhouse St *BBNW* BB2 2 A3
Foxstones Crs *BBNW* BB2 48 E1
Foxstones La *BRFD/BLYE* BB10 39 G2
Fox St *ACC* BB5 44 D1
CLI BB7 6 D2
PDHM/BLYW BB12 25 J5
Foxwell Cl *RAW/HAS* BB4 61 F1
Foxwood Cha *ACC* BB5 43 J5
Frances St *DWN* BB3 58 E1
France St *ACC* BB5 44 A1
BBNW BB2 * 2 D5
Francis Av *NLSN* BB9 8 E2
Francis St *ACC* BB5 * 34 B2
BBNW BB2 41 F6
BRFD/BLYE BB10 27 F2
COL BB8 9 H4
Franklin Rd *BBNW* BB2 41 F4
Franklin St *CLI* BB7 6 C4
DWN BB3 59 F2
PDHM/BLYW BB12 * 26 B5
Frank St *ACC* BB5 * 34 C4
Fraser St *ACC* BB5 44 C3
BRFD/BLYE BB10 27 G2
Freckleton St *BBNW* BB2 2 E6
Frederick Rw *BBN* BB1 42 B2
Frederick St *ACC* BB5 44 A3
BBNW BB2 41 J4
DWN BB3 59 F1
Freeholds Rd *WHIT* OL12 65 F5
Free La *RAW/HAS* BB4 60 D5
Free Trade St *BLY* BB11 * 5 F3
French Cl *BBNW* BB2 41 F3
French Rd *BBNW* BB2 40 E3
Freshfield Av *ACC* BB5 34 A2
Fry St *NLSN* BB9 19 F1
Fulham St *NLSN* BB9 9 F5
Fullers Ter *BCUP* OL13 64 A2
Full Vw *BBNW* BB2 49 F1
Furness Av *BBN* BB1 32 B5
Furness St *BRFD/BLYE* BB10 27 G2
Furthergate *BBN* BB1 42 B2
Further La *BBNW* BB2 30 A4

G

Gadfield St *DWN* BB3 59 G3
Gaghills Rd *RAW/HAS* BB4 62 E2
Gainsborough Av *BBNW* BB2 2 A2
BLY BB11 37 J2
Galligreaves St *BBNW* BB2 2 C7
Galligreaves Wy *BBNW* BB2 41 G4
Gambleside Cl *RAW/HAS* BB4 46 E6
Game St *GTH/LHO* BB6 22 D6
Gannow La *PDHM/BLYW* BB12 26 A5
Garbett St *ACC* BB5 44 C3
Gardeners Rw *CLI* BB7 15 H2
Garden St *ACC* BB5 34 D6
ACC BB5 43 K4
BBNW BB2 2 A5
COL BB8 9 K3
GTH/LHO BB6 33 J1
NLSN BB9 * 18 B4
NLSN BB9 18 E1
PDHM/BLYW BB12 16 D4
PDHM/BLYW BB12 25 F2
Garfield St *ACC* BB5 45 F2
Garner Av *BBNW* BB2 49 H2
Garnett Rd *CLI* BB7 6 B4
Garnett St *DWN* BB3 59 G2
NLSN BB9 8 D5
Garrick St *NLSN* BB9 9 F5
Garsdale Av *BRFD/BLYE* BB10 18 B5
Garsden Av *BBN* BB1 42 E5
Garstang St *DWN* BB3 59 F1
Garswood Cl
PDHM/BLYW BB12 26 E1
Gas St *BCUP* OL13 64 A1
BLY BB11 5 F3
RAW/HAS BB4 60 C2
Gatefield Ct *BLY* BB11 5 H6
Gate St *BBN* BB1 3 K4
Gawthorpe Rd
PDHM/BLYW BB12 26 C4
Gawthorpe St
PDHM/BLYW BB12 25 F2
Gawthorpe Vw
PDHM/BLYW BB12 * 16 D4
Geddes St *BBNW* BB2 40 D5
Genoa St *BLY* BB11 37 G1
George Av *GTH/LHO* BB6 33 H1
George La *PDHM/BLYW* BB12 23 K1
George's Rw *RAW/HAS* BB4 62 E3
George St *ACC* BB5 * 34 B2
ACC BB5 44 B3
BBN BB1 3 G6
BBN BB1 33 H4
BLY BB11 4 E4
CLI BB7 6 C5
CLI BB7 13 J4
DWN BB3 * 59 F1
GTH/LHO BB6 22 C6
NLSN BB9 * 8 D6
RAW/HAS BB4 * 53 K6
George St West *BBNW* BB2 2 B6
Gerald Ct *BLY* BB11 5 J6
Gertrude St *NLSN* BB9 9 F5
Gib Field Rd *COL* BB8 9 G4
Gib Hill La *RAW/HAS* BB4 47 F6
Gib Hill Rd *NLSN* BB9 9 H6
Gib La *BBNW* BB2 48 E2
Gibraltar St *BBNW* BB2 41 F1
Gibson St *NLSN* BB9 * 9 F5
Gilbert St *BRFD/BLYE* BB10 27 K1
RAW/HAS BB4 62 C2
Giles St *CLI* BB7 6 D4
NLSN BB9 8 E6
Gillibrand St *DWN* BB3 49 K6
Gillies St *ACC* BB5 44 E1
BBNW BB2 41 K5
Gills Cft *CLI* BB7 6 E5
Gill St *COL* BB8 9 H4
NLSN BB9 8 C6
PDHM/BLYW BB12 4 D2
Girvan Gv *BLY* BB11 4 B5
Gisburn Gv *BRFD/BLYE* BB10 27 J6
Gisburn Pl *BBNW* BB2 2 A5
Gisburn Rd *NLSN* BB9 8 D4
Gisburn St *BBNW* BB2 2 A5
Gladstone Crs *BCUP* OL13 64 B1
Gladstone St *BBN* BB1 42 B1
BCUP OL13 64 B1
GTH/LHO BB6 22 D6
Gladstone Ter *BBNW* BB2 40 D6
Glamorgan Gv
PDHM/BLYW BB12 25 K4
Glasson Cl *BBNW* BB2 41 K6
Glebe Cl *ACC* BB5 44 D2
Glebe St *BLY* BB11 5 H7
GTH/LHO BB6 22 D6
Glenborough Av *BCUP* OL13 63 H3
Glenbrook Cl *BBNW* BB2 49 F1
Glencoe Av *DWN* BB3 59 K2
Glen Crs *BCUP* OL13 63 F3
Glendale Cl *BLY* BB11 38 A2
Glendale Dr *BBNW* BB2 30 C3
Glendene Pk *BBN* BB1 20 D6
Glendor Rd *BRFD/BLYE* BB10 27 K6
Gleneagles Av *DWN* BB3 59 K2
Gleneagles Dr *GTH/LHO* BB6 12 C4
Glenfield Pk *NLSN* BB9 * 9 F6
Glenfield Rd *NLSN* BB9 9 F6
Glengreave Av *BBN* BB1 31 J2
Glenluce Crs *BBN* BB1 42 D4
Glenmore Cl *ACC* BB5 45 G5
Glen Rd *RAW/HAS* BB4 62 E3
Glenroy Av *COL* BB8 9 K1
Glenshiels Av *DWN* BB3 59 K2
Glen St *BCUP* OL13 63 K3
COL BB8 9 K1
The Glen *BBNW* BB2 49 J3
Glen View Rd *BLY* BB11 37 K3
Glen Wy *NLSN* BB9 18 B3
Gloucester Av *ACC* BB5 34 B2
ACC BB5 34 C6
Gloucester Rd *BBN* BB1 33 F4
BBN BB1 42 C2
Glynn St *ACC* BB5 34 B6
Godiva St *BRFD/BLYE* BB10 27 F2
Godley St *BLY* BB11 5 J2
Goitside *NLSN* BB9 * 8 E6
Goit St *BBNW* BB2 41 G5
RAW/HAS BB4 62 E2
Goldacre La *GTH/LHO* BB6 22 B4
Goldfield Av *BRFD/BLYE* BB10 28 A5
Goldhey St *BBN* BB1 * 32 A6
Goodshaw Av *BBN* BB1 31 J4
RAW/HAS BB4 46 E6
Goodshaw Av North
RAW/HAS BB4 46 E5
Goodshaw Cl *BBN* BB1 31 J4
Goodshaw Fold Cl
RAW/HAS BB4 46 E5
Goodshaw Fold Rd
RAW/HAS BB4 46 D5
Goodshaw La *ACC* BB5 46 A6
RAW/HAS BB4 54 E1
Goosebutts La *CLI* BB7 6 E4
Goose Green La *COL* BB8 10 D5
Goose Hill St *BCUP* OL13 57 F6
Goose House Rd *DWN* BB3 50 A5
Gooseleach La
PDHM/BLYW BB12 24 B3
Gordon Av *ACC* BB5 44 C3
Gordon Rd *NLSN* BB9 * 18 D1
Gordon St *ACC* BB5 34 C3
ACC BB5 44 A2
BCUP OL13 57 F5
BRFD/BLYE BB10 28 C5
COL BB8 10 A2
DWN BB3 50 A6
PDHM/BLYW BB12 26 E4
RAW/HAS BB4 61 J1
Gorple Gn *BRFD/BLYE* BB10 28 C6
Gorple Rd *BRFD/BLYE* BB10 28 D6
Gorple St *BRFD/BLYE* BB10 18 E6
Gorse Gv *RAW/HAS* BB4 60 D3
Gorse Rd *BBNW* BB2 41 F2
Gorse St *BBN* BB1 42 C2
Grafton Av *ACC* BB5 45 G4
BRFD/BLYE BB10 18 B4
Grafton Ct *DWN* BB3 58 E1
Grafton St *BBNW* BB2 41 H5
CLI BB7 6 E3
NLSN BB9 9 F6
Grafton Vls *BCUP* OL13 64 A2
Graham St *PDHM/BLYW* BB12 25 G4
Granby St *PDHM/BLYW* BB12 4 A2
Grane Pk *RAW/HAS* BB4 60 D1
Grane Rd *RAW/HAS* BB4 52 A6
Grane St *RAW/HAS* BB4 53 K6
Grange Av *GTH/LHO* BB6 22 D5
NLSN BB9 9 F2
RAW/HAS BB4 55 F6
Grange Cl *ACC* BB5 44 C4
GTH/LHO BB6 22 D5
RAW/HAS BB4 * 62 A1
Grange Crs *RAW/HAS* BB4 61 K1
Grange La *ACC* BB5 44 E2
Grange Park Wy
RAW/HAS BB4 60 C2
Grange Rd *BBNW* BB2 41 F5
BRFD/BLYE BB10 39 G6
RAW/HAS BB4 62 A1
Grange St *ACC* BB5 34 A2
ACC BB5 * 44 E2
BLY BB11 4 C5
Grange Ter *RAW/HAS* BB4 * 54 E6
The Grange *BBN* BB1 20 E6
Grantham St *BBNW* BB2 41 F5
Grant Rd *BBNW* BB2 * 41 F4
Grant St *ACC* BB5 * 44 C1
BLY BB11 4 C5
Granville Gdns *ACC* BB5 45 F3
Granville Rd *ACC* BB5 44 E4
BBNW BB2 41 F2
DWN BB3 58 E3
GTH/LHO BB6 22 E5
NLSN BB9 18 C3
Granville St *BRFD/BLYE* BB10 19 F6
BRFD/BLYE BB10 27 F3
COL BB8 10 A2
Grasmere Av *BBN* BB1 31 G4
PDHM/BLYW BB12 25 F1
Grasmere Cl *ACC* BB5 35 F5
BBN BB1 33 G4
Grasmere Rd *RAW/HAS* BB4 61 F3
Grasmere St *BRFD/BLYE* BB10 27 F1
Grasmere Ter *BCUP* OL13 57 F6
Grassington Dr
BRFD/BLYE BB10 18 E6
Great Bolton St *BBNW* BB2 2 C7
Great George St *COL* BB8 9 K3
Greave Cl *RAW/HAS* BB4 54 E5
Greave Clough Cl *BCUP* OL13 57 G6
Greave Clough Dr *BCUP* OL13 57 G6
Greave Rd *BCUP* OL13 57 H6
Greaves St *GTH/LHO* BB6 33 J1
RAW/HAS BB4 60 C1
Greenacre *DWN* BB3 49 K3
Greenacres *PDHM/BLYW* BB12 24 A1
Greenacre St *CLI* BB7 6 D4
Green Bank *BCUP* OL13 63 J3
Greenbank Dr
PDHM/BLYW BB12 17 J1
Greenbank Pk *RAW/HAS* BB4 62 A1
Greenbank Rd *BBN* BB1 42 C1
Greenbank St *RAW/HAS* BB4 62 A1
Greenbank Ter *DWN* BB3 49 K3
Greenbank Wy *BBN* BB1 42 C1
Greenbrook Cl
PDHM/BLYW BB12 25 J5
Greenbrook Rd
PDHM/BLYW BB12 25 J5
Greencliffe La
BRFD/BLYE BB10 39 G4
Green Cl *BLY* BB11 37 J3
Green Close Pk *BBNW* BB2 41 G5
Greendale Av *RAW/HAS* BB4 62 D2
Greendale Cl *BRFD/BLYE* BB10 39 G6
Green Dr *CLI* BB7 7 F1
Green End Cl *BCUP* OL13 * 57 G6
Greenfield Av *CLI* BB7 * 6 B3
Greenfield Rd
BRFD/BLYE BB10 38 D1
COL BB8 9 H3
Greenfields *BBNW* BB2 49 H2
Greenfield St *DWN* BB3 59 H5
RAW/HAS BB4 53 K6
RAW/HAS BB4 54 E6
Greenfield Vw *DWN* BB3 50 A2
Greenfold Dr *RAW/HAS* BB4 46 E5
Greengate Cl *PDHM/BLYW* BB12 4 A1
Greenhead Av *BBN* BB1 32 B5
Greenhead La
PDHM/BLYW BB12 17 H3
Greenhill *GTH/LHO* BB6 22 C6
Green Hill Rd *BCUP* OL13 64 B2
Green Howarth Vw *ACC* BB5 44 C4
Greenhurst Cl *BBNW* BB2 * 2 D5
Green La *BBNW* BB2 40 E6
PDHM/BLYW BB12 25 F3
Green Meadow *COL* BB8 10 D5
Greenock Cl *BLY* BB11 4 A7
Greenock St *BLY* BB11 4 A7
Green Pk *CLI* BB7 13 J4
Green Ridge Cl *NLSN* BB9 18 D4
Green Rd *COL* BB8 9 J3
Green Rw *DWN* BB3 49 F3
Greenside Av *BBNW* BB2 40 E6
Greens La *BCUP* OL13 57 G6
BCUP OL13 63 J4
RAW/HAS BB4 60 E4
Greensnook La *BCUP* OL13 57 G6
Greensnook Ter *BCUP* OL13 57 G6
Green St *ACC* BB5 43 J5
BRFD/BLYE BB10 27 G2
DWN BB3 59 F2
GTH/LHO BB6 22 C6
PDHM/BLYW BB12 25 F4
RAW/HAS BB4 55 F6
Green St East *DWN* BB3 59 F2
The Green *COL* BB8 10 B1
DWN BB3 * 59 F2
Greenway St *DWN* BB3 49 K6
The Greenwood *BBNW* BB2 49 H3
Gregory Fold *RAW/HAS* BB4 60 D4
Gregson La *BBNW* BB2 * 2 D4
Gregson St *DWN* BB3 * 59 F3
Grenada Cl *DWN* BB3 49 K3
Gresham St *RAW/HAS* BB4 62 E2
Gretna Rd *BBN* BB1 31 K4
Gretna Wk *BBN* BB1 31 K4
Greystoke Av *BBNW* BB2 48 C1
Greystones Dr
PDHM/BLYW BB12 17 H1
Grey St *BRFD/BLYE* BB10 27 F3
NLSN BB9 8 D5
Griffin Cl *ACC* BB5 35 H4
BLY BB11 26 A6
Griffin St *BBNW* BB2 41 F4
Grime St *DWN* BB3 58 E1
Grimshaw Pk *BBNW* BB2 41 K5
Grimshaw St *ACC* BB5 * 34 B3
ACC BB5 44 C2
BLY BB11 5 G4
DWN BB3 59 G4
GTH/LHO BB6 22 D6
Grindlestone Hirst *COL* BB8 9 J4
Grindleton Gv
BRFD/BLYE BB10 38 D1
Grindleton Rd *BBNW* BB2 2 A5
Grisedale Av *BBN* BB1 42 C5
Grisedale Dr
PDHM/BLYW BB12 26 A3
Grizedale Cl *ACC* BB5 34 A3
Grosvenor St *COL* BB8 10 B2
PDHM/BLYW BB12 4 E1
Grove Ct *ACC* BB5 43 J4
Grove La *PDHM/BLYW* BB12 25 H2
Grove St *ACC* BB5 43 J4
ACC BB5 44 C1
BBNW BB2 41 J5
BCUP OL13 57 G6
BLY BB11 * 4 A4
NLSN BB9 8 D4
NLSN BB9 18 E1
The Grove *ACC* BB5 44 A2
CLI BB7 6 E2
CLI BB7 13 J4
PDHM/BLYW BB12 * 26 A5
Guide La *PDHM/BLYW* BB12 16 E2
Guide Sq *BBN* BB1 50 C1
Guilford St *NLSN* BB9 18 B4
Gurney St *BBNW* BB2 41 F4
Guy St *PDHM/BLYW* BB12 25 F2
Guysyke *COL* BB8 9 J3

H

Habergham Dr
PDHM/BLYW BB12 25 J3
Habergham St
PDHM/BLYW BB12 25 F2
Hacking Cl *GTH/LHO* BB6 21 H2
Hacking St *DWN* BB3 58 E2
NLSN BB9 9 F5
Hagg St *COL* BB8 9 J3
Haldane St *BRFD/BLYE* BB10 * 27 G1
Hale St *BLY* BB11 5 H7
Halifax Rd *BRFD/BLYE* BB10 29 J2
NLSN BB9 18 C4
Hallam Crs *NLSN* BB9 19 G1
Hallam Rd *NLSN* BB9 9 F6
Hallam St *ACC* BB5 34 C4
Hall Carr Rd *RAW/HAS* BB4 61 J2
Hall Cl *RAW/HAS* BB4 54 E3
Halley Rd *DWN* BB3 49 J6
Hallfield Rd *GTH/LHO* BB6 22 E5
Halliwell St *ACC* BB5 45 G5
Hall Mdw *COL* BB8 10 D4
Hall Park Av *BRFD/BLYE* BB10 39 F1
Hall Rd *COL* BB8 10 D4
Hall St *BBNW* BB2 41 J5
BCUP OL13 57 F6
BLY BB11 5 G3
BRFD/BLYE BB10 28 B6
CLI BB7 6 D4
COL BB8 9 K3
RAW/HAS BB4 54 E6
RAW/HAS BB4 60 E1
Hallwell St *BRFD/BLYE* BB10 27 F3
Hallwood Cl *BRFD/BLYE* BB10 18 B5
Halmote Av *PDHM/BLYW* BB12 16 D4
Halstead Cl *NLSN* BB9 8 D3
Halstead La *NLSN* BB9 8 D3
Halstead St *BLY* BB11 4 E5
BRFD/BLYE BB10 28 B5
Hambledon St
PDHM/BLYW BB12 25 G3
Hambledon Vw
PDHM/BLYW BB12 24 A2
Hameldon Ap *BLY* BB11 4 A4
Hameldon Av *ACC* BB5 45 G5
Hameldon Cl *BLY* BB11 36 A2
Hameldon Rd *BLY* BB11 36 A3
RAW/HAS BB4 46 E5
Hameldon Vw *GTH/LHO* BB6 22 E6
Hamer Av *BBN* BB1 42 D2
RAW/HAS BB4 46 E6
Hamer St *DWN* BB3 59 F3
RAW/HAS BB4 61 K1
Hamilton Rd *COL* BB8 9 G5
NLSN BB9 8 C6
Hamilton St *BBNW* BB2 41 H5
Hamlet Cl *BBNW* BB2 * 2 B7
Hammerton Gn *BCUP* OL13 57 G6
Hammerton St *BCUP* OL13 57 F5
BLY BB11 5 F4

Hammond Av BCUP OL13 63 J3
Hammond Dr
PDHM/BLYW BB12 23 K1
Hammond St NLSN BB9 19 F2
Hampden Av DWN BB3 59 G4
Hampden St BLY BB11 5 J7
Hampshire Cl BBN BB1 21 F4
Hampshire Rd BBN BB1 33 G4
Hancock St BBNW BB2 2 B7
Hannah St ACC BB5 44 D2
BCUP OL13 57 G6
DWN BB3 59 G3
Hanover St COL BB8 9 K1
Hanson St GTH/LHO BB6 33 J1
Hapton Rd PDHM/BLYW BB12 25 F4
Hapton St PDHM/BLYW BB12 25 G3
Hapton Wy RAW/HAS BB4 46 E5
Harcourt Rd ACC BB5 45 F4
BBNW BB2 2 A2
Harcourt St BCUP OL13 57 F6
BLY BB11 * 4 A4
Hardman Av RAW/HAS BB4 61 K2
Hardman Cl BBN BB1 42 E3
RAW/HAS BB4 62 E4
Hardman Dr RAW/HAS BB4 62 E4
Hardman St BBNW BB2 41 G4
Hardman Wy DWN BB3 59 F2
Hardsough La RAMS BL0 61 F6
Hardy Av NLSN BB9 18 B3
Hardy Ct NLSN BB9 * 18 E1
Hardy St BBN BB1 31 K4
NLSN BB9 18 B3
Harebell Cl BBNW BB2 48 B1
Hare Clough Cl BBNW BB2 41 K4
Hareden Brook Cl BBN BB1 41 K4
Harefield Ri PDHM/BLYW BB12 26 C3
Hareholme La RAW/HAS BB4 62 C2
Harewood Av
PDHM/BLYW BB12 24 B1
Hargher St BLY BB11 4 A4
Hargreaves Ct CLI BB7 6 B4
RAW/HAS BB4 55 K3
Hargreaves Dr
RAW/HAS BB4 61 J1
Hargreaves Fold La
RAW/HAS BB4 55 K2
Hargreaves La BBNW BB2 41 J4
Hargreaves Rd ACC BB5 43 H3
Hargreaves St ACC BB5 44 E2
BLY BB11 5 F3
BRFD/BLYE BB10 19 F6
COL BB8 9 H3
NLSN BB9 18 C1
RAW/HAS BB4 53 K6
RAW/HAS BB4 55 J4
Hargrove Av
PDHM/BLYW BB12 4 A1
PDHM/BLYW BB12 25 F2
Harlech Cl RAW/HAS BB4 60 E2
Harlech Dr ACC BB5 43 J3
Harley St PDHM/BLYW BB12 26 B5
Harling St PDHM/BLYW BB12 26 A5
Harold Av BLY BB11 37 G1
Harold St BLY BB11 4 A5
COL BB8 * 9 J3
Harpers La PDHM/BLYW BB12 17 H1
Harrier Dr BBN BB1 31 H5
Harriet St BLY BB11 4 D5
Harrington St ACC BB5 34 C4
Harris Ct CLI BB7 * 6 D3
Harrison Dr COL BB8 9 J1
Harrison St BBNW BB2 2 D6
BCUP OL13 64 C3
BRFD/BLYE BB10 28 A1
Harrogate Crs
BRFD/BLYE BB10 27 J1
Harrow Av ACC BB5 34 E6
Harrow Cl PDHM/BLYW BB12 25 H5
Harrow Dr BBN BB1 42 B4
Harrow St ACC BB5 44 A3
Harry Potts Wy
BRFD/BLYE BB10 5 J3
Harry St NLSN BB9 8 D4
Hartington Rd DWN BB3 * 49 J5
Hartington St BBN BB1 * 33 G4
NLSN BB9 * 18 B4
Hartlands Cl BRFD/BLYE BB10 18 D6
Hartlet St GTH/LHO BB6 * 22 E6
Hartley Av ACC BB5 44 C4
Hartleys Ter COL BB8 10 A3
Hartley St ACC BB5 44 A3
BBN BB1 * 3 F2
BLY BB11 * 26 B6
COL BB8 9 K2
NLSN BB9 18 E2
Hartmann St ACC BB5 44 C1
Hart St BBN BB1 3 H5
BLY BB11 5 H2
Harvey St ACC BB5 43 K3
NLSN BB9 8 E6
Harwood Ga BBN BB1 3 K1
Harwood La GTH/LHO BB6 23 F5
Harwood New Rd
GTH/LHO BB6 23 F5
Harwood Rd BBN BB1 32 D1
BBN BB1 33 G3
Harwood's La DWN BB3 59 J2
Harwood St BBN BB1 32 A6
DWN BB3 58 D1
Haslam Ct BRFD/BLYE BB10 27 F2
Haslingden New Rd BBN BB1 50 D1
Haslingden Old Rd BBN BB1 42 E4
RAW/HAS BB4 61 H1
Haslingden Rd BBN BB1 50 E2
BBNW BB2 42 A5
RAW/HAS BB4 61 G2
Hastings Cl BBN BB1 42 C3
Haston Lee Av BBN BB1 31 K2
Hatfield Rd ACC BB5 35 F5
Hathaway Fold
PDHM/BLYW BB12 25 G4
Hattersley St BLY BB11 4 D2
Haugh Av PDHM/BLYW BB12 24 D2
Havelock Cl BBNW BB2 41 H4
Havelock St ACC BB5 43 K4
BBNW BB2 41 G5
PDHM/BLYW BB12 25 F2
PDHM/BLYW BB12 26 A5
Haven St BRFD/BLYE BB10 27 H6
Haverholt Cl COL BB8 9 J2
Hawarden St NLSN BB9 18 E2
Hawes Dr COL BB8 10 B1
Hawes Ter BRFD/BLYE BB10 27 G1
Haweswater Rd ACC BB5 35 F4
Hawkins St BBNW BB2 41 F5
Hawks Gv RAW/HAS BB4 61 K2
Hawkshaw Av DWN BB3 49 J6
Hawkshaw Bank Rd BBN BB1 31 H5
Hawkshead St BBNW BB2 41 F3
Hawkstone Cl ACC BB5 35 H4
Hawk St BLY BB11 5 H2
Hawkswood Gdns NLSN BB9 18 A5
Hawksworth Rd ACC BB5 34 D5
Hawley St COL BB8 9 J3
COL BB8 10 E2
Haworth Av ACC BB5 * 45 F4
RAW/HAS BB4 61 J1
Haworth Dr BCUP OL13 63 H2
Haworth St ACC BB5 * 34 D4
ACC BB5 44 A3
BBN BB1 33 G4
Hawthorn Av ACC BB5 44 A3
DWN BB3 59 H1
Hawthorn Bank ACC BB5 * 34 C2
Hawthorn Cl GTH/LHO BB6 21 J3
Hawthorn Dr BBN BB1 33 H5
Hawthorne Av
BRFD/BLYE BB10 18 B4
Hawthorne Cl NLSN BB9 8 B6
NLSN BB9 * 19 H1
Hawthorne Gv NLSN BB9 * 8 D4
Hawthorne Mdw
RAW/HAS BB4 46 E6
Hawthorne Pl CLI BB7 6 D2
Hawthorne Rd BLY BB11 4 D7
Hawthorne St BBN BB1 31 K5
Hawthorn Rd BCUP OL13 64 B1
The Hawthorns BBN BB1 20 E5
Haydock St BBN BB1 31 J4
BRFD/BLYE BB10 27 H2
Hayfield BBNW BB2 30 E6
Hayhurst Cl CLI BB7 * 13 J3
Hayhurst Farm Ter CLI BB7 6 E4
Hayhurst Rd CLI BB7 13 J3
Haywood Cl ACC BB5 * 34 D5
Haywood Rd ACC BB5 34 D6
Hazel Av ACC BB5 34 B3
DWN BB3 50 B6
Hazel Bank BBNW BB2 2 A1
Hazel Cl BBNW BB2 2 B4
Hazel Gv ACC BB5 34 C3
BBN BB1 42 E2
BCUP OL13 57 H6
CLI BB7 6 B4
RAW/HAS BB4 54 D5
The Hazels BBN BB1 20 D5
Hazel St ACC BB5 53 J1
Hazelwood Cl BBN BB1 32 A4
Hazelwood Rd NLSN BB9 19 G1
Headingley Cl ACC BB5 35 H4
Heald Cl BCUP OL13 57 G1
Heald La BCUP OL13 57 H1
Heald Rd PDHM/BLYW BB12 27 F1
Healdwood Cl
PDHM/BLYW BB12 17 K6
Healdwood Dr
PDHM/BLYW BB12 17 K6
Healey Ct BLY BB11 4 E5
Healey Mt BLY BB11 4 E5
Healey Rw BLY BB11 5 F6
Healey Wood Rd BLY BB11 5 F5
Heaning Av ACC BB5 35 F6
BBN BB1 42 D3
Heap St BRFD/BLYE BB10 27 G2
BRFD/BLYE BB10 28 B5
NLSN BB9 * 18 A4
RAW/HAS BB4 54 E1
Heartwood Cl BBNW BB2 30 E5
Heathbourne Rd BCUP OL13 63 G3
Heather Bank BLY BB11 37 G1
RAW/HAS BB4 61 J2
Heather Cl NLSN BB9 18 D5
RAW/HAS BB4 60 D3
Heatherlea Rd
PDHM/BLYW BB12 17 H1
Heatherleigh Gdns DWN BB3 49 H3
Heathfield Av BCUP OL13 63 H3
Heathfield Pk BBNW BB2 40 D1
Heathfield Rd BCUP OL13 63 H3
Heathgate PDHM/BLYW BB12 17 H1
Heath Hill Dr BCUP OL13 63 H3
Heath St BRFD/BLYE BB10 27 G3
Heatley Cl BBNW BB2 2 C7
Heaton St BBNW BB2 2 E5
Heber St BLY BB11 47 F3
Hebrew Rd BRFD/BLYE BB10 27 F3
Hebrew Sq BRFD/BLYE BB10 * 27 F3
Heckenhurst Av
BRFD/BLYE BB10 28 A5
Hector Rd DWN BB3 49 J4
The Hedgerow BBNW BB2 30 E5
Height Barn La BCUP OL13 64 B3
Height Cft NLSN BB9 18 E4
Heightside Av RAW/HAS BB4 62 D1
Height Side La RAW/HAS BB4 55 F2
Heights Rd NLSN BB9 18 D3
Helena St BRFD/BLYE BB10 5 K4
Helm Cl BLY BB11 37 H3
Helmn Wy NLSN BB9 9 F4
Helmsdale Rd NLSN BB9 9 G6
Helmshore Rd RAW/HAS BB4 60 D6
Helston Cl BLY BB11 37 F1
Helton Cl NLSN BB9 8 D3
Helvellyn Dr
PDHM/BLYW BB12 26 B3
Hempshaw Av RAW/HAS BB4 46 E5
Hemp St BCUP OL13 64 A2
Hendon Rd NLSN BB9 19 F1
Hendry La BBNW BB2 49 H1
Henrietta St BBNW BB2 * 2 B4
BCUP OL13 64 A1
Henry St ACC BB5 34 C4
ACC BB5 44 B1
ACC BB5 45 F4
BBN BB1 33 H4
COL BB8 9 J3
NLSN BB9 * 8 D6
RAW/HAS BB4 61 J1
Henry Whalley St BBNW BB2 40 E5
Henthorn Rd CLI BB7 6 B5
Herbert St BBNW BB2 41 H5
BCUP OL13 63 J3
BLY BB11 4 D5
PDHM/BLYW BB12 25 G4
Hereford Av
PDHM/BLYW BB12 26 A4
Hereford Cl ACC BB5 34 D6
Hereford Dr CLI BB7 6 E4
Hereford Rd BBN BB1 42 D2
NLSN BB9 9 G5
Hereford St NLSN BB9 18 C1
Herkomer Av BLY BB11 37 J3
Hermitage St BBN BB1 33 J4
Heron Cl BBN BB1 31 H5
Heron Ct BLY BB11 26 B6
Heron Wy ACC BB5 44 A4
Herschel Av PDHM/BLYW BB12 26 B3
Herschell St BBNW BB2 41 F6
Hertford St BBNW BB2 41 G5
Hesketh Ct GTH/LHO BB6 22 E5
Hesketh St GTH/LHO BB6 22 D6
Hesse St DWN BB3 * 59 F3
Hetton Lea NLSN BB9 8 C4
Hexham Cl ACC BB5 45 G4
Heyfold Gdns DWN BB3 49 K6
Hey Head Av RAW/HAS BB4 * 63 F2
Heyhead St NLSN BB9 18 C4
Heyhurst Rd BBNW BB2 2 C4
Heymoor Av GTH/LHO BB6 22 E5
Heys ACC BB5 44 A4
Heys Cl BBNW BB2 49 F2
RAW/HAS BB4 62 B1
Heys Ct ACC BB5 44 A4
BBNW BB2 49 G1
Heysham Crs BBNW BB2 41 K6
Heys La ACC BB5 44 A4
DWN BB3 49 F3
DWN BB3 58 E1
Heys St BCUP OL13 64 A1
GTH/LHO BB6 23 F6
RAW/HAS BB4 53 J6
RAW/HAS BB4 62 B2
Hey St NLSN BB9 8 E6
Heywood St GTH/LHO BB6 33 J1
Heyworth Av BBNW BB2 49 G2
Hibson Rd NLSN BB9 18 D3
Hibson St NLSN BB9 18 E1
Hick's Ter BBN BB1 33 H4
Hiers House La COL BB8 9 H1
Higgin St BRFD/BLYE BB10 5 K4
BRFD/BLYE BB10 28 C6
COL BB8 9 J2
Higham Hall Rd
PDHM/BLYW BB12 16 D4
Higham Rd PDHM/BLYW BB12 16 A6
Higham St PDHM/BLYW BB12 25 G2
Highbank BBN BB1 31 K4
Highbury Pl BBN BB1 2 E1
High Cl PDHM/BLYW BB12 25 H5
Higher Antley St ACC BB5 44 C2
Higher Audley St BBN BB1 3 H5
Higher Barn St BBN BB1 3 H4
Higher Booths La
RAW/HAS BB4 46 E6
Higher Cswy NLSN BB9 8 D4
Higher Commons La
BBNW BB2 30 A1
Higher Croft Rd DWN BB3 49 K1
Higher Cross Rw BCUP OL13 * 57 F6
Higher Eanam BBN BB1 3 J4
Higher Fld GTH/LHO BB6 21 H3
Higher Firs Dr ACC BB5 34 C2
Higher Gate Rd ACC BB5 35 H4
Higher House Cl BBNW BB2 49 F2
Higher La RAW/HAS BB4 53 K5
Higher Lawrence St
DWN BB3 * 58 E1
Higher London Ter DWN BB3 59 G1
Higher Mill St RAW/HAS BB4 54 E6
Higher Peel St ACC BB5 43 K4
Higher Perry St DWN BB3 59 G1
Higher Ramsgreave Rd
BBN BB1 31 G2
Higher Reedley Rd NLSN BB9 18 C5
Higher Saxifield
BRFD/BLYE BB10 18 E6
Higher South St DWN BB3 * 59 G2
Higher Tentre BLY BB11 5 J4
Higher Witton Rd BBNW BB2 41 F3
Highfield BCUP OL13 63 K1
GTH/LHO BB6 22 C6
Highfield Av BRFD/BLYE BB10 18 B6
Highfield Cl ACC BB5 44 B4
Highfield Ct RAW/HAS BB4 60 D1
Highfield Crs NLSN BB9 8 E4
Highfield Gdns BBNW BB2 41 J5
Highfield Ms DWN BB3 59 G3
Highfield Pk RAW/HAS BB4 60 D1
Highfield Rd BBN BB1 33 G4
BBNW BB2 41 J4
CLI BB7 6 D4
DWN BB3 59 G2
RAW/HAS BB4 62 C2
Highfield St DWN BB3 59 G3
Highgate NLSN BB9 18 D2
Highmoor NLSN BB9 19 F3
Highmoor Pk CLI BB7 6 E4
High St ACC BB5 44 B4
BBN BB1 3 F4
BBN BB1 33 H4
CLI BB7 6 A3
COL BB8 10 A2
DWN BB3 59 F2
NLSN BB9 * 18 B4
NLSN BB9 * 18 D2
PDHM/BLYW BB12 25 G2
RAW/HAS BB4 53 K5
Hightown Rd RAW/HAS BB4 55 J5
Highwoods Pk GTH/LHO BB6 12 C4
Higson St BBNW BB2 2 C3
Hilary St BRFD/BLYE BB10 27 F2
Hildrop Rd NLSN BB9 9 F6
Hill Crest BCUP OL13 63 J2
Hill Crest Av BRFD/BLYE BB10 39 F1
Hillcrest Rd BBNW BB2 40 D5
GTH/LHO BB6 21 H3
Hill End La RAW/HAS BB4 62 B2
Hill Houses DWN BB3 59 F3
Hillingdon Rd
BRFD/BLYE BB10 18 D6
Hillingdon Rd North
BRFD/BLYE BB10 18 C5
Hill La COL BB8 10 D1
Hill Pl NLSN BB9 18 D3
Hill Ri RAW/HAS BB4 61 F2
Hillsborough Av NLSN BB9 18 D4
Hillside BLY BB11 37 H2
Hillside Av BBN BB1 42 D3
BRFD/BLYE BB10 18 C5
Hillside Cl BLY BB11 37 H2
CLI BB7 6 D5
GTH/LHO BB6 22 D5
NLSN BB9 18 C4
Hillside Crs BCUP OL13 57 F2
Hillside Dr RAW/HAS BB4 62 D1
Hillside Gdns DWN BB3 59 F3
Hillside Rd RAW/HAS BB4 61 F1
Hillside Vw NLSN BB9 18 C4
Hillside Wk BBN BB1 42 C3
Hill St ACC BB5 * 34 C4
ACC BB5 43 K2
ACC BB5 44 E2
ACC BB5 45 F5
BBN BB1 42 B2
COL BB8 9 K3
NLSN BB9 18 B4
PDHM/BLYW BB12 17 K3
PDHM/BLYW BB12 25 F4
RAW/HAS BB4 54 E2
Hill Top NLSN BB9 8 D3
Hilltop Dr RAW/HAS BB4 61 F4
Hill Vw BBN BB1 31 J5
RAW/HAS BB4 61 J2
Hilmont Ter BBN BB1 31 K6
Hilton Rd DWN BB3 59 G3
Hilton St DWN BB3 59 F3
Hindle Fold La GTH/LHO BB6 22 D5
Hindle St ACC BB5 44 C1
BCUP OL13 63 J3
DWN BB3 58 D1
Hindley Ct NLSN BB9 8 C6
Hind St BRFD/BLYE BB10 27 G1
Hinton St BRFD/BLYE BB10 5 K4
Hippings Wy CLI BB7 6 D1
Hirst St BLY BB11 5 J7
PDHM/BLYW BB12 25 F2
Hoarstones Av
PDHM/BLYW BB12 17 H2
Hobart St BLY BB11 5 J2
Hob Gn BBNW BB2 30 D3
Hobson St RAW/HAS BB4 54 D5
Hodder Gv CLI BB7 6 B4
DWN BB3 49 J5
Hodder Pl BBN BB1 3 G1
Hodder St ACC BB5 45 F1
BBN BB1 3 F1
BRFD/BLYE BB10 18 C6
Hoddlesden Rd DWN BB3 59 K2
Hodgson St ACC BB5 44 A3
DWN BB3 59 G2
Hogarth Av BLY BB11 37 J2
Hoghton Av BCUP OL13 64 B2
Holbeck St BRFD/BLYE BB10 27 F3
Holcombe Dr BRFD/BLYE BB10 5 K2
Holcombe Rd RAW/HAS BB4 60 C3
Holden Cl NLSN BB9 8 C6
Holden Fold DWN BB3 50 B6
Holden Rd NLSN BB9 18 A4
Holden St ACC BB5 * 44 D2
BBN BB1 51 F3
BBNW BB2 2 A5
BLY BB11 5 F3
CLI BB7 6 E3
Holden Wood Dr
RAW/HAS BB4 60 C2
Hole House St BBN BB1 42 C2
Holgate St BRFD/BLYE BB10 19 F6
GTH/LHO BB6 22 D6
Holker St COL BB8 9 H3
DWN BB3 59 G3
Holland Av RAW/HAS BB4 54 D5
Holland Pl NLSN BB9 8 E5
Holland St ACC BB5 44 B1
BBN BB1 2 D2
PDHM/BLYW BB12 * 24 E3
Hollies Cl BBNW BB2 48 D1
Hollies Rd BBN BB1 21 F4
Hollin Bridge St BBNW BB2 41 H5
Hollingreave Rd BLY BB11 5 H6
Hollington St COL BB8 10 D2
Hollin Hl BLY BB11 38 B2
Hollin La RAW/HAS BB4 54 E5
Hollin Mill St NLSN BB9 18 B3
Hollins Av BRFD/BLYE BB10 39 F1
Hollins Cl ACC BB5 44 E3
Hollins Grove St DWN BB3 49 K6
Hollinshead Ter DWN BB3 58 A4
Hollins La ACC BB5 44 E3
Hollins Rd DWN BB3 49 K5
NLSN BB9 9 G5
Hollin St BBNW BB2 41 G5
Hollin Wy RAW/HAS BB4 54 E3
Hollinwood Dr RAW/HAS BB4 54 E4
Hollowhead Av BBN BB1 20 E6
Hollowhead La BBN BB1 20 E6
Holly Av RAW/HAS BB4 61 F2
Holly St ACC BB5 43 K3
BBN BB1 31 K6
BRFD/BLYE BB10 5 K4
NLSN BB9 19 F1
Holly Ter BBN BB1 31 K
Holly Tree Cl DWN BB3 59 F
Holly Tree Wy BBNW BB2 48 D
Holmbrook Cl BBNW BB2 49 K
Holmby St BRFD/BLYE BB10 27 G
Holme Bank RAW/HAS BB4 61 J
Holme Crs COL BB8 10 D
Holme End PDHM/BLYW BB12 17 K
Holme Hl CLI BB7 6 D
Holme La RAW/HAS BB4 61 H
Holme Lea ACC BB5 34 B
Holme Rd ACC BB5 34 A
PDHM/BLYW BB12 26 D
Holmes Dr BCUP OL13 57 F
Holmes La BCUP OL13 57 F
Holmes St BLY BB11 5 J
PDHM/BLYW BB12 25 G
RAW/HAS BB4 55 F
RAW/HAS BB4 56 A
Holmes Ter RAW/HAS BB4 54 D
The Holmes RAW/HAS BB4 54 D
Holmestrand Av BLY BB11 36 E
Holme St ACC BB5 44 D
BCUP OL13 63 J
COL BB8 10 D
DWN BB3 59 F
NLSN BB9 8 D
NLSN BB9 18 E
Holmeswood Pk
RAW/HAS BB4 61 H
Holmsley St BRFD/BLYE BB10 5 K
Holt Mill Rd RAW/HAS BB4 62 C
Holt Sq NLSN BB9 8 E
Holt St BBN BB1 33 J
RAW/HAS BB4 62 D
Holyoake St
PDHM/BLYW BB12 25 K
Homecare Av CLI BB7 15 H
Homer St BLY BB11 26 B
Homevale RAW/HAS BB4 60 D
Honey Hole BBNW BB2 41 J
Honey Holme La
BRFD/BLYE BB10 39 F
Honister Rd BRFD/BLYE BB10 18 B
Honiton Av BBNW BB2 49 G
Hood House St BLY BB11 4 D
Hood St ACC BB5 34 E
Hope St ACC BB5 44 D
BBNW BB2 2 C
BCUP OL13 57 F
BRFD/BLYE BB10 28 B
DWN BB3 58 E
GTH/LHO BB6 33 J
NLSN BB9 18 B
PDHM/BLYW BB12 * 25 G
RAW/HAS BB4 60 E
RAW/HAS BB4 62 B
Hope Ter BBNW BB2 2 A
Hopkinson St COL BB8 * 10 D
Hopwood St ACC BB5 44 C
BLY BB11 * 4 D
Horace St PDHM/BLYW BB12 * 4 B
Horden Rake BBNW BB2 48 C
Horden Vw BBNW BB2 48 C
Hordley St PDHM/BLYW BB12 25 K
Hornby Ct BBNW BB2 2 A
Hornby St ACC BB5 44 A
BLY BB11 5 H
Horncliffe Cl RAW/HAS BB4 61 H
Horncliffe Vw RAW/HAS BB4 60 E
Horne St ACC BB5 34 E
Horning Crs BRFD/BLYE BB10 27 J
Horsfall Cl ACC BB5 34 D
Horsfield Cl COL BB8 10 B
Horton Av BRFD/BLYE BB10 18 B
Howard Cl ACC BB5 44 B
Howard St BBN BB1 33 G
BLY BB11 4 A
NLSN BB9 * 18 C
Howarth Av ACC BB5 34 B
Howarth Cl BLY BB11 38 A
Howarth's St RAW/HAS BB4 55 K
Howe Cft CLI BB7 6 E
Howe Wk BLY BB11 5 G
Howgill Cl NLSN BB9 19 F
Howorth Rd BLY BB11 38 A
Howsin St BRFD/BLYE BB10 27 F
Hoyle St ACC BB5 53 J
BCUP OL13 63 K
Hozier St BBN BB1 42 C
Hubie St PDHM/BLYW BB12 26 E
Hud Hey Rd RAW/HAS BB4 53 J
Hud Rake RAW/HAS BB4 53 K
Hudson Cl BBNW BB2 31 F
Hudson St ACC BB5 44 E
BLY BB11 4 B
NLSN BB9 * 18 B
Hufling Ct BLY BB11 5 J
Hufling La BLY BB11 5 J
Hughes St BLY BB11 5 G
Hugh Rake RAW/HAS BB4 54 D
Hull St BLY BB11 5 J
Hulton Dr NLSN BB9 18 E
Humphrey St NLSN BB9 18 B
Hunslet St BLY BB11 5 J
NLSN BB9 19 F
Hunters Dr PDHM/BLYW BB12 26 C
Hunters Ldg BBNW BB2 40 D
Huntington Dr DWN BB3 59 F
Huntroyde Av
PDHM/BLYW BB12 24 E
Huntroyde Cl
PDHM/BLYW BB12 26 C
Hurst Crs RAW/HAS BB4 55 F
Hurstead St ACC BB5 45 G
Hurst La RAW/HAS BB4 55 F
Hurstwood Av BBNW BB2 40 E
BRFD/BLYE BB10 27 J
Hurstwood Gdns NLSN BB9 18 D
Hurstwood La
BRFD/BLYE BB10 39 H
Hurtley St BRFD/BLYE BB10 27 F
Hutch Bank Rd RAW/HAS BB4 60 C
Hutchinson Ct DWN BB3 58 E
Hutchinson St BBNW BB2 * 41 J

uttock End La BCUP OL13 63 J3
utton Dr PDHM/BLYW BB12 26 D4
utton St BBN BB1 3 K3
yacinth Cl RAW/HAS BB4 60 C3
yndburn Br GTH/LHO BB6 23 G6
yndburn Dr DWN BB3 49 H5
yndburn Rd ACC BB5 44 B1
GTH/LHO BB6 23 F6
yndburn St ACC BB5 44 B1
he Hynings GTH/LHO BB6 22 C5
ythe Cl BBN BB1 42 C3

I

conhurst Cl ACC BB5 45 F5
e St BBN BB1 31 J6
stone Cl BBNW BB2 50 A1
htenhill Park La
PDHM/BLYW BB12 26 B1
htenhill Park Ms
PDHM/BLYW BB12 26 B4
htenhill St
PDHM/BLYW BB12 25 F2
hten Rd PDHM/BLYW BB12 4 A1
ston Ms NLSN BB9 * 18 B4
ch Fld BRFD/BLYE BB10 28 C5
dia St ACC BB5 44 B1
DWN BB3 59 G3
dustrial Pl BCUP OL13 64 A1
dustrial St BCUP OL13 64 B1
dustry St DWN BB3 59 G1
fant St ACC BB5 44 E1
firmary Cl BBNW BB2 * 41 H5
firmary Rd BBNW BB2 41 H5
firmary St BBNW BB2 41 J5
g Dene Av COL BB8 9 H3
g Dene Cl COL BB8 9 H3
gham St NLSN BB9 8 D4
glehurst Rd BLY BB11 26 A6
gle Nook BRFD/BLYE BB10 39 F1
gleton Cl ACC BB5 45 F2
glewhite Fold
PDHM/BLYW BB12 25 G4
kerman St BBN BB1 3 F1
BCUP OL13 64 B1
PDHM/BLYW BB12 * 25 F3
skip St PDHM/BLYW BB12 25 F3
stitute St PDHM/BLYW BB12 25 G3
take Crs COL BB8 10 B1
verness Rd DWN BB3 58 E3
ene Pl BBNW BB2 41 F2
ene St BRFD/BLYE BB10 27 H6
on St BBNW BB2 41 H4
vine St NLSN BB9 * 9 F5
ving Pl BBNW BB2 41 F2
well St BCUP OL13 64 A1
PDHM/BLYW BB12 25 K5
well Ter BCUP OL13 57 F6
well Vale Rd RAW/HAS BB4 61 F5
well Valley Wy BCUP OL13 57 F4
BCUP OL13 63 J3
RAW/HAS BB4 61 G4
herwood St BBNW BB2 41 H6
le of Man BBN BB1 31 J1
le of Man St RAW/HAS BB4 55 K2
lington BBNW BB2 2 E7
lington Cl BRFD/BLYE BB10 18 D6
an St BRFD/BLYE BB10 27 G1
egate COL BB8 9 K2
inson Rd DWN BB3 50 B6
ory St PDHM/BLYW BB12 26 B5
y Av RAW/HAS BB4 54 A6
y St BBNW BB2 41 H5
BRFD/BLYE BB10 27 G2
NLSN BB9 9 G5
RAW/HAS BB4 62 E3
y Ter DWN BB3 59 G5

J

cks Key Dr DWN BB3 59 H6
ckson Heights Rd BBN BB1 51 H5
ckson St ACC BB5 * 34 B2
ACC BB5 * 44 A2
BRFD/BLYE BB10 * 27 F3
ck Walker Wy BBNW BB2 49 H2
cob St ACC BB5 44 E2
mes Av GTH/LHO BB6 22 C6
mes St ACC BB5 34 B2
ACC BB5 35 G3
ACC BB5 43 K3
BBN BB1 3 F3
BBN BB1 * 33 J4
BBN BB1 51 F3
BCUP OL13 * 63 F4
BRFD/BLYE BB10 27 F2
COL BB8 * 10 A2
DWN BB3 58 E2
GTH/LHO BB6 22 C6
RAW/HAS BB4 61 K1
mes St West DWN BB3 59 F2
ne St WHIT OL12 65 F5
nnat Cl ACC BB5 * 44 D2
sper St BBN BB1 31 K4
nny St NLSN BB9 18 D3
pson St DWN BB3 59 F3
rsey St BBNW BB2 41 F6
ssel St BBNW BB2 41 F5
bling St COL BB8 * 9 H4
ckey St BLY BB11 26 B6
e Connolly Wy
RAW/HAS BB4 62 D3
hnny Barn Cl RAW/HAS BB4 62 D1
hn O'Gaunt St
PDHM/BLYW BB12 25 F2
hnson New Rd DWN BB3 50 E6
hnson Rd DWN BB3 50 D5
hnston Cl BBNW BB2 2 B4
hnston St BBNW BB2 2 B4
John St ACC BB5 34 A6
ACC BB5 34 B2
ACC BB5 43 K4
COL BB8 9 J3
DWN BB3 58 E1
NLSN BB9 8 E3
NLSN BB9 18 B3
RAW/HAS BB4 62 E2
Joiners Aly GTH/LHO BB6 * 22 D6
Joiner's Rw BBN BB1 3 F7
Jonathan Cl RAW/HAS BB4 60 D3
Joseph St DWN BB3 59 F2
NLSN BB9 8 D5
Jubilee Cl DWN BB3 59 H2
RAW/HAS BB4 60 D2
Jubilee Rd ACC BB5 34 B6
RAW/HAS BB4 60 D2
Jubilee St ACC BB5 * 34 C4
ACC BB5 44 A3
BBN BB1 3 F5
BRFD/BLYE BB10 19 F6
DWN BB3 59 F2
PDHM/BLYW BB12 * 24 A1
Jude St NLSN BB9 18 D1
Judge Flds COL BB8 9 K1
Junction St DWN BB3 59 G4
NLSN BB9 9 G5
NLSN BB9 18 B3
PDHM/BLYW BB12 4 C2
June St BBN BB1 3 K6
Juniper St BBN BB1 32 A6
Juno St NLSN BB9 9 F5

K

Kateholm BCUP OL13 57 G2
Kay Gdns BLY BB11 5 H5
Kay St ACC BB5 43 K3
BBNW BB2 41 J4
CLI BB7 6 C4
DWN BB3 59 G2
PDHM/BLYW BB12 25 G2
RAW/HAS BB4 61 K1
Keats Cl ACC BB5 45 G5
COL BB8 9 K1
Keats Fold PDHM/BLYW BB12 25 J4
Keele Wk BBN BB1 3 H6
Keighley Av COL BB8 9 K1
Keighley Rd COL BB8 10 B2
Keirby Wk BLY BB11 5 H3
Keith St PDHM/BLYW BB12 26 B5
Kelbrook Dr BLY BB11 37 J2
Kelsall Av BBN BB1 32 B5
Kelswick Dr NLSN BB9 18 E3
Kelvin St DWN BB3 58 E2
Kemp Ct BBN BB1 31 K2
Kemple Vw CLI BB7 6 B5
Kempton Ri BBN BB1 41 K4
Kendal Av NLSN BB9 8 D3
Kendall Cl BBNW BB2 49 H1
Kendal Rw BBN BB1 51 F3
Kendal St BBN BB1 3 F2
CLI BB7 6 E2
NLSN BB9 8 D6
Kenilworth Cl
PDHM/BLYW BB12 25 H3
Kenilworth Dr CLI BB7 6 B5
Kensington Pl BLY BB11 4 B6
Kensington St NLSN BB9 18 C2
Kent Ct NLSN BB9 8 D3
Kent Dr BBN BB1 42 E3
Kentmere Cl
PDHM/BLYW BB12 26 A3
Kentmere Dr BBNW BB2 48 C1
Kent St BBN BB1 3 G6
PDHM/BLYW BB12 26 E4
Kent Wk RAW/HAS BB4 60 D3
Kenworthy St BBN BB1 3 H1
Kenyon Rd NLSN BB9 18 A2
Kenyon St ACC BB5 44 D1
BBN BB1 42 C1
BCUP OL13 64 C3
RAW/HAS BB4 54 E6
Keppel Pl BLY BB11 4 C4
Kershaw Cl RAW/HAS BB4 54 E2
Kershaw St ACC BB5 44 A1
BCUP OL13 * 64 A1
Kestrel Cl BBN BB1 31 H5
Keswick Cl ACC BB5 35 F4
Keswick Dr BBNW BB2 48 C1
Keswick Rd BRFD/BLYE BB10 27 F1
Keynsham Gv
PDHM/BLYW BB12 26 C4
Key Vw DWN BB3 59 H6
Khyber St COL BB8 9 J3
Kibble Crs BRFD/BLYE BB10 18 C6
Kibble Gv NLSN BB9 18 D5
Kidder St BBNW BB2 49 H1
Kiddrow La PDHM/BLYW BB12 25 K5
Kielder Dr PDHM/BLYW BB12 26 C4
Killington St BRFD/BLYE BB10 27 H1
Kiln Cl CLI BB7 7 F1
Kiln Hl PDHM/BLYW BB12 16 D3
Kiln House Wy ACC BB5 44 C4
The Kilns BLY BB11 38 B2
Kiln St NLSN BB9 18 D1
Kimberley Cl BRFD/BLYE BB10 19 F6
Kimberley St BCUP OL13 * 63 F4
BRFD/BLYE BB10 19 F6
Kime St PDHM/BLYW BB12 26 B5
King Edward St ACC BB5 43 J4
Kingfisher Bank BLY BB11 37 F1
Kingfisher Cl BBN BB1 31 J5
King La CLI BB7 6 D3
Kings Av RAW/HAS BB4 61 K2
King's Bridge Cl BBNW BB2 41 F6
King's Bridge St BBNW BB2 41 F6
Kingsbridge Whf BBNW BB2 41 F6
King's Cswy NLSN BB9 18 D4
Kingsdale Av BRFD/BLYE BB10 18 B6
Kings Dr DWN BB3 59 K2
PDHM/BLYW BB12 25 H5
King's Hwy ACC BB5 35 H5
ACC BB5 53 K1
Kingshotte Gdns NLSN BB9 8 C4
Kingsland Gv BLY BB11 5 J7
Kingsland Rd BLY BB11 38 B2
Kingsley Av PDHM/BLYW BB12 25 H4
Kingsley Cl ACC BB5 34 B6
Kingsley Rd COL BB8 11 F1
Kingsley St NLSN BB9 9 F5
Kingsmead BBN BB1 42 D3
Kingsmill Av CLI BB7 13 G1
King's Rd ACC BB5 34 D5
BBNW BB2 49 F1
Kingston Av ACC BB5 44 C3
Kingston Crs RAW/HAS BB4 60 C4
Kingston Pl DWN BB3 49 J2
King St ACC BB5 * 34 B3
ACC BB5 44 D1
BBNW BB2 2 D5
BCUP OL13 64 A1
BRFD/BLYE BB10 19 F6
CLI BB7 6 D3
CLI BB7 13 J5
COL BB8 10 A2
GTH/LHO BB6 22 D6
NLSN BB9 18 A4
PDHM/BLYW BB12 25 F3
RAW/HAS BB4 53 K5
RAW/HAS BB4 62 D3
Kingsway ACC BB5 34 C5
ACC BB5 35 H4
BLY BB11 5 G2
BLY BB11 36 A2
DWN BB3 50 A2
GTH/LHO BB6 23 G5
King William St BBN BB1 2 E4
Kinross Cl BBN BB1 3 K5
Kinross St BLY BB11 4 B5
Kinross Wk BBN BB1 3 K5
Kipling Pl GTH/LHO BB6 33 H1
Kirby Rd BBNW BB2 41 H6
NLSN BB9 18 B1
Kirk Av CLI BB7 6 B3
Kirkdale Av RAW/HAS BB4 62 D2
Kirkdale Cl DWN BB3 59 H5
Kirkdale Rd GTH/LHO BB6 21 H3
Kirkfell Dr PDHM/BLYW BB12 26 B3
Kirkgate BLY BB11 5 J6
Kirkhill Av RAW/HAS BB4 54 A6
Kirk Hill Rd RAW/HAS BB4 54 A6
Kirkmoor Cl CLI BB7 6 C2
Kirkmoor Rd CLI BB7 6 C2
Kirk Rd ACC BB5 34 A6
Kirkstall Av PDHM/BLYW BB12 24 A2
Kirkstone Av BBNW BB2 48 C1
Kirk Vw RAW/HAS BB4 63 F2
Knighton Av BBNW BB2 31 G5
Knightsbridge Av COL BB8 9 H2
Knott Hill St WHIT OL12 65 F5
Knotts Dr COL BB8 9 J4
Knotts La COL BB8 9 J3
PDHM/BLYW BB12 25 J5
Knotts Mt COL BB8 9 J4
Knott St DWN BB3 59 F2
Knowle La DWN BB3 50 A6
Knowlesly Rd DWN BB3 59 G5
Knowles St BBN BB1 33 H4
Knowl Gap Av RAW/HAS BB4 60 D2
Knowl Meadow RAW/HAS BB4 60 D5
Knowlmere St ACC BB5 44 D1
Knowsley Crs WHIT OL12 65 F5
Knowsley Park Wy
RAW/HAS BB4 60 E3
Knowsley Rd BBN BB1 20 E6
RAW/HAS BB4 60 E3
Knowsley Rd West BBN BB1 20 D5
Knowsley St COL BB8 * 9 K3
Knuck Knowles Dr CLI BB7 6 D1
Kyan St BRFD/BLYE BB10 27 G1

L

Laburnum Cl BLY BB11 4 B7
Laburnum Dr ACC BB5 44 B4
Laburnum Rd BBN BB1 32 A5
Laburnum St RAW/HAS BB4 53 J6
Lachman Rd COL BB8 10 D4
Ladbrooke Gv BLY BB11 37 J3
Lady Cl DWN BB3 50 A3
Lady Hartley Ct COL BB8 11 F1
Laithe St BLY BB11 5 F6
COL BB8 9 J3
Lakeland Cl CLI BB7 13 G6
Lakeland Wy
PDHM/BLYW BB12 26 A3
Lambert St COL BB8 10 E5
Lambeth Cl BBN BB1 3 K5
Lambeth St BBN BB1 3 K4
COL BB8 10 D2
Lambton Gates RAW/HAS BB4 62 B1
Lamlash Rd BBN BB1 42 D3
Lammack Rd BBN BB1 31 H5
Lanark St BLY BB11 4 A6
Lancaster Av ACC BB5 34 C6
RAW/HAS BB4 60 D3
Lancaster Dr ACC BB5 34 B2
CLI BB7 6 B3
PDHM/BLYW BB12 25 G5
Lancaster Ga NLSN BB9 18 C2
Lancaster Pl BBNW BB2 41 F2
Lancaster St ACC BB5 43 J4
BBNW BB2 2 A6
COL BB8 9 K2
Lancing Pl BBNW BB2 2 A7
Land Ga WHIT OL12 65 F6
Landseer Cl BLY BB11 37 J2
Lane End La BCUP OL13 64 B2
Lane End Rd BCUP OL13 64 B3
Lane Head La BCUP OL13 57 F6
Lane House Cl BBNW BB2 * 49 F1
Lane House La COL BB8 10 E5
Laneshaw Cl DWN BB3 49 J5
Laneside ACC BB5 24 A5
Laneside Av ACC BB5 34 D5
PDHM/BLYW BB12 16 D3
Laneside Rd RAW/HAS BB4 60 E1
Langdale Av CLI BB7 6 B4
RAW/HAS BB4 61 H1
Langdale Cl ACC BB5 35 F4
BBNW BB2 48 C1
Langdale Ri COL BB8 10 B1
Langdale Rd BBNW BB2 48 B2
PDHM/BLYW BB12 25 F1
Langfield BRFD/BLYE BB10 28 C5
Langford St ACC BB5 45 G6
Langham Av ACC BB5 34 D5
Langham Rd BBN BB1 31 H6
Langham St
PDHM/BLYW BB12 26 A5
Langholme Cl NLSN BB9 8 C6
Langholme St NLSN BB9 18 E3
Langho St BBNW BB2 41 G6
Langroyd Rd COL BB8 10 A2
Langshaw Dr CLI BB7 6 D5
Lang St ACC BB5 44 C1
Langwyth Rd
BRFD/BLYE BB10 27 K6
Lansbury Pl NLSN BB9 9 F5
Lansdowne Cl BLY BB11 4 E6
Lansdowne St BBNW BB2 41 F4
Larch Av ACC BB5 44 B4
Larch Cl BBNW BB2 48 D1
RAW/HAS BB4 61 J3
The Larches BBN BB1 31 K6
Larch St NLSN BB9 19 F1
PDHM/BLYW BB12 * 26 B4
Largs Rd BBN BB1 42 C5
Lark Hl BBN BB1 3 G2
Larkhill GTH/LHO BB6 12 C4
Lark Hl RAW/HAS BB4 54 E6
Larkhill Av BRFD/BLYE BB10 18 C4
Larkspur Cl BBNW BB2 48 B1
Lark St COL BB8 10 A1
DWN BB3 59 G6
PDHM/BLYW BB12 26 B4
Latham St BRFD/BLYE BB10 27 G2
Laund Ga PDHM/BLYW BB12 17 H1
Laund Gv ACC BB5 45 F4
Laund Hey Vw RAW/HAS BB4 60 E2
Laund La RAW/HAS BB4 54 A6
Laund Rd ACC BB5 45 F5
Laund St RAW/HAS BB4 54 D5
Laurel Av DWN BB3 59 G1
Laurel St BCUP OL13 57 F6
BLY BB11 * 5 J6
Laurier Rd BRFD/BLYE BB10 18 B6
Lavender Hl RAW/HAS BB4 61 J2
Lawley Rd BBNW BB2 40 E2
Lawn St BRFD/BLYE BB10 27 F3
Lawrence Av BLY BB11 26 B6
PDHM/BLYW BB12 24 B2
Lawrence St BBNW BB2 2 B5
PDHM/BLYW BB12 25 G2
RAW/HAS BB4 55 K5
Lawson St RAW/HAS BB4 54 E1
Law St RAW/HAS BB4 62 E2
Laxey Rd BBNW BB2 41 J6
Lea Bank RAW/HAS BB4 62 C1
Leach St BBNW BB2 41 J5
COL BB8 9 J3
Leacroft DWN BB3 50 A3
Lea Dr BBNW BB2 49 J3
Leamington Av
BRFD/BLYE BB10 27 H2
Leamington Rd BBNW BB2 41 F1
Leamington St NLSN BB9 18 E2
Leaverholme Cl
BRFD/BLYE BB10 39 G6
Leaver St PDHM/BLYW BB12 25 K5
Lebanon St BRFD/BLYE BB10 27 H6
Lee Brook Cl RAW/HAS BB4 54 E5
Leebrook Rd RAW/HAS BB4 54 D5
Leeds Cl BBN BB1 3 J6
Leeds Rd NLSN BB9 9 G5
Lee Green St BRFD/BLYE BB10 27 G3
Lee Gv BRFD/BLYE BB10 39 F1
Lee La BBN BB1 33 G2
Lee Rd BCUP OL13 63 K4
NLSN BB9 9 F5
Lees Ct DWN BB3 * 49 J5
Lee's St BCUP OL13 64 D3
The Lees BRFD/BLYE BB10 39 G6
Lee St ACC BB5 44 E1
BCUP OL13 64 A1
BRFD/BLYE BB10 27 F3
NLSN BB9 8 D4
Leet Rd PDHM/BLYW BB12 16 D4
Leeward Cl DWN BB3 49 K3
Leicester Rd BBN BB1 42 C2
Leigh Pk BLY BB11 36 A2
Lemonious St ACC BB5 44 E3
Lenches Fold COL BB8 9 K4
Lenches Rd COL BB8 9 K4
Lench Rd RAW/HAS BB4 62 C3
Lench St RAW/HAS BB4 62 E3
Lennox St BRFD/BLYE BB10 28 B5
Leonard St NLSN BB9 18 E2
Leopold Rd BBNW BB2 41 F1
Leopold St COL BB8 9 H3
Leopold Wy BBNW BB2 50 A1
Levant St PDHM/BLYW BB12 25 F4
Leven Gv DWN BB3 49 J3
Levens Cl BBNW BB2 49 K1
Leven St BLY BB11 5 K6
Lever St RAW/HAS BB4 62 A1
Lewis St GTH/LHO BB6 22 E6
Leyburn Cl ACC BB5 45 G2
Leyburn Rd BBNW BB2 49 F2
Leyland Cl COL BB8 10 D4
Leyland Rd BLY BB11 5 J5
Leyland St ACC BB5 44 B2
Leys Cl CLI BB7 6 E2
Ley St ACC BB5 45 G5
Library St ACC BB5 44 A1
Liddesdale Rd NLSN BB9 9 H5
Liddington Cl BBNW BB2 50 A1
Lightbown St DWN BB3 50 A6
Lilac Gv CLI BB7 6 B4
DWN BB3 50 B6
Lilac Rd BBN BB1 32 A5
Lilac St COL BB8 10 B1
Lilac Ter BCUP OL13 63 J3
Lilford Rd BBN BB1 2 C1
Lily St BCUP OL13 64 A1
DWN BB3 59 G2
NLSN BB9 19 F3
Limbrick BBN BB1 2 E2
Lime Av ACC BB5 43 K5
Limefield BBNW BB2 2 A3
Limefield Av CLI BB7 13 J4
NLSN BB9 18 C3
Limefield St ACC BB5 45 F2
Lime Rd ACC BB5 34 D6
RAW/HAS BB4 54 A6
Limers La GTH/LHO BB6 22 B5
Limes Av DWN BB3 58 E3
Lime St BBN BB1 2 E2
CLI BB7 6 E2
COL BB8 10 A1
GTH/LHO BB6 22 D5
NLSN BB9 18 C1
Lime Tree Gv RAW/HAS BB4 54 E5
Limewood Cl ACC BB5 45 F1
RAW/HAS BB4 60 D4
Limey La BLY BB11 47 J1
Lina St ACC BB5 44 B1
Linby St BRFD/BLYE BB10 5 K5
Lincoln Cl BBN BB1 42 B3
Lincoln Pl RAW/HAS BB4 53 J6
Lincoln Rd BBN BB1 42 B3
Lincoln St BLY BB11 5 G6
Lincoln Wy CLI BB7 7 F2
Lindadale Av ACC BB5 44 C4
Lindadale Cl ACC BB5 44 C4
Lindale Crs BRFD/BLYE BB10 27 F1
Linden Av BBN BB1 2 D1
Linden Cl NLSN BB9 8 B6
Linden Dr CLI BB7 6 E4
Linden Lea BBNW BB2 48 D1
RAW/HAS BB4 61 J3
Linden Rd COL BB8 9 K2
Linden St BRFD/BLYE BB10 5 K5
Lindisfarne Av BBNW BB2 41 K6
Lindisfarne Cl
PDHM/BLYW BB12 26 D4
Lindley St BBNW BB2 41 F5
Lindon Park Rd RAW/HAS BB4 61 F4
Lindred Rd NLSN BB9 18 B1
Lindsay Pk BRFD/BLYE BB10 28 A6
Lindsay St BLY BB11 5 H2
Linedred La NLSN BB9 18 B2
Line St BCUP OL13 63 J3
Lingfield Av CLI BB7 6 D5
Lingfield Wy BBNW BB2 48 B1
Lingmoor Dr
PDHM/BLYW BB12 25 K3
Linkside Av NLSN BB9 19 H1
Links Rd BBNW BB2 48 A1
Linton Dr BLY BB11 37 H2
Linton Gdns NLSN BB9 8 C4
Lion Ct ACC BB5 44 A1
Lionel St PDHM/BLYW BB12 26 B5
Lions Dr BBN BB1 50 D1
Lion St ACC BB5 34 A6
Lisbon Dr BLY BB11 4 D4
DWN BB3 59 H2
Lisbon Drive BLY BB11 4 D3
Lister St ACC BB5 44 C1
Littlemoor Rd CLI BB7 6 D5
Little Moor Vw CLI BB7 6 D5
Little Peel St BBNW BB2 2 C4
Little Queen St COL BB8 * 9 J3
Little St ACC BB5 44 C1
Little Toms La
BRFD/BLYE BB10 18 D6
Littondale BBNW BB2 48 B2
Littondale Gdn BBNW BB2 * 48 B2
Liverpool Rd
PDHM/BLYW BB12 25 K5
Livesey Branch Rd BBNW BB2 48 B2
Livesey Hall Cl BBNW BB2 40 C6
Livesey St BBN BB1 33 H3
PDHM/BLYW BB12 25 F3
Livingstone Rd ACC BB5 34 D5
BBNW BB2 41 F3
Livingstone St NLSN BB9 18 B4
Lloyd Cl NLSN BB9 18 E1
Lloyd St DWN BB3 49 K6
Lock Ga RAW/HAS BB4 61 F2
Lockside BBNW BB2 41 H5
Lock St ACC BB5 * 44 A3
Lockyer Av PDHM/BLYW BB12 26 A5
Lodge La BCUP OL13 64 A2
Lodgeside ACC BB5 34 B2
Lodge St ACC BB5 44 E1
Lodge Ter ACC BB5 44 A2
The Lodge GTH/LHO BB6 22 C6
Logwood St BBN BB1 31 K6
Lois Pl BBNW BB2 * 2 B3
Lomas La RAW/HAS BB4 61 J2
Lomax Cl GTH/LHO BB6 22 E5
Lomax St GTH/LHO BB6 22 D6
Lomeshaye Rd NLSN BB9 18 D2
Lomeshaye Wy NLSN BB9 18 C1
London Rd BBN BB1 2 E1
London Ter DWN BB3 59 G1
London Wk BBN BB1 2 E1
The Long Cswy
BRFD/BLYE BB10 39 G3
Long Cl CLI BB7 6 E1
Longholme Rd RAW/HAS BB4 61 K1
Long La DWN BB3 48 D6
Long Meadow COL BB8 * 10 C2
Longridge Heath
BRFD/BLYE BB10 18 D5
Longshaw La BBNW BB2 41 H5
Longshaw St BBNW BB2 41 H6
Longsight Av ACC BB5 35 H5
CLI BB7 6 E2
Longsight Rd BBNW BB2 30 A2
GTH/LHO BB6 21 J1
Longton Cl BBN BB1 42 C2

Longton Rd PDHM/BLYW BB12 26 C3
Longton St BBN BB1 42 B2
Longworth Av
BRFD/BLYE BB10 27 J5
Longworth Rd CLI BB7 13 H5
Lonsdale Gdns NLSN BB9 8 D4
Lonsdale St ACC BB5 44 B1
NLSN BB9 9 F6
PDHM/BLYW BB12 * 26 B4
Lord Av BCUP OL13 63 H3
Lord's Crs DWN BB3 50 A3
Lord Sq BBN BB1 2 E4
Lord St ACC BB5 44 A3
BBN BB1 33 H4
BBNW BB2 2 E4
BCUP OL13 64 A1
COL BB8 9 J2
DWN BB3 59 F1
GTH/LHO BB6 33 J1
NLSN BB9 18 A4
RAW/HAS BB4 54 D2
RAW/HAS BB4 61 K1
Lord Street Ml BBN BB1 2 E4
Lord St West BBNW BB2 2 E4
Lorne St DWN BB3 58 E1
Lorton Cl PDHM/BLYW BB12 26 A3
Lothersdale Cl
BRFD/BLYE BB10 18 D6
Lottice La BBN BB1 43 F6
Loughrigg Cl
PDHM/BLYW BB12 26 A3
Louis Pollard Crs
GTH/LHO BB6 22 E5
Louis St RAMS BL0 61 G6
Love Clough Rd RAW/HAS BB4 46 D5
Lovely Hall La BBN BB1 20 C3
Low Bank PDHM/BLYW BB12 25 H5
Lower Antley St ACC BB5 44 B2
Lower Ashworth Cl BBNW BB2 2 B5
Lower Audley St BBN BB1 3 F6
Lower Barnes St ACC BB5 34 A1
Lower Barn St DWN BB3 59 H4
Lower Clough St NLSN BB9 8 C5
Lower Clowes Rd
RAW/HAS BB4 61 H3
Lower Cockcroft BBNW BB2 2 E4
Lower Cribden Av
RAW/HAS BB4 61 H1
Lower Cross St DWN BB3 59 F2
Lower Eccleshill Rd DWN BB3 50 A4
Lowerfield GTH/LHO BB6 21 G3
Lowerfields PDHM/BLYW BB12 25 J5
Lowerfold GTH/LHO BB6 22 D5
Lowerfold Rd GTH/LHO BB6 22 D5
Lowergate CLI BB7 6 D3
Lower Gate Rd ACC BB5 35 H3
Lower Hazel Cl BBNW BB2 2 B5
Lower Hollin Bank St
BBNW BB2 41 H5
Lowerhouse Crs
PDHM/BLYW BB12 25 K5
Lower House Gn
RAW/HAS BB4 55 K1
Lowerhouse La
PDHM/BLYW BB12 25 K5
Lower Laithe Dr NLSN BB9 8 C4
Lower La RAW/HAS BB4 53 K5
Lower Manor La
PDHM/BLYW BB12 26 E1
Lower Mead Dr
PDHM/BLYW BB12 26 E1
Lower Parrock Rd NLSN BB9 8 C6
Lower Philips Rd BBN BB1 32 B5
Lower Ridge Cl
BRFD/BLYE BB10 5 K2
Lower Rosegrove La
PDHM/BLYW BB12 25 J6
Lower School St COL BB8 9 K3
Lower Tentre BLY BB11 5 J4
Lower Timber Hill La BLY BB11 38 A2
Lower Wilworth BBN BB1 31 J4
Loweswater Cl ACC BB5 35 G5
Loweswater Crs
PDHM/BLYW BB12 26 A3
Lowe Vw RAW/HAS BB4 62 E2
Lowood Pl BBNW BB2 40 E1
Lowther Pl BBN BB1 32 A5
Lowther St NLSN BB9 18 C1
Lowthwaite Dr NLSN BB9 18 E3
Loxley Gdns
PDHM/BLYW BB12 25 J5
Lubbock St PDHM/BLYW BB12 26 B5
Lucy St NLSN BB9 8 D4
Luke St BCUP OL13 63 H3
Lumb Holes La RAW/HAS BB4 62 D4
Lumb La RAW/HAS BB4 55 K5
Lumb Scar BCUP OL13 64 A1
Lund St BBNW BB2 2 A5
Lune St COL BB8 10 A3
PDHM/BLYW BB12 25 H3
Lupin Cl ACC BB5 34 C6
Lupin Rd ACC BB5 34 D6
Lupton Dr NLSN BB9 8 D3
Lutner St BLY BB11 5 H5
Lydgate BRFD/BLYE BB10 27 K1
Lydia St ACC BB5 44 D3
Lyndale Av BBN BB1 21 F4
RAW/HAS BB4 60 E1
Lyndale Cl BBN BB1 * 21 F4
RAW/HAS BB4 54 E2
Lyndale Rd BLY BB11 36 A2
Lyndhurst Av BBN BB1 42 E2
Lyndhurst Gv GTH/LHO BB6 23 F5
Lyndhurst Rd BBNW BB2 41 J5
BRFD/BLYE BB10 27 H6
DWN BB3 49 J6
Lyndon Av GTH/LHO BB6 23 F5
Lyndon Ct GTH/LHO BB6 23 F5
Lynfield Rd GTH/LHO BB6 23 F5
Lynthorpe Rd BBNW BB2 41 J5
NLSN BB9 9 G6
Lynton Rd ACC BB5 44 B3
Lynwood Av ACC BB5 34 B1
DWN BB3 49 J6
Lynwood Cl ACC BB5 34 B1
DWN BB3 49 J6
Lynwood Rd ACC BB5 35 G3
BBNW BB2 41 F1
Lytham Rd BBNW BB2 49 K1
BRFD/BLYE BB10 27 H1
Lytton St PDHM/BLYW BB12 25 J4

M

Mabel St COL BB8 10 B2
Macaulay St BLY BB11 26 B6
Macleod St NLSN BB9 18 D1
Maden Rd BCUP OL13 63 J1
Maden St ACC BB5 44 A1
Maden Wy BCUP OL13 64 A1
Magpie Cl BLY BB11 26 B6
Maiden St RAW/HAS BB4 53 K3
Maitland Pl RAW/HAS BB4 61 K2
Maitland St BCUP OL13 64 A1
Major St ACC BB5 44 D3
RAW/HAS BB4 54 E2
Malham Av ACC BB5 44 B3
Malham Gdns BBN BB1 3 H7
Malham Rd BRFD/BLYE BB10 18 D6
Malham Wend NLSN BB9 8 C4
The Mall BLY BB11 5 F3
Malt St ACC BB5 34 D6
Malvern Av ACC BB5 44 A4
BBNW BB2 41 H6
PDHM/BLYW BB12 25 G5
Malvern Ct NLSN BB9 * 9 F6
Malvern Rd NLSN BB9 9 F6
Malvern Wy RAW/HAS BB4 60 D4
Manchester Rd ACC BB5 44 E2
BLY BB11 5 F5
BLY BB11 47 G2
NLSN BB9 18 D1
PDHM/BLYW BB12 36 A1
RAW/HAS BB4 60 E1
Mancknols St NLSN BB9 19 F2
Mandella Ct BBN BB1 3 F1
Manitoba Cl BBNW BB2 31 F5
Manner Sutton St BBN BB1 3 H3
Manor Brook ACC BB5 44 E1
Manor Flds CLI BB7 13 J4
Manor Pl ACC BB5 34 B6
Manor Rd BBNW BB2 41 F2
CLI BB7 * 6 C4
CLI BB7 13 J4
DWN BB3 58 E3
PDHM/BLYW BB12 26 A4
Manor St ACC BB5 35 F6
BCUP OL13 64 A2
NLSN BB9 19 F2
Mansergh St
BRFD/BLYE BB10 * 27 H1
Mansfield Cl GTH/LHO BB6 12 B4
Mansfield Crs NLSN BB9 18 C3
Mansfield Gv NLSN BB9 18 C3
Mansion St South ACC BB5 * 45 F1
Manxman Rd BBNW BB2 41 K6
Maple Av RAW/HAS BB4 54 A6
Maple Bank
BRFD/BLYE BB10 27 H4
Maple Cl BBN BB1 20 D5
CLI BB7 13 K3
Maple Crs BBN BB1 33 H5
Maple Dr ACC BB5 44 B4
Maple St ACC BB5 44 B4
BBN BB1 32 A6
BBN BB1 33 H4
GTH/LHO BB6 22 E6
Marabou Dr DWN BB3 49 H6
Marble St ACC BB5 44 A2
March St PDHM/BLYW BB12 26 E3
Margaret St ACC BB5 43 J5
BBN BB1 42 D3
BRFD/BLYE BB10 * 27 F3
RAW/HAS BB4 54 D5
Maria St DWN BB3 59 G5
Maricourt Av BBN BB1 42 D2
Marine Av BLY BB11 37 G1
Market Pl COL BB8 10 A2
Market Prom BLY BB11 5 G3
Market Sq BLY BB11 5 G3
NLSN BB9 18 D1
Market St ACC BB5 44 A2
BCUP OL13 64 A1
BCUP OL13 64 E4
COL BB8 9 K2
DWN BB3 59 F2
RAW/HAS BB4 62 E3
Market Street La BBNW BB2 2 E5
Market Wy BBN BB1 2 E3
Markham Rd BBNW BB2 41 F4
Markross St RAW/HAS BB4 61 K1
Mark St BCUP OL13 63 H3
BRFD/BLYE BB10 27 G2
Marlborough Rd ACC BB5 34 E6
Marlborough St BLY BB11 5 G6
Marles Ct BRFD/BLYE BB10 27 G3
Marlin St NLSN BB9 9 F5
Marlowe Av ACC BB5 45 G5
PDHM/BLYW BB12 25 H4
Marl Pits RAW/HAS BB4 55 F6
Marl Pl ACC BB5 * 35 F4
Marlton Rd BBNW BB2 41 H6
Marquis Cl DWN BB3 49 K3
Marsden Ct BRFD/BLYE BB10 18 C6
Marsden Crs NLSN BB9 19 G1
Marsden Dr NLSN BB9 18 D3
Marsden Gv NLSN BB9 18 C4
Marsden Hall Rd NLSN BB9 19 G1
Marsden Hall Rd North
NLSN BB9 9 G6
Marsden Height Cl NLSN BB9 18 E4
Marsden Ml NLSN BB9 * 19 F3
Marsden Rd BRFD/BLYE BB10 18 C6
Marsden St ACC BB5 44 D3
BBNW BB2 41 F5
Marshall Av ACC BB5 35 G3
Marsham Gv DWN BB3 59 H2
Marsh Ga DWN BB3 59 H2
Marsh House La DWN BB3 59 H2
Marsh St BBN BB1 3 F1
Marsh Ter DWN BB3 59 F1
Martholme Av ACC BB5 34 C2
Martholme Cl GTH/LHO BB6 22 E5
Martholme La GTH/LHO BB6 23 G3
Martin Croft Rd RAW/HAS BB4 53 J4
Martindale Cl BBN BB1 * 42 C5
Martin Dr DWN BB3 59 H5
Martinfields BRFD/BLYE BB10 18 C5
Martinique Dr DWN BB3 49 K3
Martin St BRFD/BLYE BB10 27 G2
Marton Dr BLY BB11 37 J2
Mary Ct BBN BB1 * 33 H4
Maryport Cl BBNW BB2 49 K1
Mary St BBN BB1 3 K5
BBN BB1 33 H4
BRFD/BLYE BB10 5 K4
COL BB8 9 J3
Mary Towneley Fold
BRFD/BLYE BB10 38 C1
Masefield Av
PDHM/BLYW BB12 25 H4
Masefield Cl GTH/LHO BB6 33 H1
Mason St ACC BB5 43 K4
ACC BB5 * 44 E1
COL BB8 9 K2
Massey La NLSN BB9 18 A4
Massey St BLY BB11 * 5 H3
NLSN BB9 18 A5
Masterson Av
PDHM/BLYW BB12 24 A1
Mather Av ACC BB5 34 D5
Matlock Gv BRFD/BLYE BB10 27 H1
Matthew Cl COL BB8 10 A3
Matthew St BBNW BB2 41 F5
Maudsley St ACC BB5 44 E1
BBN BB1 * 3 H4
Maud St NLSN BB9 8 D5
Maurice St NLSN BB9 18 C1
Mavis Rd BBNW BB2 40 E2
Maybury Av
PDHM/BLYW BB12 26 A4
Mayfair Cl RAW/HAS BB4 60 D4
Mayfair Crs BBN BB1 20 E6
Mayfair Rd
BRFD/BLYE BB10 27 K6
NLSN BB9 9 F6
Mayfield Av ACC BB5 44 B3
CLI BB7 6 E4
RAW/HAS BB4 60 D2
Mayfield Fold BLY BB11 38 B2
Mayfield Rd BBN BB1 31 J2
Mayfield St BBNW BB2 41 J4
Mayflower St BBNW BB2 41 F5
Maylands Pl NLSN BB9 8 C4
Mayson St BBN BB1 3 F6
May St BBN BB1 3 K6
BLY BB11 5 J6
NLSN BB9 8 D5
Mayville Rd NLSN BB9 18 B3
Meadoway ACC BB5 34 B6
Meadow Bank Av
BRFD/BLYE BB10 * 18 B4
Meadow Bank Rd NLSN BB9 18 C2
Meadow Cl ACC BB5 35 H4
BRFD/BLYE BB10 18 B5
CLI BB7 13 G6
Meadowcroft DWN BB3 50 A3
Meadowcroft Cl
RAW/HAS BB4 54 E4
Meadowfield Cl CLI BB7 13 G2
Meadow Head La DWN BB3 49 F5
Meadow Pk RAW/HAS BB4 61 F6
Meadow Ri BBNW BB2 48 E2
Meadows Av BCUP OL13 57 F5
RAW/HAS BB4 60 E1
Meadows Dr RAW/HAS BB4 46 E6
Meadowside Av ACC BB5 34 A2
The Meadows ACC BB5 44 B4
CLI BB7 13 G5
COL BB8 9 K1
DWN BB3 49 J4
PDHM/BLYW BB12 26 C3
Meadow St ACC BB5 44 E1
BLY BB11 * 5 F3
DWN BB3 59 G4
GTH/LHO BB6 33 J1
PDHM/BLYW BB12 25 F2
Meadow V DWN BB3 49 J3
Meadow Vw CLI BB7 6 B3
Meadow Wy BCUP OL13 63 K1
Meadway PDHM/BLYW BB12 24 E4
Mearley Brook Fold CLI BB7 6 E4
Mearley St CLI BB7 6 D4
Mearley Syke CLI BB7 6 E3
Medina Cl ACC BB5 * 44 D2
Meins Cft BBNW BB2 40 E2
Meins Rd BBNW BB2 40 C1
Melbourne St ACC BB5 34 C4
ACC BB5 * 43 K4
DWN BB3 * 59 G5
PDHM/BLYW BB12 25 G4
RAW/HAS BB4 62 E2
Melia Cl RAW/HAS BB4 61 J1
Melita St DWN BB3 59 G3
Mellor Brow BBNW BB2 30 A2
Mellor Cl BLY BB11 37 H2
Mellor La BBNW BB2 30 C3
Melrose Av ACC BB5 44 B4
BLY BB11 4 A6
Melrose St DWN BB3 58 E1
Melville Dr BBNW BB2 2 C3
Melville Gdns DWN BB3 59 F3
Melville St BRFD/BLYE BB10 27 H2
DWN BB3 59 F3
Mercer Crs RAW/HAS BB4 60 D3
Mercer St ACC BB5 [illegible]
GTH/LHO BB6 22 E6
PDHM/BLYW BB12 25 J4
Merchants House BBN BB1 * 3 H6
Merchants Landing BBN BB1 3 G7
Merchants Quay BBN BB1 3 H7
Merclesden Av NLSN BB9 9 H6
Mere Ct BLY BB11 37 F1
Meredith St NLSN BB9 18 E2
Merlin Dr ACC BB5 43 K4
Merlin Gv
PDHM/BLYW BB12 25 H5
Merlin Rd BBNW BB2 41 F1
Mersey Av DWN BB3 49 H5
Mersey St BCUP OL13 64 B2
PDHM/BLYW BB12 25 K5
Merton St NLSN BB9 * 8 D6
PDHM/BLYW BB12 * 26 E4
Messenger St NLSN BB9 19 F2
Meta St BBNW BB2 41 J5
Metcalf Dr ACC BB5 24 A5
Metcalfe Cl BBNW BB2 49 H1
Metcalfe St
PDHM/BLYW BB12 26 A6
Mettle Cote BCUP OL13 64 B2
The Mews PDHM/BLYW BB12 * 25 F3
Micklehurst Crs BLY BB11 37 H3
Middlegate Gn RAW/HAS BB4 46 E6
Middlesex Av
PDHM/BLYW BB12 25 K4
Middle St COL BB8 9 J3
Middleton Dr NLSN BB9 8 E1
Midfield GTH/LHO BB6 21 H3
Midgley St COL BB8 10 A3
Midland St ACC BB5 44 E2
NLSN BB9 8 E6
Midsummer St BBNW BB2 2 B3
Milbrook Cl BLY BB11 26 A6
Mile End Rw BBNW BB2 41 F1
Miles Av BCUP OL13 63 J3
Milford St COL BB8 9 J2
Milking La DWN BB3 50 A3
Millar Barn La RAW/HAS BB4 62 E3
Millbrook PDHM/BLYW BB12 17 J1
Millbrook St DWN BB3 49 K2
Mill Entrance ACC BB5 34 B3
Miller Cl ACC BB5 43 J2
Miller Fold Av ACC BB5 44 D4
Mill Fld ACC BB5 34 B1
Millgate Rd RAW/HAS BB4 54 E6
Mill Gn COL BB8 9 K3
Millham St BBN BB1 3 F1
Mill Hl ACC BB5 43 K3
Mill Hill Bridge St BBNW BB2 41 F5
Mill Hill La BLY BB11 35 J3
Mill Hill St BBNW BB2 41 F5
Mill La BBNW BB2 2 E5
GTH/LHO BB6 23 G5
Mill Rw RAW/HAS BB4 54 D4
Mill St ACC BB5 34 B3
ACC BB5 43 K4
ACC BB5 45 G6
BCUP OL13 57 F6
GTH/LHO BB6 22 D6
NLSN BB9 8 D3
PDHM/BLYW BB12 25 F3
RAW/HAS BB4 53 K5
Millthorne Av CLI BB7 6 C4
Millwood Cl BBNW BB2 40 E6
Milner Rd DWN BB3 49 J5
Milner St BRFD/BLYE BB10 27 F3
Milne St RAW/HAS BB4 61 F6
Milnshaw Gdns ACC BB5 34 C6
Milnshaw La ACC BB5 44 D1
Milton Av CLI BB7 6 D2
Milton Cl DWN BB3 59 H2
GTH/LHO BB6 33 H1
RAW/HAS BB4 60 D4
Milton Rd COL BB8 9 K2
Milton St ACC BB5 34 B2
ACC BB5 43 K3
ACC BB5 44 D1
BBN BB1 3 J3
BRFD/BLYE BB10 18 E6
NLSN BB9 8 D3
NLSN BB9 * 18 B4
PDHM/BLYW BB12 25 H4
Mincing La BBNW BB2 2 E5
Minehead Av BRFD/BLYE BB10 27 J1
Minnie Ter BBNW BB2 2 A1
Minor St RAW/HAS BB4 54 E2
Minster Crs DWN BB3 59 H3
Mint Av NLSN BB9 8 D3
Mire Ash Brow BBNW BB2 30 B4
Mire Rdg COL BB8 10 C4
Mitchell St CLI BB7 6 C4
COL BB8 9 K2
PDHM/BLYW BB12 26 B5
Mitella St BRFD/BLYE BB10 27 H6
Mitre St BLY BB11 4 C3
Mitton Av NLSN BB9 9 F1
RAW/HAS BB4 54 E5
Mitton Cl BBNW BB2 49 G1
Mitton Gv BRFD/BLYE BB10 27 J6
Mitton St BBN BB1 31 K6
Mizpah St BRFD/BLYE BB10 27 H6
Moleside Cl ACC BB5 45 F1
Mollington Rd BBNW BB2 31 F6
Molly Wood La
PDHM/BLYW BB12 25 J6
Monarch St ACC BB5 44 A3
Mona Rd BBNW BB2 41 J6
Monk Hall St BRFD/BLYE BB10 27 F3
Monk St ACC BB5 44 C1
CLI BB7 6 C4
Monmouth Rd BBN BB1 42 D2
Monmouth St COL BB8 10 C2
PDHM/BLYW BB12 4 A2
Montague Cl BBNW BB2 2 C5
Montague Rd BLY BB11 4 D5
Montague St BBNW BB2 2 C3
CLI BB7 6 C3
COL BB8 10 A1
NLSN BB9 18 B4
Montford Rd
PDHM/BLYW BB12 17 K4
Montgomery Gv
PDHM/BLYW BB12 26 B4
Monton Rd DWN BB3 49 J5
Montreal Rd BBNW BB2 31 G5
Montrose St BBNW BB2 2 A7
BLY BB11 4 E7
NLSN BB9 18 B
Moor Cl DWN BB3 59 J
Moorcroft DWN BB3 50 A
Moor Edge CLI BB7 13 H
Moore Dr PDHM/BLYW BB12 16 D
Moorend CLI BB7 6 E
Moore St COL BB8 * 9 J
NLSN BB9 19 F
PDHM/BLYW BB12 25 J
Moor Fld CLI BB7 13 H
Moorfield Av ACC BB5 35 H
BBN BB1 31 J
Moorfield Cl ACC BB5 34 D
Moorfield Dr ACC BB5 34 D
Moorfield Wy ACC BB5 34 D
Moorgate ACC BB5 44 D
Moorgate Gdns BBNW BB2 41 G
Moorgate St BBNW BB2 41 G
Moorhead St COL BB8 9 J
Moorhouse Av ACC BB5 44 C
Moorhouse Cl ACC BB5 44 C
Moorhouse St ACC BB5 44 C
BLY BB11 26 B
Moorings Cl BBNW BB2 41 H
The Moorings
PDHM/BLYW BB12 4 C
Moorland Av BBNW BB2 48 B
CLI BB7 6 E
DWN BB3 58 C
Moorland Cl NLSN BB9 8 E
Moorland Crs CLI BB7 6 E
Moorland Dr NLSN BB9 18 D
Moorland Ri RAW/HAS BB4 54 A
Moorland Rd BBNW BB2 49 G
BLY BB11 37 J
CLI BB7 6 E
GTH/LHO BB6 21 H
Moorlands Ter BCUP OL13 64 B
The Moorlands BCUP OL13 57 G
Moorland Vw DWN BB3 * 50 A
NLSN BB9 18 E
Moor La CLI BB7 6 D
CLI BB7 13 H
CLI BB7 14 B
CLI BB7 22 A
DWN BB3 50 A
PDHM/BLYW BB12 25 F
RAW/HAS BB4 53 G
Moor Rd RAW/HAS BB4 60 D
Moorside Av BBN BB1 42 C
NLSN BB9 18 D
Moorside Crs BCUP OL13 57 G
Moorside Dr ACC BB5 34 C
Moor Side La CLI BB7 14 B
Moor St ACC BB5 34 B
Moorthorpe Cl DWN BB3 59 F
Moor Vw BCUP OL13 57 G
BCUP OL13 * 63 G
Moorview Cl BRFD/BLYE BB10 27 K
Morecambe Rd BBNW BB2 41 K
Moreton St ACC BB5 44 D
Morley Av BBNW BB2 40 E
Morley St BLY BB11 5 J
PDHM/BLYW BB12 25 F
Morse St BRFD/BLYE BB10 27 H
Morton St BBN BB1 2 E
Moscow Mill St ACC BB5 44 A
Mosedale Dr
PDHM/BLYW BB12 26 A
Moseley Rd BLY BB11 38 A
Mosley St BBNW BB2 41 J
NLSN BB9 18 D
Mosman Pl NLSN BB9 8 C
Mossbank BBN BB1 * 3 J
Moss Cl RAW/HAS BB4 60 D
Mossdale BBN BB1 3 J
Moss Fold Rd DWN BB3 49 J
Moss Ga BBN BB1 3 K
Moss Hall Rd ACC BB5 34 D
Moss La BBN BB1 43 F
Moss Side St WHIT OL12 65 F
Moss St BBN BB1 3 K
CLI BB7 6 C
GTH/LHO BB6 33 J
Mostyn St DWN BB3 49 J
Moulding Cl BBNW BB2 41 F
Mountain La ACC BB5 44 E
Mount Av RAW/HAS BB4 62 E
Mount Crs BRFD/BLYE BB10 39 G
Mount La BRFD/BLYE BB10 38 E
Mount Pleasant BBN BB1 3 G
RAW/HAS BB4 61 H
Mount Pleasant St
ACC BB5 * 44 A
BLY BB11 * 5 F
Mount Rd BLY BB11 4 E
Mount St ACC BB5 34 C
ACC BB5 44 D
GTH/LHO BB6 22 D
NLSN BB9 8 D
NLSN BB9 18 B
RAW/HAS BB4 61 H
Mount Ter RAW/HAS BB4 61 K
The Mount BBNW BB2 2 B
Mount Trinity BBN BB1 3 G
Mowbray Av BBNW BB2 41 K
Mulberry St BBN BB1 42 B
Mulberry Wk BBN BB1 * 42 B
Murdock St BBNW BB2 * 41 F
Murray St BRFD/BLYE BB10 27 G
Musbury Crs RAW/HAS BB4 61 J
Musbury Ms RAW/HAS BB4 60 C
Musbury Rd RAW/HAS BB4 60 B
Musden Av RAW/HAS BB4 60 D
Museum St BBN BB1 2 E
Myerscough Smithy Rd
BBNW BB2 30 A
Myers St BRFD/BLYE BB10 27 F
Myrtle Av BLY BB11 * 4 A
Myrtle Bank Rd BBNW BB2 * 49 G
BCUP OL13 57 F
Myrtle Gv BRFD/BLYE BB10 39 F
RAW/HAS BB4 60 D
Mytton St PDHM/BLYW BB12 25 G
Mytton Vw CLI BB7 6 B

N

arian Ct BBN BB1 .....31 K6
ab La ACC BB5 .....43 H3
BBNW BB2 .....2 D4
airne St BLY BB11 .....4 B4
ancy St DWN BB3 .....59 F2
ansen Rd BBNW BB2 .....41 F5
apier St ACC BB5 .....44 E2
NLSN BB9 .....18 E3
aples Av BLY BB11 * 4 A6
aples Rd DWN BB3 .....59 H2
arcissus Av RAW/HAS BB4 .....60 C3
ares Rd BBNW BB2 .....41 F4
arvik Av BLY BB11 .....37 F1
ave Cl DWN BB3 .....59 H2
avigation Wy BBN BB1 .....3 G7
aze Rd RAW/HAS BB4 .....62 D2
aze View Av RAW/HAS BB4 .....62 E1
eath Cl BBN BB1 .....31 J6
eddy La CLI BB7 .....13 G5
elson Rd BRFD/BLYE BB10 .....19 F5
elson Sq BLY BB11 .....5 F4
elson St ACC BB5 .....44 E2
BCUP OL13 .....64 D3
CLI BB7 .....6 A3
DWN BB3 .....58 E1
GTH/LHO BB6 * 22 E5
eptune St BLY BB11 .....4 E3
etherby St BLY BB11 .....4 B6
etherfield Cl
PDHM/BLYW BB12 .....4 A1
etherfield Rd NLSN BB9 .....18 E1
etherheys Cl COL BB8 .....9 H2
ethertown Cl CLI BB7 .....13 H3
etherwood Gdns
GTH/LHO BB6 .....12 B4
etherwood Rd
BRFD/BLYE BB10 .....27 H3
etherwood St
BRFD/BLYE BB10 * 27 K1
ewark St ACC BB5 .....44 B2
ew Bank Rd BBNW BB2 .....41 F1
ew Barn RAW/HAS BB4 .....60 D5
ew Barn Ct BBNW BB2 .....41 K5
ew Barn La RAW/HAS BB4 .....61 K3
ew Bath St COL BB8 .....10 A2
ewbigging Av RAW/HAS BB4 .....62 E1
ew Brown St NLSN BB9 * 8 D6
ew Bury Cl ACC BB5 .....43 J4
ewby Cl BLY BB11 .....37 H3
ewcastle St BBNW BB2 .....41 G4
ew Chapel St BBNW BB2 .....41 F5
ew Church Cl ACC BB5 * 34 B2
ewchurch Cl BBNW BB2 .....41 K5
ewchurch Old Rd BCUP OL13 .....63 J2
ewchurch Rd BCUP OL13 .....63 G3
RAW/HAS BB4 .....55 F6
ewfield Dr BBNW BB2 .....50 A1
NLSN BB9 .....18 E1
ew Garden Flds
RAW/HAS BB4 .....55 K2
ew Garden St BBNW BB2 * 41 H4
ew Ground Ct
BRFD/BLYE BB10 .....18 C6
ew Hall Hey Rd
RAW/HAS BB4 .....61 J2
ew Hall St PDHM/BLYW BB12 .....26 E2
ewhouse Rd ACC BB5 .....34 E5
ewington Av BBN BB1 .....31 K2
ewlands Av CLI BB7 .....6 B4
ewlands Cl BBNW BB2 .....48 C1
ew La ACC BB5 .....43 J5
ew Line BCUP OL13 .....64 B3
ewman St BRFD/BLYE BB10 .....27 F2
ew Market St CLI BB7 .....6 D3
COL BB8 .....9 K2
ew Mill St BBN BB1 .....3 G1
ew Oxford St COL BB8 .....10 A2
ew Park St BBNW BB2 .....2 D3
ewport St NLSN BB9 .....8 E6
ew Rd BLY BB11 .....37 K3
RAW/HAS BB4 .....62 E1
ew Rw COL BB8 .....10 E3
ew Scotland Rd NLSN BB9 .....8 E6
ew St NLSN BB9 .....9 F6
PDHM/BLYW BB12 * 24 E3
RAW/HAS BB4 .....53 K6
ew Taylor Fold
BRFD/BLYE BB10 * 19 F6
ewton Dr ACC BB5 .....45 F4
BRFD/BLYE BB10 .....39 F6
ewton St ACC BB5 * 43 H2
BBN BB1 .....42 B2
CLI BB7 .....6 C4
DWN BB3 .....59 G1
PDHM/BLYW BB12 .....26 B4
ewtown St COL BB8 .....10 A3
ew Wellington Cl BBNW BB2 .....41 G6
ew Wellington St BBNW BB2 .....41 G6
icholas St BLY BB11 .....5 G4
BRFD/BLYE BB10 .....18 E6
COL BB8 .....9 J3
DWN BB3 .....58 E2
icholl St BRFD/BLYE BB10 .....27 F3
ickey La BBNW BB2 .....30 D3
icola Cl BCUP OL13 .....57 G2
ightingale Cl BBN BB1 .....42 B6
CLI BB7 .....13 G2
ightingale Crs BLY BB11 * 26 B6
ile St NLSN BB9 * 8 D6
ixon Cl RAW/HAS BB4 * 61 F2
oble St BBN BB1 .....33 H4
DWN BB3 .....59 F3
GTH/LHO BB6 .....33 J1
oblett St BBN BB1 .....3 G3
oggarth Rd
PDHM/BLYW BB12 .....17 H1
ook La ACC BB5 .....43 H5
BBNW BB2 .....40 D6
ook Ter BBNW BB2 .....40 E6
ora St NLSN BB9 .....8 D5
Norbreck Cl BBNW BB2 .....49 K1
Norfolk Av PDHM/BLYW BB12 .....25 G5
PDHM/BLYW BB12 .....26 A4
Norfolk Cl ACC BB5 .....34 B2
Norfolk Gv ACC BB5 .....34 C6
Norfolk St ACC BB5 .....34 E6
BBN BB1 .....33 G4
BBNW BB2 .....41 G5
COL BB8 .....10 A2
DWN BB3 .....59 G2
NLSN BB9 .....8 D6
Norham Cl PDHM/BLYW BB12 .....26 D4
Norman Rd ACC BB5 .....43 J2
Norman St BBNW BB2 .....2 A7
BRFD/BLYE BB10 .....27 F4
Norris St DWN BB3 .....59 G2
North Bank Av BBN BB1 .....31 J4
Northcliffe GTH/LHO BB6 .....22 C5
Northcote Rd GTH/LHO BB6 .....12 C6
Northcote St DWN BB3 .....59 G5
Northfield Rd ACC BB5 .....53 K1
BBN BB1 .....31 J6
Northgate BBNW BB2 .....2 E4
North Park Av NLSN BB9 .....8 C6
North Rd BBN BB1 .....42 C4
RAW/HAS BB4 .....62 B1
North St BRFD/BLYE BB10 .....19 F6
BRFD/BLYE BB10 .....27 F2
CLI BB7 .....6 E2
COL BB8 .....9 K1
NLSN BB9 .....8 D6
PDHM/BLYW BB12 .....25 F2
PDHM/BLYW BB12 .....25 F6
RAW/HAS BB4 .....56 A1
RAW/HAS BB4 .....61 F2
RAW/HAS BB4 .....61 K1
RAW/HAS BB4 .....62 D2
Northumberland Cl DWN BB3 .....59 H5
North Valley Rd COL BB8 .....9 K2
Northwood Cl
PDHM/BLYW BB12 .....26 C3
Norton St PDHM/BLYW BB12 .....36 A1
Norwood Av BBNW BB2 .....41 J5
NLSN BB9 .....9 F5
Notre Dame Gdns BBN BB1 .....3 J1
Nottingham St BBN BB1 .....3 K6
Nova Scotia Whf BBNW BB2 * 41 H5
Nowell Gv PDHM/BLYW BB12 .....24 A1
Nowell St GTH/LHO BB6 * 22 D6
Nuttall Av GTH/LHO BB6 .....33 J1
Nuttall St ACC BB5 .....44 E3
BBNW BB2 .....41 H6
BCUP OL13 .....57 H6
BLY BB11 * 5 K7
Nutter Crs PDHM/BLYW BB12 .....16 D4
Nutter Rd ACC BB5 .....34 E6

O

Oak Av ACC BB5 .....53 J1
Oak Cl BBN BB1 .....33 H5
Oakdene Av ACC BB5 .....35 G4
Oaken Bank BRFD/BLYE BB10 .....18 E6
Oaken Cl BCUP OL13 .....57 H6
Oakenclough Rd BCUP OL13 .....57 H6
Oakeneaves Av BLY BB11 .....37 H3
Oakenhead Wood Old Rd
RAW/HAS BB4 .....54 C6
Oakenhurst Rd BBNW BB2 .....2 C5
Oakfield Av ACC BB5 .....34 A2
ACC BB5 .....35 G4
Oakfield Crs ACC BB5 .....44 B3
Oakfield Rd BBNW BB2 .....49 H2
Oak Gv DWN BB3 .....59 G1
Oak Hill Cl ACC BB5 .....44 E3
Oakhurst Av ACC BB5 .....35 G4
Oaklands Av NLSN BB9 .....8 D4
Oaklands Dr RAW/HAS BB4 .....61 H1
Oaklands Ter BBN BB1 .....31 K6
Oakland St NLSN BB9 .....18 E1
Oak La ACC BB5 .....45 F2
Oakley Rd RAW/HAS BB4 .....61 J1
Oakley St RAW/HAS BB4 .....61 H1
Oakmere Cl DWN BB3 .....49 H3
Oaks Brow BBN BB1 .....20 B4
Oak St ACC BB5 .....34 B4
ACC BB5 * 43 K4
ACC BB5 .....44 E2
BBN BB1 .....31 K6
BLY BB11 .....47 F3
COL BB8 .....10 B1
GTH/LHO BB6 .....22 D5
NLSN BB9 .....8 E6
NLSN BB9 .....18 B3
PDHM/BLYW BB12 .....26 B5
WHIT OL12 .....64 E6
Oak Ter COL BB8 * 11 G1
Oakwood Av BBN BB1 .....32 A4
Oakwood Cl BRFD/BLYE BB10 .....18 D6
Oakwood Rd ACC BB5 .....45 F4
Oat St PDHM/BLYW BB12 .....25 F4
Oban Dr BBN BB1 .....42 C4
Oban St BRFD/BLYE BB10 .....27 H2
Observatory Rd BBNW BB2 .....42 A5
Oddfellows Ter
RAW/HAS BB4 .....55 K6
Old Back La CLI BB7 .....14 B2
Old Bank La BBN BB1 .....42 A5
BBNW BB2 .....41 K5
Old Bank St BBNW BB2 .....2 E5
Old Farmside BBNW BB2 .....49 H2
Oldfield Av DWN BB3 .....49 J6
Old Gates Dr BBNW BB2 .....40 D6
Old Hall Cl NLSN BB9 .....8 A2
Old Hall Dr ACC BB5 .....35 H4
Old Hall La BBNW BB2 .....40 B5
Old Hall Sq BRFD/BLYE BB10 .....28 B6
Old Hall St BRFD/BLYE BB10 .....27 F3
Oldham St BLY BB11 * 5 F6
Old Kiln BCUP OL13 .....63 J3
Old La WHIT OL12 .....65 F5
Old Langho Rd GTH/LHO BB6 .....12 B6
Old Laund St
PDHM/BLYW BB12 .....17 J1
Old Meadows Rd BCUP OL13 .....57 G5
Old Mill Dr COL BB8 .....10 B3
Old Mill St BBN BB1 .....3 G1
Old Parsonage La
PDHM/BLYW BB12 .....24 E3
Old Roman Rd
PDHM/BLYW BB12 .....14 D6
Old School Ms BCUP OL13 .....63 H3
RAW/HAS BB4 * 53 K6
Old Station Ct CLI BB7 .....6 D3
Old St RAW/HAS BB4 .....62 D2
Olivant St PDHM/BLYW BB12 .....26 B4
Olive La DWN BB3 .....59 G1
Oliver St BCUP OL13 .....63 H3
Olive St BCUP OL13 .....63 K3
Olympia St BRFD/BLYE BB10 .....27 H6
Onchan Dr BCUP OL13 .....64 C2
Onchan Rd BBNW BB2 .....41 J6
Ontario Cl BBNW BB2 .....30 E5
Oozebooth Ter BBN BB1 .....31 H6
Oozehead La BBNW BB2 .....41 F2
Openshaw Dr BBN BB1 .....31 J5
Oporto Cl BLY BB11 .....4 D4
Orange St ACC BB5 .....34 D6
Orchard Br BLY BB11 * 5 F3
Orchard Cl BBNW BB2 .....49 H3
Orchard Dr ACC BB5 .....44 B2
Orchard St GTH/LHO BB6 .....33 J1
Ordnance St BBN BB1 .....3 K3
Oriole Cl BBN BB1 .....3 F2
Orkney Cl BBN BB1 .....42 C4
Ormerod Rd BLY BB11 .....5 H1
Ormerod St ACC BB5 .....44 C3
BLY BB11 .....5 G4
BRFD/BLYE BB10 .....28 B6
COL BB8 .....9 J3
NLSN BB9 * 19 F1
RAW/HAS BB4 .....53 K2
RAW/HAS BB4 .....61 K1
Orpen Av BLY BB11 .....37 K2
Orton Ct NLSN BB9 .....8 D3
Osborne Rd BBNW BB2 .....41 F1
Osborne Ter BCUP OL13 .....63 J3
DWN BB3 .....58 D1
RAW/HAS BB4 .....55 J5
Osborne Wy RAW/HAS BB4 .....60 D2
Oslo Rd BLY BB11 .....26 A6
Osprey Cl BBN BB1 .....31 H5
Oswald St ACC BB5 .....43 J4
ACC BB5 .....45 F1
BBN BB1 .....2 E1
BBN BB1 .....33 J3
PDHM/BLYW BB12 .....26 E3
Ottawa Cl BBNW BB2 .....30 E5
Otterburn Gv BRFD/BLYE BB10 .....27 J5
Otterburn Rd BBNW BB2 .....49 G2
Ottershaw Gdns BBN BB1 .....31 J5
Ouseburn Rd BBNW BB2 .....49 G1
Outram La BBN BB1 .....31 J4
Outwood Rd BLY BB11 .....5 K7
Owen Ct ACC BB5 .....34 B2
Owen St ACC BB5 .....34 D6
PDHM/BLYW BB12 .....25 K6
Owlet Hall Rd DWN BB3 .....58 D1
Oxford Av ACC BB5 .....34 C2
Oxford Cl BBN BB1 .....3 H5
PDHM/BLYW BB12 .....25 G5
Oxford Dr BBN BB1 .....42 E3
Oxford Pl BLY BB11 .....5 J5
Oxford Rd BLY BB11 .....5 J4
NLSN BB9 .....9 G5
Oxford St ACC BB5 * 44 D1
COL BB8 .....10 A2
DWN BB3 .....49 K5
NLSN BB9 .....18 B4
Ox Hey ACC BB5 .....34 B1
Oxhey Cl BRFD/BLYE BB10 .....28 A5

P

Paddock St ACC BB5 * 44 A3
The Paddock BBNW BB2 .....30 E5
Padgate Pl BLY BB11 .....37 F1
Padiham Rd CLI BB7 .....15 J3
PDHM/BLYW BB12 .....4 B2
Pagefield Crs CLI BB7 .....7 F4
Paignton Rd BBN BB1 .....31 H6
Paisley St BLY BB11 .....4 B5
Palace Gdns
PDHM/BLYW BB12 .....26 A4
Palace St PDHM/BLYW BB12 * 26 B4
Palatine Rd BBNW BB2 .....2 A4
Palatine Sq BLY BB11 .....4 D5
Palmer Rd BBN BB1 .....2 C1
Palmerston St
PDHM/BLYW BB12 .....25 G4
Palmer St BBN BB1 .....2 D1
Palm St BBN BB1 .....31 K6
BLY BB11 .....4 A4
Pansy St North ACC BB5 .....34 D6
Pansy St South ACC BB5 * 34 D6
Paradise La BBNW BB2 .....2 D4
Paradise St ACC BB5 .....44 D2
BBNW BB2 .....2 D5
BLY BB11 .....5 F3
NLSN BB9 .....8 E2
RAW/HAS BB4 .....62 E1
Paris BBN BB1 .....31 J1
Parish St PDHM/BLYW BB12 .....25 F2
Park Av BBN BB1 .....2 C1
BLY BB11 .....4 D7
CLI BB7 .....6 D2
GTH/LHO BB6 .....22 E5
NLSN BB9 .....8 C6
RAW/HAS BB4 .....60 E2
Park Bridge Rd
BRFD/BLYE BB10 .....38 D2
Park Crs ACC BB5 .....44 C3
BBNW BB2 .....2 A1
RAW/HAS BB4 .....60 E2
Parkdale Gdns DWN BB3 .....49 H3
Park Dr NLSN BB9 .....18 C4
Parker Av CLI BB7 .....6 C5
Parker La BLY BB11 .....5 G4
Parker St ACC BB5 .....35 F5
ACC BB5 .....45 F5
BBN BB1 .....33 H3
BLY BB11 .....5 G2
BRFD/BLYE BB10 * 19 F6
COL BB8 .....9 J2
NLSN BB9 * 9 F5
Parkes Wy BBNW BB2 .....49 G2
Park Farm Rd BBNW BB2 .....48 B1
Park Gate Rd BBN BB1 .....20 B2
Parkhurst Cl BBN BB1 .....42 B6
Parkinson St BBNW BB2 .....41 F5
BLY BB11 .....5 H6
RAW/HAS BB4 .....53 J6
Parklands Wy BBNW BB2 .....49 F2
Parkland Vw BLY BB11 .....37 J3
Park La ACC BB5 .....44 A4
BRFD/BLYE BB10 .....18 C4
GTH/LHO BB6 .....22 E5
Park Lee Rd BBNW BB2 .....41 J6
Park Pl BBNW BB2 .....48 B2
Park Rd ACC BB5 .....44 C1
BBN BB1 .....33 J4
BBNW BB2 .....3 F7
BCUP OL13 .....64 A2
BRFD/BLYE BB10 .....38 E4
DWN BB3 .....59 G5
GTH/LHO BB6 .....22 E5
PDHM/BLYW BB12 .....25 F3
RAW/HAS BB4 .....60 B3
RAW/HAS BB4 .....62 E2
Parkside Rd NLSN BB9 .....19 H1
Park St ACC BB5 .....44 E1
CLI BB7 .....6 D4
GTH/LHO BB6 .....22 E6
NLSN BB9 .....8 E3
RAW/HAS BB4 .....53 K6
RAW/HAS BB4 .....60 C4
Park St East NLSN BB9 .....8 E3
Park Ter BBN BB1 .....31 H6
Park Vw PDHM/BLYW BB12 .....25 F3
RAW/HAS BB4 .....62 E2
Park View Cl NLSN BB9 .....18 B2
Park Wy COL BB8 .....9 J2
Parkwood Av
PDHM/BLYW BB12 .....4 A1
Park Wood Dr RAW/HAS BB4 .....61 H1
Parkwood Rd BBN BB1 .....42 B3
Parliament St BLY BB11 .....5 J5
DWN BB3 * 59 F2
Parramatta St RAW/HAS BB4 .....61 K1
Parrock Rd NLSN BB9 .....8 B5
Parrock St NLSN BB9 .....18 E1
RAW/HAS BB4 .....54 E2
Parsonage Dr
BRFD/BLYE BB10 .....18 C4
Parsonage Rd BBN BB1 .....31 K2
Parsonage St ACC BB5 .....44 A2
COL BB8 .....9 J3
Parson La CLI BB7 .....6 D3
Partridge Dr ACC BB5 .....45 G6
Partridge Hl
PDHM/BLYW BB12 .....25 G2
Partridge Hill St
PDHM/BLYW BB12 * 25 G3
Pasture Cl BLY BB11 .....37 J2
Pasturegate BLY BB11 .....4 B7
Pasturegate Av BLY BB11 .....4 B7
Pasture Gv CLI BB7 .....13 G2
Pasturelands Dr CLI BB7 .....13 G6
Pasture La NLSN BB9 .....8 C3
The Pastures BBNW BB2 .....30 E5
Paterson St BBNW BB2 .....41 J4
Patrick Av PDHM/BLYW BB12 .....24 A1
Patrick Crs RAW/HAS BB4 .....62 B1
Patten St BBN BB1 .....42 C2
Patterdale Av ACC BB5 .....43 K2
BBN BB1 .....42 C4
Patterdale Cl BRFD/BLYE BB10 .....18 C5
Paulhan St BRFD/BLYE BB10 .....27 G1
Paxton St ACC BB5 .....44 D1
Paynter Cl ACC BB5 .....34 C3
Paythorne Av
BRFD/BLYE BB10 .....27 J6
Peabody St DWN BB3 .....59 F1
Peace St BLY BB11 .....4 A4
Pearl St ACC BB5 .....44 B2
BBN BB1 .....31 K4
Pearson St BBNW BB2 .....2 D6
Peart St BRFD/BLYE BB10 .....27 G1
Peebles Gv BLY BB11 .....37 H2
Peel Bank Rd ACC BB5 .....43 H3
Peel Cl BBNW BB2 .....49 J1
Peel Dr BCUP OL13 .....64 C2
Peel Gdns COL BB8 .....9 J2
Peel Mt BBN BB1 .....42 E3
Peel Mount Cl BBN BB1 .....43 F3
Peel Park Av ACC BB5 .....35 F6
CLI BB7 .....6 E4
Peel Park Cl ACC BB5 .....35 F6
CLI BB7 .....6 E4
Peel Pl NLSN BB9 .....8 E1
Peel Rd COL BB8 .....9 H3
Peel St ACC BB5 .....43 K4
ACC BB5 .....44 E1
BBNW BB2 .....41 G5
CLI BB7 .....6 E3
PDHM/BLYW BB12 .....25 G3
RAW/HAS BB4 .....62 B1
Peers Clough Rd
RAW/HAS BB4 .....55 K1
Pelham St BBN BB1 .....3 J1
Pemberton St BBN BB1 .....31 J4
Pembroke St ACC BB5 .....44 E1
BBNW BB2 .....2 E7
BRFD/BLYE BB10 .....27 G2
Pendle Av ACC BB5 .....34 B1
BCUP OL13 .....57 G5
Pendle Cl BCUP OL13 .....64 B1
Pendle Dr BBNW BB2 .....41 K5
CLI BB7 .....13 G2
Pendle Flds PDHM/BLYW BB12 .....17 H2
Pendlehurst St BLY BB11 .....4 D7
Pendlemist Vw COL BB8 .....9 J4
Pendle Rd CLI BB7 .....6 E3
GTH/LHO BB6 .....23 F5
NLSN BB9 .....18 A4
Pendleside Cl CLI BB7 .....15 J2
Pendle St ACC BB5 .....44 C3
BBN BB1 .....3 K4
NLSN BB9 .....8 D6
PDHM/BLYW BB12 .....25 G4
Pendle St East CLI BB7 .....15 H2
Pendle St West CLI BB7 .....15 H2
Pendleton Av ACC BB5 .....44 B3
RAW/HAS BB4 .....54 E5
Pendle Vw ACC BB5 * 35 H3
GTH/LHO BB6 .....12 C3
Pendle Wy COL BB8 .....11 G2
NLSN BB9 .....8 A1
PDHM/BLYW BB12 .....17 G5
PDHM/BLYW BB12 .....26 C3
Penistone St
PDHM/BLYW BB12 .....4 A2
Pennine Crs NLSN BB9 .....18 C4
Pennine Gv PDHM/BLYW BB12 .....25 F1
Pennine Rd BCUP OL13 .....64 B1
Pennine Wy NLSN BB9 .....18 C4
Penny House La ACC BB5 .....34 E6
Penny St BBN BB1 .....3 F4
Penrith Crs COL BB8 .....9 H5
Penrith Rd COL BB8 * 9 G4
Penshaw Cl BBN BB1 .....31 J4
Penzance St BBNW BB2 * 41 F5
Percival St ACC BB5 .....44 B1
BBN BB1 .....31 K6
DWN BB3 .....49 K6
Percy St ACC BB5 .....43 H2
ACC BB5 .....44 E1
BBNW BB2 .....41 F5
COL BB8 .....10 A1
NLSN BB9 .....18 D2
WHIT OL12 .....65 F5
Peregrine Dr DWN BB3 .....49 H6
Peridot Cl BBN BB1 .....31 K3
Peronne Crs BBN BB1 .....42 D2
Perry St DWN BB3 .....59 F1
Persia St ACC BB5 .....44 B1
Perth St ACC BB5 .....44 C2
BBNW BB2 .....41 G4
BLY BB11 .....4 A4
NLSN BB9 .....9 F6
Peters Rw BBN BB1 * 33 J4
Peter St ACC BB5 .....44 C2
BBN BB1 .....3 J2
COL BB8 * 10 A3
NLSN BB9 * 8 D3
RAW/HAS BB4 .....61 K1
Petre Crs BBN BB1 .....33 H5
Petrel Cl BBN BB1 .....31 H5
Petre Rd ACC BB5 .....34 B3
Pheasantford Gn
BRFD/BLYE BB10 .....27 G3
Pheasantford St
BRFD/BLYE BB10 .....27 G3
Philips Rd BBN BB1 .....32 B6
BCUP OL13 .....57 G2
Philip St DWN BB3 .....59 G2
Phillips La COL BB8 .....9 H3
Phoenix Pk BBN BB1 .....32 C4
Phoenix Wy BLY BB11 .....26 B6
Piccadilly Rd BLY BB11 .....4 C4
Piccadilly Sq BLY BB11 .....4 D4
Piccadilly St RAW/HAS BB4 .....53 K6
Pickering Fold BBN BB1 .....50 B2
Pickering St NLSN BB9 * 18 B4
Pickles St PDHM/BLYW BB12 .....4 B1
Pickup Fold Rd DWN BB3 .....59 H4
Pickup Rd BBN BB1 .....33 G5
Pickup St ACC BB5 .....34 B3
ACC BB5 .....44 B3
BBN BB1 .....3 H2
BCUP OL13 * 57 G6
Picton St BBNW BB2 * 49 F1
Pierce Cl PDHM/BLYW BB12 .....24 E2
Piercy Rd RAW/HAS BB4 .....55 K6
Pilgrim St NLSN BB9 .....19 F3
Pilkington Dr ACC BB5 .....34 C2
Pilkington St BBN BB1 .....3 F5
Pilling Av ACC BB5 .....45 G5
Pilling St RAW/HAS BB4 .....53 K3
RAW/HAS BB4 .....62 E3
Pilmuir Rd BBNW BB2 .....41 J6
Pilot St ACC BB5 .....34 D6
Pimlico Link Rd CLI BB7 .....7 G1
Pimlico Rd CLI BB7 .....6 E2
Pinch Clough Rd
RAW/HAS BB4 .....55 K4
Pinder St NLSN BB9 .....9 F5
Pine Cl BBN BB1 .....33 H5
Pine Crs ACC BB5 .....44 B5
Pine St BBN BB1 .....32 A6
BLY BB11 .....5 J4
DWN BB3 .....59 G3
NLSN BB9 .....19 F1
Pinewood BBNW BB2 .....48 D1
Pinewood Dr ACC BB5 .....35 F6
Pinfold NLSN BB9 .....8 E2
Pinfold Pl NLSN BB9 .....9 H6
Pink Pl BBNW BB2 .....41 F4
Pink St PDHM/BLYW BB12 .....26 B5
Pinner La RAW/HAS BB4 .....54 D2
Piper Lea RAW/HAS BB4 .....62 E2
Pitt St PDHM/BLYW BB12 * 25 G3
Pitville St DWN BB3 .....49 K6
Plain Pl BBNW BB2 .....2 E7
Plane St BBN BB1 .....32 A6
BCUP OL13 .....57 F5
Plane Tree Cl BLY BB11 .....37 H3
Plane Tree Rd BBN BB1 * 32 A6
Plantation Rd ACC BB5 .....45 F1
BBNW BB2 .....41 F6
Plantation Sq ACC BB5 .....45 F1
Plantation St ACC BB5 .....44 E2
BCUP OL13 .....63 H3
BRFD/BLYE BB10 * 27 F4

NLSN BB9 8 E6
RAW/HAS BB4 62 A1
Plant St ACC BB5 43 K4
Platt Cl ACC BB5 44 C2
Pleasant Pl BLY BB11 * 5 F4
Pleasant Vw RAW/HAS BB4 62 E2
Pleasington Cl BBNW BB2 41 F3
Pleasington Gv
BRFD/BLYE BB10 27 J6
Pleasington La BBNW BB2 48 A1
Pleasington Rd BBNW BB2 40 A5
Pleasington St BBNW BB2 41 F3
Pleck Farm Av BBN BB1 31 J5
Pleckgate Fold BBN BB1 31 H4
Pleckgate Rd BBN BB1 31 H5
Pleck Rd ACC BB5 44 E1
Plover St PDHM/BLYW BB12 4 A2
Plover Vw PDHM/BLYW BB12 4 A2
Plumbe St BLY BB11 5 H5
Pocklington St ACC BB5 45 F5
Poets' Rd PDHM/BLYW BB12 25 J4
Poland St ACC BB5 44 B2
Pole La DWN BB3 59 H4
Police St DWN BB3 59 F2
Pollard St ACC BB5 34 E6
BLY BB11 4 A4
Pomfret St BBNW BB2 41 H4
BLY BB11 4 C3
Pont St NLSN BB9 18 D2
Poole St BBN BB1 42 C2
Poplar Av GTH/LHO BB6 22 E5
Poplar Cl ACC BB5 44 B4
BBN BB1 33 H5
Poplar St BBN BB1 31 K6
NLSN BB9 9 F6
RAW/HAS BB4 53 K6
Portal Gv PDHM/BLYW BB12 26 A5
Porter St ACC BB5 44 B1
Portfield La CLI BB7 14 B6
Portfield Rd CLI BB7 14 A5
Portland Rd GTH/LHO BB6 21 H3
Portland St ACC BB5 44 C1
BBNW BB2 2 A7
COL BB8 10 B2
DWN BB3 59 G5
NLSN BB9 8 D4
NLSN BB9 18 D1
Portree Crs BBN BB1 42 D4
Portsmouth Av
BRFD/BLYE BB10 27 K1
Pot House La ACC BB5 44 B6
DWN BB3 50 C6
Poulton Av ACC BB5 34 C5
Powell St BLY BB11 4 D6
DWN BB3 59 F1
Powys Cl RAW/HAS BB4 60 E2
Prairie Crs BRFD/BLYE BB10 18 B6
Pratt St BRFD/BLYE BB10 27 F2
Prescott St BRFD/BLYE BB10 5 K4
Preston New Rd BBNW BB2 2 A3
Preston Old Rd BBNW BB2 48 B1
Preston St DWN BB3 49 K6
Prestwich St BLY BB11 4 B6
Priestfield Av COL BB8 9 H2
Primet Br COL BB8 9 J3
Primet Hts COL BB8 9 H4
Primet Hl COL BB8 9 J3
Primet St COL BB8 9 J3
Primrose Bank BBN BB1 3 G2
Primrose Cl BBNW BB2 41 F5
Primrose Dr BBN BB1 3 G3
Primrose Hl BBNW BB2 30 E2
Primrose Rd CLI BB7 6 C5
Primrose St ACC BB5 44 C3
BRFD/BLYE BB10 * 27 H2
CLI BB7 6 C4
DWN BB3 59 G3
NLSN BB9 18 B4
NLSN BB9 18 E1
Primrose Ter BBNW BB2 41 F5
Primula Dr DWN BB3 50 A2
Prince Lee Mdw DWN BB3 59 G3
Princess Gdns BBNW BB2 48 B2
Princess St ACC BB5 44 B1
BBNW BB2 41 G5
BCUP OL13 57 F6
CLI BB7 13 J4
COL BB8 9 J2
GTH/LHO BB6 22 E6
NLSN BB9 18 D2
PDHM/BLYW BB12 24 E3
Princes St BBN BB1 33 H4
BBNW BB2 2 D5
Princess Wy PDHM/BLYW BB12 5 F2
Prince St BCUP OL13 64 E4
BLY BB11 4 C5
DWN BB3 58 E2
Pringle St BBN BB1 3 H7
Prinny Hill Rd RAW/HAS BB4 53 J6
Printers Fold
PDHM/BLYW BB12 25 H5
Priory Cl RAW/HAS BB4 62 D2
Priory Ct BBNW BB2 40 A5
BLY BB11 38 B3
Priory Dr DWN BB3 59 H3
Priory Gra DWN BB3 59 H3
Priory Pl DWN BB3 59 H3
Priory St NLSN BB9 9 F6
Pritchard St BBNW BB2 41 J5
BLY BB11 4 C6
Procter St BBNW BB2 41 K4
Proctor Cl NLSN BB9 19 F4
Progress Av BBN BB1 * 32 A6
Progress Rd NLSN BB9 9 F4
Progress St DWN BB3 59 G2
Prospect Av DWN BB3 58 D1
Prospect Hl RAW/HAS BB4 60 D1
Prospect Rd RAW/HAS BB4 54 D6
Prospect St GTH/LHO BB6 22 D6
RAW/HAS BB4 62 E2
Prospect Ter NLSN BB9 * 8 D3
Provence Av GTH/LHO BB6 12 C3
Providence St BBN BB1 32 A5
Prunella Dr DWN BB3 50 A2
Pump St BBNW BB2 2 B6
BLY BB11 4 C3
CLI BB7 6 C3
Punstock Rd DWN BB3 58 E2

Q

Quakerfields DWN BB3 59 F1
Quaker La DWN BB3 59 F1
Quarry Bank St
PDHM/BLYW BB12 26 B4
Quarry St ACC BB5 44 E2
BBN BB1 3 H3
BCUP OL13 64 B1
PDHM/BLYW BB12 25 G2
WHIT OL12 65 F6
Quebec Rd BBNW BB2 31 F5
Queen Elizabeth Crs
ACC BB5 45 F2
Queensberry Rd BLY BB11 4 C5
Queensborough Rd
ACC BB5 34 D6
Queen's Dr ACC BB5 44 B4
Queensgate NLSN BB9 18 C2
Queen's Lancashire Wy
BLY BB11 4 E3
Queen's Park Rd BBN BB1 3 K6
BRFD/BLYE BB10 27 G3
Queen's Rd ACC BB5 34 E6
BBN BB1 42 B4
BRFD/BLYE BB10 27 G1
CLI BB7 6 D4
DWN BB3 59 G6
Queens Rd West ACC BB5 34 C6
Queen's Ter BBNW BB2 41 F6
BCUP OL13 63 K3
Queen St ACC BB5 34 B2
ACC BB5 44 A3
ACC BB5 * 44 E1
BCUP OL13 64 A1
BLY BB11 4 E3
BRFD/BLYE BB10 19 F6
CLI BB7 6 B3
COL BB8 9 J2
DWN BB3 58 E1
GTH/LHO BB6 22 D6
NLSN BB9 8 D3
NLSN BB9 8 E6
PDHM/BLYW BB12 25 F3
RAW/HAS BB4 61 K1
Queensway ACC BB5 34 C6
BBNW BB2 48 E1
CLI BB7 6 D4
RAW/HAS BB4 62 D2
Queen Victoria Rd BLY BB11 5 J1
BRFD/BLYE BB10 27 G2
Queen Victoria St BBNW BB2 41 F5

R

Raby St RAW/HAS BB4 61 K1
Radeclyffe St CLI BB7 6 D2
Radfield Rd DWN BB3 58 E3
Radford Gdns DWN BB3 59 F4
Radford St DWN BB3 59 F3
Radnor Av PDHM/BLYW BB12 25 K4
Radnor Cl ACC BB5 43 J3
Radnor St ACC BB5 34 D6
Raeburn Av BLY BB11 37 J2
Raedale Av BRFD/BLYE BB10 18 B5
Raglan Rd BLY BB11 4 C6
Raglan St COL BB8 * 9 K3
NLSN BB9 8 D6
Railgate BCUP OL13 64 E2
Railton Av BBNW BB2 48 E1
Railway Gv BBN BB1 * 32 A6
Railway Rd BBN BB1 3 F4
DWN BB3 59 F2
RAW/HAS BB4 * 53 K5
Railway St BCUP OL13 63 G3
BLY BB11 5 F2
NLSN BB9 18 A4
NLSN BB9 18 E1
Railway Ter GTH/LHO BB6 33 J1
NLSN BB9 18 A4
Railway Vw ACC BB5 * 34 E6
BBNW BB2 41 F5
Railway View Av CLI BB7 * 6 D2
Railway View Rd CLI BB7 6 D2
Rake Foot RAW/HAS BB4 53 K6
Rakehead La BCUP OL13 63 G3
Rakes Br DWN BB3 50 A2
Rakes House Rd NLSN BB9 8 E5
Rake Top Av
PDHM/BLYW BB12 16 D3
Raleigh St PDHM/BLYW BB12 25 G3
Ralph St ACC BB5 34 E5
Ramsbottom St ACC BB5 34 D6
RAW/HAS BB4 62 D3
Rams Clough La ACC BB5 52 C2
Ramsey Av BCUP OL13 64 B2
Ramsey Gv BRFD/BLYE BB10 27 H1
Ramsey Rd BBNW BB2 41 H6
Ramsgreave Dr BBN BB1 31 G4
Ramsgreave Rd BBN BB1 31 J2
Randall St BRFD/BLYE BB10 27 G2
Randal St BBN BB1 2 E3
Randolph St BBN BB1 3 K6
Ranger St ACC BB5 44 C2
Rankin Dr DWN BB3 59 K3
Rannoch Dr BBNW BB2 40 D6
Ratcliffe Fold RAW/HAS BB4 53 K6
Ratcliffe St DWN BB3 59 G3
RAW/HAS BB4 53 J6
Raven Av RAW/HAS BB4 60 E4
Raven Cft RAW/HAS BB4 60 E3
Ravenglass Cl BBNW BB2 42 A6
Raven Oak La
BRFD/BLYE BB10 28 C6
Raven Pk RAW/HAS BB4 60 E3
Raven Rd BBNW BB2 * 41 F2
Ravenscroft Cl BBN BB1 32 A4
Ravens Gv BRFD/BLYE BB10 18 C5
Raven St NLSN BB9 9 F6
Ravenswing Av BBNW BB2 31 F6
Ravenswood GTH/LHO BB6 22 C5
Rawcliffe St BLY BB11 * 5 H2
Rawlinson St DWN BB3 * 59 G5
Raws Ct BLY BB11 * 5 G2
Rawson Av ACC BB5 44 C3
Rawson St BRFD/BLYE BB10 27 G2
Raws St BLY BB11 * 5 G2
Rawsthorne Av
RAW/HAS BB4 60 D1
Rawstorne St BBNW BB2 2 A5
Raygill Av BLY BB11 37 H2
Raynor St BBNW BB2 2 D3
Read Hall Ct
PDHM/BLYW BB12 * 23 J1
Reading Cl BBN BB1 * 3 J6
Read St ACC BB5 34 C4
Rectory Cl DWN BB3 59 H3
RAW/HAS BB4 62 C2
Rectory Rd PDHM/BLYW BB12 26 E4
Redearth Rd DWN BB3 59 F3
Redearth St DWN BB3 59 F3
Redgate Cl BLY BB11 38 B2
Redlam BBNW BB2 41 F4
Redlam Brow BBNW BB2 2 A7
Red Lees Av BRFD/BLYE BB10 39 F1
Red Lees Rd BRFD/BLYE BB10 39 F1
Red Lion St BLY BB11 5 G4
Redman Rd BRFD/BLYE BB10 18 B5
Redness Cl NLSN BB9 18 E3
Red Rake BBN BB1 31 G6
Redruth St PDHM/BLYW BB12 4 A2
Red Scar St COL BB8 * 9 J3
Red Shell La ACC BB5 43 H6
Red Spar Rd BRFD/BLYE BB10 27 J1
Redvers Rd DWN BB3 49 J4
Redvers St BRFD/BLYE BB10 27 G2
Redwing Av GTH/LHO BB6 22 C5
Redwood Dr RAW/HAS BB4 61 J3
Reedfield BRFD/BLYE BB10 18 C5
Reedley Dr BRFD/BLYE BB10 18 C5
Reedley Gv BRFD/BLYE BB10 18 B6
Reedley Rd BRFD/BLYE BB10 18 B5
Reeds Cl RAW/HAS BB4 54 E3
Reedsholme Cl RAW/HAS BB4 54 E3
Reeds La RAW/HAS BB4 54 E3
Reed St BCUP OL13 57 G6
BLY BB11 5 H6
Reedyford Rd NLSN BB9 8 E5
Reeford Gv CLI BB7 6 C4
Refuge Buildings BBN BB1 * 3 F3
Regency Cl CLI BB7 13 G2
Regent Av COL BB8 10 A1
Regent Pl NLSN BB9 8 E5
Regent Rd ACC BB5 34 B6
Regents Cl BBNW BB2 40 A5
Regent St BBN BB1 3 F3
BCUP OL13 64 B1
NLSN BB9 8 E6
NLSN BB9 18 B4
RAW/HAS BB4 53 J6
Regents Vw BBN BB1 31 J4
Reginald St COL BB8 9 H2
Rendel St PDHM/BLYW BB12 26 B4
Rennie St BRFD/BLYE BB10 27 H6
Renshaw St BRFD/BLYE BB10 27 G2
Reservoir St BLY BB11 5 F6
DWN BB3 58 E2
Revidge Rd BBNW BB2 41 F1
Rewe Cl BBNW BB2 * 49 G1
Reynolds St BLY BB11 37 J2
Rhoda St NLSN BB9 19 F1
Rhoden Rd ACC BB5 43 K5
Rhodes Av BBN BB1 31 H5
RAW/HAS BB4 60 D4
Rhuddlan Cl RAW/HAS BB4 60 E2
Rhyddings St ACC BB5 44 A3
Rhyl Av BBN BB1 31 J6
Ribble Av BRFD/BLYE BB10 27 H1
DWN BB3 49 J5
Ribblesdale Av ACC BB5 34 D5
BBN BB1 21 F4
CLI BB7 6 D2
Ribblesdale Pl BBNW BB2 2 A4
NLSN BB9 8 E2
Ribblesdale St
BRFD/BLYE BB10 27 G3
Ribble St BBN BB1 3 F1
BCUP OL13 64 B3
Ribbleton Dr ACC BB5 34 E5
Ribbleton Gv CLI BB7 13 G2
Ribble Wy CLI BB7 6 B3
CLI BB7 12 C2
Ribchester Av
BRFD/BLYE BB10 27 J6
Ribchester Rd BBN BB1 20 D5
Ribchester Wy NLSN BB9 18 C5
Richard St BBNW BB2 2 C6
BCUP OL13 57 F2
BLY BB11 5 J5
NLSN BB9 18 B4
Richmond Av BRFD/BLYE BB10 39 F2
RAW/HAS BB4 61 F1
Richmond Crs BBN BB1 42 E2
Richmond Hl BBN BB1 * 2 E3
Richmond Hill St ACC BB5 44 C2
Richmond Pk DWN BB3 59 F1
Richmond Rd ACC BB5 44 B3
NLSN BB9 8 C6
Richmond St ACC BB5 44 D2
BLY BB11 4 B5
Richmond Ter BBN BB1 2 E3
CLI BB7 6 C4
DWN BB3 59 F1
Rickard Rd NLSN BB9 10 C3
Ridding La CLI BB7 13 H4
Riddings Av BRFD/BLYE BB10 28 A5
Riddings La CLI BB7 13 J4
Ridehalgh La BRFD/BLYE BB10 29 H1
Ridehalgh St COL BB8 9 H4
Ridge Av BRFD/BLYE BB10 27 J5
Ridge Ct BRFD/BLYE BB10 27 H5
Ridge Rd BLY BB11 5 J3
Ridge Rw BRFD/BLYE BB10 27 J5
Ridgeway GTH/LHO BB6 22 C5
NLSN BB9 8 D4
Ridgeway Av BBNW BB2 50 A1
Ridgeways RAW/HAS BB4 61 F1
The Ridgeway NLSN BB9 18 D2
Riding Barn St ACC BB5 44 B1
The Ridings
PDHM/BLYW BB12 26 C3
Riding St BLY BB11 4 C4
Rifle St RAW/HAS BB4 60 E1
Rigby St COL BB8 9 J3
NLSN BB9 18 D1
Rigg St NLSN BB9 18 E1
Riley St ACC BB5 44 D3
BCUP OL13 57 F4
BLY BB11 * 5 J7
NLSN BB9 18 B4
Rimington Av ACC BB5 44 C4
BRFD/BLYE BB10 27 J6
COL BB8 9 J1
Rimington Cl BBNW BB2 41 K5
Rimington Pl NLSN BB9 9 H6
Rings Nook RAW/HAS BB4 * 46 E5
Rings St RAW/HAS BB4 46 E5
Ringstone Crs NLSN BB9 19 H1
Ringwood Cl ACC BB5 34 D4
Ripon Rd ACC BB5 43 J2
Ripon St BBN BB1 3 K6
NLSN BB9 18 D2
Risedale Gv BBNW BB2 48 E1
Rishton Rd ACC BB5 34 A2
BBN BB1 21 H6
Rising Bridge Rd
RAW/HAS BB4 53 J2
River Dr PDHM/BLYW BB12 25 H3
River Lea Gdns CLI BB7 6 E2
Riverside Vw ACC BB5 34 A1
River St BBN BB1 3 G5
BCUP OL13 64 A2
COL BB8 9 K3
COL BB8 10 E4
DWN BB3 58 E1
Riversway Dr DWN BB3 49 K3
River Wy NLSN BB9 8 D3
Rivington St BBN BB1 42 B3
Roberts St NLSN BB9 19 F1
RAW/HAS BB4 54 E6
Robert St ACC BB5 34 E6
ACC BB5 43 K4
BBNW BB2 41 J4
COL BB8 10 A2
DWN BB3 58 E2
GTH/LHO BB6 * 22 E6
RAW/HAS BB4 62 E1
Robin Bank Rd DWN BB3 59 F1
Robin House La
BRFD/BLYE BB10 19 J5
Robinson La
PDHM/BLYW BB12 18 A5
Robinson St BBN BB1 32 A6
BRFD/BLYE BB10 27 F2
Robson St NLSN BB9 * 18 B3
Rochdale Rd BCUP OL13 64 B2
Rochester Cl BCUP OL13 57 G2
Rochester Dr
BRFD/BLYE BB10 18 C6
Rock Bridge Fold
RAW/HAS BB4 55 J4
Rockcliffe Av BCUP OL13 63 K2
Rockcliffe Dr BCUP OL13 63 K2
Rockcliffe Rd BCUP OL13 64 A2
Rockfield St BBNW BB2 41 J5
Rock Hall Rd RAW/HAS BB4 53 K6
Rock La BLY BB11 38 B2
DWN BB3 48 E6
Rockliffe La BCUP OL13 64 B2
Rockliffe St BBNW BB2 41 J5
RAW/HAS BB4 54 E6
Rock St ACC BB5 45 G5
CLI BB7 6 D3
RAW/HAS BB4 53 K6
Rock Ter CLI BB7 * 22 B1
RAW/HAS BB4 54 E2
Rockwood Cl
BRFD/BLYE BB10 18 E6
Rodney St BBNW BB2 41 G4
Roebuck Cl BBNW BB2 41 H4
Roe Greave Rd ACC BB5 43 K4
Roe Lee Pk BBN BB1 31 K3
Rogersfield GTH/LHO BB6 21 H3
Rolleston Rd BBNW BB2 41 F3
Roman Rd BBNW BB2 41 K5
Roman Wy CLI BB7 6 E3
Rome Av BLY BB11 37 G1
Romford St
PDHM/BLYW BB12 26 B4
Romney Av BLY BB11 37 J2
NLSN BB9 8 D4
Romney St NLSN BB9 18 D2
Romney Wk BBN BB1 42 C3
Ronald St BBN BB1 42 C2
PDHM/BLYW BB12 25 K6
Ronaldsway Cl BCUP OL13 64 B2
Ronbury Cl NLSN BB9 * 8 C6
Roney St BBNW BB2 2 B3
Rookery Nook Vls
BCUP OL13 * 57 F5
Rook Hill Rd BCUP OL13 63 G3
Rook St COL BB8 9 K2
NLSN BB9 8 D6
Rooley Moor Rd
BCUP OL13 63 F5
Rooley Vw BCUP OL13 63 K2
Rose Av BLY BB11 4 D7
Rose Bank RAW/HAS BB4 54 E6
Rose Bank St BCUP OL13 57 F6
Rosebay Av BBNW BB2 48 B1
Rosebery St
BRFD/BLYE BB10 27 G1
Rosegrove La
PDHM/BLYW BB12 26 A6
Rose Hill Av BBN BB1 3 J5
Rosehill Av BLY BB11 4
NLSN BB9 * 19
Rosehill Mt BLY BB11 4
Rose Hill Rd BBNW BB2 40
Rosehill Rd BLY BB11 4
COL BB8 9
Rose Hill St BCUP OL13 64
DWN BB3 59
RAW/HAS BB4 46
Roseland Av NLSN BB9 18
Rosemount BCUP OL13 57
Rosemount Av BLY BB11 4
Rosendale Cl BCUP OL13 57
Rosendale Crs BCUP OL13 57
Rose St ACC BB5 44
BCUP OL13 64
DWN BB3 59
RAW/HAS BB4 62
Rose Vale St RAW/HAS BB4 62
Roseway NLSN BB9 18
Rosewood Av BBN BB1 31
BLY BB11 37
RAW/HAS BB4 54
Rosley St COL BB8 10
Rossall Cl PDHM/BLYW BB12 25
Rossall Ter BBNW BB2 41
Rossendale Av BLY BB11 37
Rossendale Rd BLY BB11 37
Rossendale Wy BCUP OL13 57
BCUP OL13 65
RAW/HAS BB4 62
Rosser Ct NLSN BB9 8
Rossetti Av BLY BB11 37
Ross St DWN BB3 59
NLSN BB9 * 18
Rothesay Rd BBN BB1 42
NLSN BB9 18
Rothwell Av ACC BB5 44
Roughlee Gv BRFD/BLYE BB10 27
Rough Lee Rd ACC BB5 44
Roughlee St NLSN BB9 8
Roundel St BRFD/BLYE BB10 * 27
Roundhill La RAW/HAS BB4 53
Round Hill Pl
BRFD/BLYE BB10 * 38
Roundhill Rd ACC BB5 53
Roundhill Vw ACC BB5 53
Roundwood Av
BRFD/BLYE BB10 18
Rowan Av ACC BB5 43
Rowan Cl BBN BB1 32
Rowan Gv BRFD/BLYE BB10 27
Rowan Tree Cl ACC BB5 * 35
Rowen Pk BBNW BB2 30
Rowland Av NLSN BB9 19
Rowland St ACC BB5 44
Rowley La BRFD/BLYE BB10 27
Royal Oak Av BBN BB1 31
Royds Av ACC BB5 44
Royds Rd BCUP OL13 63
Royds St ACC BB5 44
Royle Rd PDHM/BLYW BB12 4
Royshaw Av BBN BB1 31
Royshaw Cl BBN BB1 31
Ruby St BBN BB1 * 31
Rudyard Dr DWN BB3 59
Rugby Av ACC BB5 34
Rumley Rd BLY BB11 5
Rumley's Fold BLY BB11 37
Rupert St NLSN BB9 18
Rushbed Dr RAW/HAS BB4 54
Rushes Farm Cl ACC BB5 43
Rushey Cl RAW/HAS BB4 54
Rushton Cl NLSN BB9 9
Rushton St BCUP OL13 63
GTH/LHO BB6 33
NLSN BB9 8
Rushworth St East
BRFD/BLYE BB10 27
Rushworth St West
BRFD/BLYE BB10 * 27
Rushy Fld ACC BB5 23
Ruskin Av ACC BB5 43
COL BB8 9
PDHM/BLYW BB12 25
Ruskin Gv BLY BB11 36
Ruskin St BRFD/BLYE BB10 27
Russell Ct BLY BB11 5
Russell Pl GTH/LHO BB6 22
Russell St ACC BB5 44
BBNW BB2 2
NLSN BB9 8
Russell Ter PDHM/BLYW BB12 25
Russel St BCUP OL13 57
Russia St ACC BB5 44
Ruthin Cl BBN BB1 31
Rutland Av BBN BB1 42
PDHM/BLYW BB12 25
Rutland Cl ACC BB5 * 34
Rutland Pl PDHM/BLYW BB12 25
Rutland St ACC BB5 44
BBNW BB2 41
COL BB8 10
NLSN BB9 8
Ryburn Av BBNW BB2 41
Rycliffe St PDHM/BLYW BB12 25
Rydal Av DWN BB3 59
Rydal Cl ACC BB5 35
BRFD/BLYE BB10 18
PDHM/BLYW BB12 25
Rydal Mt BBN BB1 51
Rydal Pl COL BB8 10
Rydal Rd BBN BB1 32
RAW/HAS BB4 61
Rydal St BRFD/BLYE BB10 27
Ryde Cl RAW/HAS BB4 61
Ryden Rd BBN BB1 20
The Rydings GTH/LHO BB6 21
Ryefield Av RAW/HAS BB4 60
Ryefield Av West
RAW/HAS BB4 60
Ryefield Ct RAW/HAS BB4 * 60
Ryefield Pl RAW/HAS BB4 60
Rye Gdns BBNW BB2 49
Rylands St BRFD/BLYE BB10 27

S

bden Brook Ct CLI BB7 15 J1
bden Rd CLI BB7 14 B5
PDHM/BLYW BB12 15 K3
PDHM/BLYW BB12 16 D3
ccary La BBN BB1 30 E1
ckville St BLY BB11 4 E5
NLSN BB9 18 B4
NLSN BB9 19 F3
dler St ACC BB5 * 44 A2
ffron Cl NLSN BB9 8 C6
gar Holme Ter
RAW/HAS BB4 55 J4
gar St NLSN BB9 18 E1
hara Fold BBN BB1 32 A6
Aidan's Av BBNW BB2 41 G6
DWN BB3 59 G3
Aidan's Cl BBNW BB2 41 G6
Albans Ct BBN BB1 3 H2
Albans Rd BBN BB1 33 G5
DWN BB3 49 J5
Andrew's Cl ACC BB5 43 K3
Andrews Rd GTH/LHO BB6 12 C3
Andrew's St BBN BB1 2 D2
BRFD/BLYE BB10 * 27 G2
Annes Cl ACC BB5 * 44 A2
BBN BB1 3 H7
Anne's Crs RAW/HAS BB4 55 K6
Anne's Dr
PDHM/BLYW BB12 17 H2
Anne's St
PDHM/BLYW BB12 25 F4
Anne's Wy
PDHM/BLYW BB12 17 H2
Ann's Sq CLI BB7 6 A3
Ann's St BBNW BB2 41 J4
Barnabas St BBNW BB2 2 A4
DWN BB3 * 59 G5
Bedes Pk DWN BB3 49 J4
Bee's Cl BBNW BB2 41 K6
Cecilia St GTH/LHO BB6 22 E6
Charles' Rd BBN BB1 * 33 G4
Clement Cl BBN BB1 42 B3
Clement St BBN BB1 42 B2
Crispin Wy RAW/HAS BB4 60 D1
Cuthberts Cl DWN BB3 * 49 J6
Cuthbert St
BRFD/BLYE BB10 27 G1
David's Av BBNW BB2 48 B2
Edmund's St GTH/LHO BB6 22 E6
Francis' Rd BBNW BB2 40 E5
Gabriel's Av BBN BB1 31 K2
George's Av BBNW BB2 41 F6
Georges Cl COL BB8 9 J4
Georges Rd NLSN BB9 19 F2
Georges Ter DWN BB3 * 58 E2
RAW/HAS BB4 * 63 F5
Giles St PDHM/BLYW BB12 25 F2
Helens Cl ACC BB5 44 B4
Helier Cl BBNW BB2 49 F1
Hubert's Rd GTH/LHO BB6 33 J1
Hubert's St GTH/LHO BB6 22 E6
Ives Rd BBN BB1 42 D3
James Cl ACC BB5 34 A6
RAW/HAS BB4 * 53 K6
James Ct BBN BB1 31 H6
James' Crs DWN BB3 * 59 F1
James Ms ACC BB5 34 A6
James Rd ACC BB5 33 K6
BBN BB1 31 J6
James Rw RAW/HAS BB4 * 54 E6
James's La BLY BB11 * 5 G3
James's Pl BBN BB1 31 J6
James's Rw BLY BB11 5 F3
James's St BLY BB11 5 F3
CLI BB7 6 D4
James' St ACC BB5 44 D2
BBNW BB2 41 G6
BCUP OL13 64 A1
NLSN BB9 18 B4
RAW/HAS BB4 62 D3
Johns BBNW BB2 2 D2
John's Av DWN BB3 59 G3
John's Cl ACC BB5 45 G5
PDHM/BLYW BB12 23 K1
RAW/HAS BB4 54 D2
John's Pl NLSN BB9 19 G1
John's Rd
PDHM/BLYW BB12 25 F5
PDHM/BLYW BB12 26 B5
John's St DWN BB3 59 G3
GTH/LHO BB6 33 J1
RAW/HAS BB4 * 62 E3
John St BCUP OL13 57 F6
Kitts Cl DWN BB3 49 J3
Lawrence Av BBNW BB2 31 F5
Lawrence St GTH/LHO BB6 22 D6
Leonard's St
PDHM/BLYW BB12 25 F2
Lucia Cl DWN BB3 49 J3
Margarets Ct BBN BB1 42 B2
Margaret's Gdns BLY BB11 36 A1
Margarets Wy BBN BB1 42 B2
Mark's Pl BBNW BB2 * 41 F3
Mark's Rd BBNW BB2 41 F3
Martin's Dr BBNW BB2 48 B2
Marys Cl BBN BB1 * 42 B3
Mary's Ct ACC BB5 34 B3
BBNW BB2 * 30 B2
RAW/HAS BB4 61 J1
Mary's Dr GTH/LHO BB6 21 H3
Mary's Gdns BBNW BB2 30 C3
Mary's Ga BLY BB11 5 J4
Mary's Pl RAW/HAS BB4 61 K1
Mary's St CLI BB7 6 D2
NLSN BB9 18 C1
Mary's Ter RAW/HAS BB4 61 K1
Mary's Whf RAW/HAS BB4 61 K1
Marys Wharfe BBNW BB2 41 K4
Matthews Ct BLY BB11 4 D5
Matthew St BLY BB11 4 C5
St Michael's Cl BBNW BB2 48 C2
St Michaels Ct BBN BB1 3 H1
NLSN BB9 8 C5
St Michael's St BBN BB1 31 K6
St Nicholas' Av CLI BB7 15 H2
St Nicholas Rd ACC BB5 * 34 B6
St Oswald's Cl BBN BB1 42 E3
St Oswald's Rd BBN BB1 42 E3
St Paul's Av BBNW BB2 2 D4
St Paul's Cl CLI BB7 6 B3
St Paul's Ct BLY BB11 * 5 F4
St Paul's Rd BBN BB1 * 33 G4
NLSN BB9 18 D3
St Paul's St ACC BB5 44 A3
BBNW BB2 2 C4
CLI BB7 6 B3
St Paul's Ter CLI BB7 6 B3
St Peter's Av RAW/HAS BB4 60 E1
St Peter's Cl BBN BB1 20 C5
DWN BB3 59 G3
St Peter's Rd RAW/HAS BB4 62 D1
St Peter St BBN BB1 33 G4
BBNW BB2 2 E5
St Philip's St BBNW BB2 41 F4
NLSN BB9 8 E6
St Philip St BRFD/BLYE BB10 27 F2
St Silas's Rd BBNW BB2 41 F2
St Stephen's Rd BBN BB1 32 A6
St Stephen's St BLY BB11 5 K6
St Stephen's Wy COL BB8 10 B2
St Thomas's Rd RAW/HAS BB4 54 E2
St Thomas St BBN BB1 42 B3
St Vincents Cl DWN BB3 49 J3
Salem St RAW/HAS BB4 53 K6
Salerno St BLY BB11 26 B6
Salesbury Cl BBN BB1 31 K1
Salford BBN BB1 3 F4
Salisbury Rd DWN BB3 49 J6
Salisbury St GTH/LHO BB6 22 E5
Saltburn St
PDHM/BLYW BB12 * 26 A5
Salterford La BRFD/BLYE BB10 39 G2
Salthill Rd CLI BB7 6 E3
Salus St BRFD/BLYE BB10 27 H2
Sand Beds La WHIT OL12 62 A6
Sandfield Rd BCUP OL13 64 B2
Sandhill St DWN BB3 59 G6
Sandhurst St BLY BB11 5 J2
Sandiway Dr BRFD/BLYE BB10 19 F6
Sandon St BBNW BB2 41 G4
DWN BB3 59 G1
Sandon Ter BBNW BB2 41 G4
Sandown Rd RAW/HAS BB4 61 F1
Sandpiper Cl BBN BB1 3 G2
Sandpiper Sq BLY BB11 26 A6
Sandringham Cl CLI BB7 13 G2
NLSN BB9 8 B6
Sandringham Gv
RAW/HAS BB4 60 D2
Sandringham Rd DWN BB3 49 J5
Sands Rd BBN BB1 33 H3
The Sands CLI BB7 13 H4
Sandwich Cl BBN BB1 42 C3
Sandybeds Cl ACC BB5 45 F5
Sandygate BLY BB11 4 D3
Sandyhall La NLSN BB9 8 A5
Sandy La ACC BB5 44 E2
BBNW BB2 40 A5
DWN BB3 49 J3
NLSN BB9 8 D5
Sangara Dr DWN BB3 49 K2
Sansbury Crs NLSN BB9 9 G5
Sapphire St BBN BB1 31 K4
Sarah St BCUP OL13 64 D3
DWN BB3 59 G2
Sark Gdns BBNW BB2 41 K6
Saunder Bank BLY BB11 5 F4
Saunder Height La
RAW/HAS BB4 55 H6
Saunders Cl RAW/HAS BB4 54 E2
Saunders Rd BBNW BB2 2 A4
Savoy St ACC BB5 44 B2
Sawley Av ACC BB5 35 F6
PDHM/BLYW BB12 24 A2
Sawley Cl DWN BB3 59 H3
Sawley Dr GTH/LHO BB6 23 F6
Sawrey Ct ACC BB5 34 A2
Saxifield St BRFD/BLYE BB10 18 E6
Saxon Cl ACC BB5 43 J2
Saxon St BRFD/BLYE BB10 27 F4
Scafell Cl PDHM/BLYW BB12 26 B3
Scaitcliffe St ACC BB5 44 D2
Scarborough Rd BBNW BB2 42 A6
Scarlett St BLY BB11 4 C5
Scarr La BBNW BB2 40 E1
Scar St BBNW BB2 41 F4
Scarth La PDHM/BLYW BB12 35 K1
Schofield Cl RAW/HAS BB4 61 J1
Schofield Rd RAW/HAS BB4 61 J1
Schofield St DWN BB3 58 E1
RAW/HAS BB4 60 D5
RAW/HAS BB4 62 D3
Scholefield Av NLSN BB9 18 E4
Scholefield La NLSN BB9 19 F4
Scholes St DWN BB3 58 E2
Scholey Head La
BRFD/BLYE BB10 39 G5
Schoolhouse Fold BLY BB11 36 A2
School House La ACC BB5 44 D5
School La BBN BB1 50 D1
BLY BB11 5 G2
BRFD/BLYE BB10 39 G4
COL BB8 11 G1
PDHM/BLYW BB12 24 B2
School St ACC BB5 44 D1
BBN BB1 33 H4
BCUP OL13 63 G3
DWN BB3 60 F2
GTH/LHO BB6 33 J1
NLSN BB9 18 C1
RAW/HAS BB4 54 E1
RAW/HAS BB4 55 K5
Scotland Bank Ter BBNW BB2 49 F1
Scotland Rd NLSN BB9 8 D6
Scott Av ACC BB5 45 G5
PDHM/BLYW BB12 24 B2
Scott Cl ACC BB5 43 K2
Scott Park Rd BLY BB11 4 C6
Scott's Ter BLY BB11 4 A3
Scott St ACC BB5 34 B2
NLSN BB9 8 D6
PDHM/BLYW BB12 25 J4
Scout Rd RAW/HAS BB4 55 J6
Seacole Cl BBN BB1 42 B6
Seascale Cl BBNW BB2 41 K6
Second Av ACC BB5 34 C5
Sedbergh Cl ACC BB5 45 F2
Sedburgh St
BRFD/BLYE BB10 27 H1
Seedall Av CLI BB7 6 B3
Seedhill Ter NLSN BB9 * 8 D6
Sefton Av BLY BB11 * 4 D4
Sefton Cl ACC BB5 34 C2
DWN BB3 59 H5
Sefton St COL BB8 10 B2
NLSN BB9 18 B4
Sefton Ter BLY BB11 4 D4
Segar St GTH/LHO BB6 * 22 D6
Selborne St BBNW BB2 41 F4
Selby Cl ACC BB5 45 G4
Selby St COL BB8 9 J2
NLSN BB9 18 E2
Seldon St COL BB8 * 9 K3
NLSN BB9 8 E6
Selkirk Cl BBN BB1 3 K5
Selkirk St BLY BB11 4 A7
Selous Rd BBNW BB2 41 F4
Serpentine Rd BLY BB11 4 E6
Sett End Rd North BBN BB1 42 D6
Sett End Rd West BBN BB1 42 C6
Settle Ter BRFD/BLYE BB10 27 H1
Seven Trees Av BBN BB1 * 32 A5
Shackleton St
BRFD/BLYE BB10 27 G3
Shadsworth Cl BBN BB1 42 C3
Shadsworth Rd BBN BB1 42 C4
Shaftesbury Av BLY BB11 37 K1
DWN BB3 49 J6
GTH/LHO BB6 23 F5
Shakeshaft St BBN BB1 3 K5
Shakespeare Av
GTH/LHO BB6 33 H1
Shakespeare St
PDHM/BLYW BB12 25 G4
Shakespeare Wy BBNW BB2 2 B7
Shale St PDHM/BLYW BB12 4 A2
Shap Cl ACC BB5 45 G4
NLSN BB9 8 D3
Shap Gv BRFD/BLYE BB10 18 A6
Sharples St ACC BB5 44 B2
BBNW BB2 41 H4
Sharp St BRFD/BLYE BB10 27 G1
NLSN BB9 8 D4
Shawbridge Ct CLI BB7 6 E3
Shaw Bridge St CLI BB7 6 E3
Shaw Brook Cl BBN BB1 33 G5
Shawcliffe La GTH/LHO BB6 22 B3
Shaw Cl BBNW BB2 2 B4
Shaw Clough Rd
RAW/HAS BB4 55 K6
Shaw Clough St
RAW/HAS BB4 * 55 K6
Shawfield RAW/HAS BB4 61 J2
Shaw St BBNW BB2 2 B3
COL BB8 9 J3
RAW/HAS BB4 53 K3
Shays Dr CLI BB7 6 E5
Shear Bank Cl BBN BB1 2 C1
Shear Bank Gdns BBN BB1 2 C1
Shear Bank Rd BBN BB1 2 C1
Shear Brow BBN BB1 2 D1
Shearwater Dr BBN BB1 3 G2
Sheddon Gv BRFD/BLYE BB10 27 K6
Shed St ACC BB5 43 K4
COL BB8 9 J3
Sheep Gn RAW/HAS BB4 53 K6
Sheffield Rd NLSN BB9 9 H6
Shelley Dr ACC BB5 45 G5
Shelley Gdns GTH/LHO BB6 33 H1
Shelley Gv DWN BB3 59 H2
Shepherd St BCUP OL13 57 F6
DWN BB3 59 F4
Sherbourne Rd ACC BB5 45 G4
Sheridan Rd COL BB8 11 F1
Sheridan St NLSN BB9 9 F5
Sherwood Ct BRFD/BLYE BB10 27 H6
Sherwood Rd BBN BB1 42 B3
Sherwood Wy ACC BB5 34 C4
Shetland Cl BBN BB1 20 E5
BBN BB1 42 C4
Shireburn Av CLI BB7 6 B4
The Shires DWN BB3 49 H3
Shop La ACC BB5 45 F2
Shore Av BRFD/BLYE BB10 27 K1
Shorey Bank BLY BB11 5 H1
Shorrock La BBNW BB2 41 F6
Shorrock St DWN BB3 59 F3
Short Clough Cl RAW/HAS BB4 54 E3
Short Clough La RAW/HAS BB4 54 E3
Shorten Brook Dr ACC BB5 24 B5
Shorten Brook Wy ACC BB5 24 B5
The Shortlands
PDHM/BLYW BB12 25 F1
Short St BCUP OL13 63 G3
COL BB8 9 K3
Showfield BRFD/BLYE BB10 28 C5
Shropshire Dr BBN BB1 20 E5
Shuttle Cl ACC BB5 44 C1
Shuttleworth Md
PDHM/BLYW BB12 * 24 A2
Shuttleworth St BBN BB1 33 H3
BRFD/BLYE BB10 * 27 G1
Siddows Av CLI BB7 6 B4
Sidebeet La BBN BB1 32 E5
The Sidings BCUP OL13 64 B3
CLI BB7 13 J3
DWN BB3 59 G4
Siding St BCUP OL13 63 H3
Sidmouth Av RAW/HAS BB4 61 F1
Silbury Cl BBNW BB2 50 A1
Silloth Cl BBNW BB2 41 K6
Silverdale Cl ACC BB5 34 A3
BBNW BB2 49 K1
BRFD/BLYE BB10 18 B6
Simmonds Wy NLSN BB9 18 B2
Simmons' St BBNW BB2 2 D3
Simmons Wy ACC BB5 34 C2
Simonstone La
PDHM/BLYW BB12 24 B3
Simonstone Rd CLI BB7 15 H3
Simpson St ACC BB5 43 K4
PDHM/BLYW BB12 36 A1
Singleton Av
PDHM/BLYW BB12 24 A1
Skelshaw Cl BBN BB1 * 42 A4
Skelton St COL BB8 10 A2
Skiddaw Cl
PDHM/BLYW BB12 26 B2
Skiddaw St BBN BB1 3 K4
Skipton Rd COL BB8 10 A1
Skye Crs BBN BB1 42 D4
Slack PDHM/BLYW BB12 16 D3
Slade La PDHM/BLYW BB12 25 F1
Slaidburn Av BRFD/BLYE BB10 38 D1
RAW/HAS BB4 54 E5
Slaidburn Dr ACC BB5 44 B3
Slater Av COL BB8 9 K1
Slater St BBNW BB2 41 G6
Sliven Clod Rd RAW/HAS BB4 46 C5
Smalley St BLY BB11 5 K6
Smalley Wy BBNW BB2 41 J5
Smallshaw La BLY BB11 26 A6
Smirthwaite St BLY BB11 4 A5
Smith St BRFD/BLYE BB10 28 C6
COL BB8 9 J3
NLSN BB9 18 E1
PDHM/BLYW BB12 4 D2
Smithy Bridge St ACC BB5 43 K4
Smithyfield Av
BRFD/BLYE BB10 28 A5
The Smithy CLI BB7 * 13 J4
Snaefell Rd BBNW BB2 41 J6
Snape St DWN BB3 49 K6
Snell Gv COL BB8 10 B1
Sniddle Hill La DWN BB3 58 D3
Snodworth Rd GTH/LHO BB6 21 J4
Snowden St
PDHM/BLYW BB12 26 A5
Snowdon Av BBN BB1 31 J6
Snowdrop Cl RAW/HAS BB4 60 C3
Snow St BBN BB1 3 G1
Solway Av BBNW BB2 40 D6
Somerford Cl
PDHM/BLYW BB12 26 C4
Somerset Av BBN BB1 20 E5
CLI BB7 6 E1
DWN BB3 49 K6
Somerset Cl ACC BB5 44 B4
Somerset Gv ACC BB5 34 B6
Somerset Pl NLSN BB9 9 G6
Somerset Rd BBN BB1 33 F4
Somerset St BLY BB11 * 5 H7
Somerset Wk RAW/HAS BB4 60 E3
Soudan St BRFD/BLYE BB10 * 27 G1
Sough La BBN BB1 43 F6
Sough Rd DWN BB3 59 G3
Soulby Cl BBNW BB2 41 G6
Southcliffe GTH/LHO BB6 22 C5
Southcliffe Av
PDHM/BLYW BB12 26 B4
South Dr PDHM/BLYW BB12 25 H3
Southern Av
PDHM/BLYW BB12 26 B4
Southey St BLY BB11 4 C3
Southfield La
BRFD/BLYE BB10 19 J1
COL BB8 9 K6
Southfield Sq NLSN BB9 * 19 F1
Southfield St NLSN BB9 19 F2
South Shore St ACC BB5 44 A2
RAW/HAS BB4 53 J6
South St ACC BB5 35 G5
ACC BB5 44 E2
BCUP OL13 64 B1
BLY BB11 5 G2
DWN BB3 59 F2
RAW/HAS BB4 54 E6
RAW/HAS BB4 61 F2
RAW/HAS BB4 62 D2
South Valley Dr COL BB8 9 J4
South Vw NLSN BB9 18 D2
PDHM/BLYW BB12 * 15 G6
Southwood Dr ACC BB5 45 G4
Southworth St BBNW BB2 41 H5
Sow Clough Rd BCUP OL13 63 J2
Sowerby St
PDHM/BLYW BB12 25 F3
Spa Garth CLI BB7 6 E3
Sparth Av ACC BB5 34 B2
Sparth Rd ACC BB5 34 B2
Spa St PDHM/BLYW BB12 4 C1
PDHM/BLYW BB12 25 G3
Speedie Cl BBNW BB2 49 H1
Speedwell St BBNW BB2 41 F5
Speke St BBNW BB2 41 F5
Spencer Gv GTH/LHO BB6 22 C6
Spencer St ACC BB5 45 F1
BRFD/BLYE BB10 27 F2
RAW/HAS BB4 54 E2
Spenser Cl BRFD/BLYE BB10 39 J1
Spenser St PDHM/BLYW BB12 25 G4
Spindle Berry Ct ACC BB5 * 44 E3
The Spinney BBNW BB2 30 E5
PDHM/BLYW BB12 26 C3
Spinning Av BBN BB1 50 D1
Spouthouse La ACC BB5 35 H4
Spread Eagle St ACC BB5 43 H2
Spring Av GTH/LHO BB6 22 D5
Springbank Gdns
RAW/HAS BB4 46 D5
Spring Bank Ter BBNW BB2 41 G5
Springdale Rd GTH/LHO BB6 21 H3
Springfield Av ACC BB5 44 B3
BBNW BB2 40 C6
BCUP OL13 57 G6
Springfield Bank BLY BB11 5 H5
Springfield Cl CLI BB7 13 K2
Springfield Dr RAW/HAS BB4 62 D2
Springfield Rd BLY BB11 5 H6
GTH/LHO BB6 33 H1
NLSN BB9 18 D3
RAW/HAS BB4 55 F6
Springfield St ACC BB5 43 K4
BBNW BB2 41 F4
DWN BB3 59 F3
Springfield Ter BBNW BB2 40 D6
Springfield Vw BLY BB11 47 G2
Spring Gdns ACC BB5 44 E2
BCUP OL13 57 G6
DWN BB3 59 F3
PDHM/BLYW BB12 25 F2
Spring Gardens Rd COL BB8 9 K3
Spring Gardens St
RAW/HAS BB4 62 E3
Spring Gv COL BB8 10 E1
Spring Hall ACC BB5 23 G6
Spring Hl BBN BB1 2 E4
Springhill Av BCUP OL13 63 H4
Spring Hill Rd ACC BB5 44 B3
BLY BB11 4 E5
Springhill Vls BCUP OL13 63 J3
Spring La BBNW BB2 41 F4
COL BB8 9 K2
RAW/HAS BB4 53 K5
Spring Mdw ACC BB5 34 C2
DWN BB3 59 H4
Spring Rw COL BB8 * 10 E1
Spring St ACC BB5 44 B3
BBN BB1 33 H3
BCUP OL13 * 64 A2
NLSN BB9 18 C2
RAW/HAS BB4 54 E1
Springthorpe St DWN BB3 59 G5
Springvale ACC BB5 44 B3
Spring Vale Garden Vil
DWN BB3 59 H5
Springvale Ml RAW/HAS BB4 * 60 D1
Spring Vale Rd DWN BB3 59 G4
Spring Vw BBNW BB2 2 B3
Springwood Rd
BRFD/BLYE BB10 27 K6
Spring Yd COL BB8 9 K2
Sprucewood Cl ACC BB5 45 F1
Squire Rd NLSN BB9 19 F1
Squirrels Cl ACC BB5 35 G5
Stables Cl RAW/HAS BB4 54 E3
Stable Yd ACC BB5 * 44 B1
Stack La BCUP OL13 64 C3
Staffa Crs BBN BB1 42 D3
Stafford St BRFD/BLYE BB10 27 F4
DWN BB3 49 K5
NLSN BB9 19 G1
Staghills Rd RAW/HAS BB4 62 C2
Stainton Dr PDHM/BLYW BB12 26 D3
Stakes Hall Pl BBNW BB2 41 G5
Stamford Pl CLI BB7 6 E2
Stanbury Dr BRFD/BLYE BB10 27 K1
Stancliffe St BBNW BB2 41 F4
Standen Hall Cl
BRFD/BLYE BB10 * 18 E6
Standen Hall Dr
BRFD/BLYE BB10 18 D6
Standen Rd CLI BB7 6 E4
Standish St BLY BB11 5 G2
Standroyd Dr COL BB8 10 C2
Standroyd Rd COL BB8 10 C2
Stanford Gdns BBNW BB2 42 A6
Stanhill La ACC BB5 43 H3
Stanhill Rd BBN BB1 43 F3
Stanhope St DWN BB3 59 F1
PDHM/BLYW BB12 * 5 F1
Stanley Dr DWN BB3 59 G5
Stanley Ga BBNW BB2 30 C3
Stanley Mt BCUP OL13 57 F6
Stanley Range BBNW BB2 41 F5
Stanley St ACC BB5 43 K4
ACC BB5 45 F1
BBN BB1 3 K2
BLY BB11 5 F5
COL BB8 9 K2
NLSN BB9 * 18 B4
NLSN BB9 18 D1
Stansfeld St BBNW BB2 2 B7
Stansfield Rd RAW/HAS BB4 62 D3
Stansfield St BLY BB11 26 A6
DWN BB3 59 F3
NLSN BB9 8 E6
Stanthorpe Wk
BRFD/BLYE BB10 27 F2
Stanworth Rd NLSN BB9 18 D1
Stanworth St
BRFD/BLYE BB10 * 28 C6
Star Bank BCUP OL13 * 63 J4
Starkie St BBN BB1 3 G4
BLY BB11 4 C4
DWN BB3 59 G3
Star St ACC BB5 44 B2
DWN BB3 59 G2
Station Cl BBN BB1 31 K1
BBN BB1 33 G5
Station Ct RAW/HAS BB4 * 61 J2
Station Rd ACC BB5 35 G3
BBN BB1 33 G5
CLI BB7 6 D3
CLI BB7 13 J4
GTH/LHO BB6 22 E6
PDHM/BLYW BB12 25 F3
RAW/HAS BB4 53 K5
RAW/HAS BB4 60 D4
Sted Ter BBN BB1 2 D1
Steer St BRFD/BLYE BB10 27 G2
Steiner's La ACC BB5 44 A1
Steiner St ACC BB5 44 C1
Stephenson Dr
PDHM/BLYW BB12 26 B4
Stephen St BBNW BB2 41 F5
Stevenson St East ACC BB5 44 B2
Stevenson St West ACC BB5 44 B3
Stewart St BBNW BB2 49 H1
BLY BB11 5 K7

Stirling Cl CLI BB7 ....6 B5
Stirling Ct BRFD/BLYE BB10 ....19 H5
Stirling Dr BBN BB1 ....3 H6
Stirling St BBNW BB2 ....41 F6
Stockbridge Dr
PDHM/BLYW BB12 ....25 J2
Stockbridge Rd
PDHM/BLYW BB12 ....25 G3
Stockclough La BBNW BB2 ....48 B2
Stockholm St BLY BB11 ....26 A6
Stockwood Cl BBNW BB2 ....30 E5
Stone Bridge La ACC BB5 ....43 K4
Stone Edge Rd NLSN BB9 ....8 E1
Stone Hill Dr BBN BB1 ....32 A4
Stoneholme Rd
RAW/HAS BB4 ....54 E1
Stone St RAW/HAS BB4 ....60 C1
RAW/HAS BB4 ....62 E3
Stoneyhurst Av
BRFD/BLYE BB10 ....27 J6
Stoneyhurst Height
NLSN BB9 ....18 D5
Stoney St BLY BB11 ....38 B2
Stonybutts BBNW BB2 ....2 E4
Stonyhurst Cl BBNW BB2 * 2 C6
PDHM/BLYW BB12 ....25 G5
Stonyhurst Rd BBNW BB2 ....2 C5
Stoops Fold BBNW BB2 ....30 C2
Stoop St BLY BB11 ....26 B6
Stopes Brow DWN BB3 ....50 A2
Stopping Hey BBN BB1 * 21 G6
Store St DWN BB3 ....50 A2
Stork St DWN BB3 ....59 J3
Stott St NLSN BB9 ....18 D1
Stourton St BBN BB1 ....33 G3
Stout St BBNW BB2 * 2 C6
Straits ACC BB5 ....44 A3
Straits La PDHM/BLYW BB12 ....15 F6
Strange St BLY BB11 ....5 J7
Strathclyde Rd BBN BB1 ....3 J5
Stratton Ct NLSN BB9 ....18 E3
Strawberry Bank BBNW BB2 ....2 D3
Stroyan St BRFD/BLYE BB10 ....27 H6
Stuart Av BCUP OL13 ....63 J3
Stuart St ACC BB5 ....34 D6
Stubbins La CLI BB7 ....15 J2
Stubbylee La BCUP OL13 ....64 A3
Stump Hall Rd
PDHM/BLYW BB12 ....16 C2
Stunstead Rd COL BB8 ....10 E4
Sudell Cl DWN BB3 ....59 H2
Sudell Cross BBNW BB2 * 2 E3
Sudell Rd DWN BB3 ....59 F2
Sudellside St DWN BB3 ....59 G1
Suffolk Av PDHM/BLYW BB12 ....25 K5
Suffolk St BBNW BB2 ....41 G5
Sulby Rd BBNW BB2 ....41 J6
Sullivan Dr BBNW BB2 ....42 A6
Sultan St ACC BB5 ....44 E1
Summer St NLSN BB9 ....18 C2
Summerville Wk BBNW BB2 ....2 C3
Sumner St BBNW BB2 ....2 E7
Suncliffe Rd NLSN BB9 ....18 D5
Sunderland St
PDHM/BLYW BB12 ....26 A6
Sunnindale Av RAW/HAS BB4 ....63 F2
Sunningdale Gdns
BRFD/BLYE BB10 ....18 D6
Sunny Bank BCUP OL13 * 57 J4
Sunny Bank Cl RAW/HAS BB4 ....60 D5
Sunnybank Dr ACC BB5 ....43 J5
Sunny Bank Rd BBNW BB2 ....41 H6
RAW/HAS BB4 ....60 D5
Sunnybank St DWN BB3 * 59 F2
RAW/HAS BB4 ....53 J6
Sunny Bower Cl BBN BB1 ....32 B4
Sunnyfield Av
BRFD/BLYE BB10 ....39 G5
Sunnyhill Cl DWN BB3 ....58 C1
Sunnyhurst Cl DWN BB3 ....58 C1
Sunnyhurst La DWN BB3 ....58 C1
Sunnyhurst Rd BBNW BB2 ....2 C5
Sunny Lea St RAW/HAS BB4 ....54 D4
Sunnymere Dr DWN BB3 ....58 D1
Sunnyside Av BBN BB1 ....21 F4
BBNW BB2 ....40 C6
CLI BB7 ....13 H4
Sunnyside Cl RAW/HAS BB4 ....54 E3
Sun St ACC BB5 ....44 A3
CLI BB7 ....6 D4
COL BB8 ....10 A2
NLSN BB9 ....18 C1
Super St ACC BB5 ....34 A1
Surrey Av DWN BB3 ....49 K6
PDHM/BLYW BB12 ....26 A4
Surrey Rd BBN BB1 ....42 D1
NLSN BB9 ....8 D5
Surrey St ACC BB5 ....45 F1
Sussex Cl ACC BB5 ....34 B6
Sussex Dr BBN BB1 ....3 J6
RAW/HAS BB4 ....60 D3
Sussex Rd BBN BB1 ....33 F5
Sussex St BLY BB11 ....5 J7
NLSN BB9 ....8 E6
Sutcliffe St BCUP OL13 ....64 D3
BLY BB11 ....5 F3
BRFD/BLYE BB10 ....19 F6
Sutherland Cl BBN BB1 ....21 F4
Sutherland St COL BB8 ....9 J3
Sutton Av BRFD/BLYE BB10 ....27 J1
Sutton Crs ACC BB5 ....35 H4
Sutton St BBNW BB2 ....48 B1
Swainbank St BLY BB11 * 5 J5
Swaine St NLSN BB9 ....18 C1
Swallow Dr BBN BB1 ....3 F2
Swallowfields BBN BB1 ....31 H5
Swallow Pk BLY BB11 ....26 B6
Swanage Rd
BRFD/BLYE BB10 ....27 H2
Swan Ctyd CLI BB7 * 6 D3
Swan Farm Cl DWN BB3 ....49 K2
Swan Meadow CLI BB7 ....6 C2
Swan St BBNW BB2 ....41 J4
DWN BB3 ....59 G5
Swift Cl BBN BB1 ....3 G3
Swinburne Cl ACC BB5 ....45 G5
Swinden Hall Rd NLSN BB9 ....8 E5
Swinden La COL BB8 ....9 G5
Swindon St BLY BB11 ....4 B5
Swinless St BRFD/BLYE BB10 ....27 G2
Swinshaw Cl RAW/HAS BB4 ....46 E5
Swiss St ACC BB5 ....44 B1
Sycamore Av
PDHM/BLYW BB12 ....25 K4
Sycamore Cl BBN BB1 * 31 K5
BBN BB1 ....33 H5
PDHM/BLYW BB12 ....26 B5
Sycamore Crs ACC BB5 ....34 B1
Sycamore Gdns COL BB8 ....9 J1
Sycamore Gv ACC BB5 ....45 G4
DWN BB3 ....59 G1
Sycamore Rd BBN BB1 ....31 K5
Sydney Av CLI BB7 ....13 K4
Sydney St ACC BB5 ....34 C4
ACC BB5 ....44 E1
BLY BB11 ....5 F2
DWN BB3 ....59 G4
Sykefield NLSN BB9 ....18 A4
Syke Side Dr ACC BB5 ....24 B5
Sylvan Dr BLY BB11 ....36 E1

T

Tabor St PDHM/BLYW BB12 ....26 B4
Tadema Gv BLY BB11 ....37 K3
Talbot Av ACC BB5 ....34 B3
Talbot Cl CLI BB7 ....6 E4
RAW/HAS BB4 ....61 H3
Talbot Dr BRFD/BLYE BB10 ....28 A1
Talbot Rd ACC BB5 ....34 C5
Talbot St BBN BB1 ....33 J4
BLY BB11 ....5 J2
BRFD/BLYE BB10 ....28 A1
COL BB8 ....9 K1
Tanner St BLY BB11 * 5 F3
Tanpits Rd ACC BB5 ....44 A1
Tapestry St BBNW BB2 ....41 H6
Tarbert Crs BBN BB1 ....42 D3
Tarleton Av BLY BB11 ....5 K6
Tarleton St BLY BB11 ....5 K6
Tarn Av ACC BB5 ....34 B1
Tarn Brook Cl ACC BB5 ....35 H4
Tarvin Cl BRFD/BLYE BB10 ....19 F6
Tasker St ACC BB5 ....44 E1
Tattersall St ACC BB5 ....43 K3
BBNW BB2 * 2 E6
RAW/HAS BB4 ....53 K3
Tatton St COL BB8 ....9 H4
Taunton Rd BBNW BB2 ....41 F2
Tavistock St NLSN BB9 ....19 F1
Taylor Av RAW/HAS BB4 ....62 E1
Taylor Cl BBNW BB2 ....2 B7
Taylor Ct RAW/HAS BB4 ....53 J6
Taylor St BBNW BB2 ....41 H4
BRFD/BLYE BB10 ....27 F3
CLI BB7 ....6 E3
DWN BB3 ....59 F3
NLSN BB9 ....18 B3
RAW/HAS BB4 * 53 K3
RAW/HAS BB4 ....54 E6
Taylor St West ACC BB5 * 44 D1
Tay St BLY BB11 ....4 B4
Teal Cl BBN BB1 ....31 H5
Tedder Av
PDHM/BLYW BB12 ....26 A5
Telford St
PDHM/BLYW BB12 ....26 B4
Temple Cl BBN BB1 ....42 B3
Temple Dr BBN BB1 ....42 B3
Temple St BLY BB11 ....5 J4
COL BB8 ....10 A1
NLSN BB9 ....19 F1
Templeton Cl DWN BB3 ....59 F1
Tenby Cl BBN BB1 ....31 J6
Tennis St BRFD/BLYE BB10 ....27 F3
Tennyson Av ACC BB5 ....43 J3
PDHM/BLYW BB12 ....23 K1
PDHM/BLYW BB12 ....25 H4
Tennyson Pl GTH/LHO BB6 ....33 H1
Tennyson Rd COL BB8 ....9 K2
Tennyson St
BRFD/BLYE BB10 * 19 F6
PDHM/BLYW BB12 ....36 A1
Tenterfield St RAW/HAS BB4 ....62 E3
Terry St NLSN BB9 ....9 G5
Tetbury Cl BBNW BB2 ....48 C1
Tewkesbury Cl ACC BB5 ....45 F4
Tewksbury St BBNW BB2 ....41 F6
Thames Av BRFD/BLYE BB10 ....18 C6
Thanet Lee Cl
BRFD/BLYE BB10 ....38 E4
Thirlmere Av BRFD/BLYE BB10 ....27 F1
COL BB8 ....10 B1
PDHM/BLYW BB12 ....25 F1
RAW/HAS BB4 ....61 F3
Thirlmere Cl ACC BB5 ....35 F4
BBN BB1 * 3 H2
Thirlmere Dr DWN BB3 ....59 H1
Thirlmere Rd
BRFD/BLYE BB10 ....27 K6
Thistlemount Av
RAW/HAS BB4 ....62 E2
Thistle St BCUP OL13 ....64 A1
Thomas St ACC BB5 * 43 K4
BBNW BB2 ....2 C6
BLY BB11 ....5 G4
COL BB8 ....9 J3
NLSN BB9 * 18 A4
NLSN BB9 ....18 E2
Thompson St DWN BB3 ....59 G4
PDHM/BLYW BB12 ....25 F3
Thorn Bank BCUP OL13 ....64 B1
Thornber Ct BRFD/BLYE BB10 ....27 H2
Thornber St BBNW BB2 ....41 G5
Thorncliffe Dr DWN BB3 ....59 J3
Thorn Crs BCUP OL13 ....64 B1
Thorn Dr BCUP OL13 ....64 B1
Thorne St NLSN BB9 ....9 G5
Thorney Bank St BLY BB11 * 4 E5
Thorneyholme Rd ACC BB5 ....34 E6
Thornfield Av RAW/HAS BB4 ....62 D2
Thorn Gdns BCUP OL13 * 64 B1
Thorn Gv COL BB8 ....10 B1
Thornhill Av BBN BB1 ....33 G5
Thorn Hill Cl BBN BB1 ....3 J4
Thornley Av BBN BB1 ....42 C1
Thorn St BCUP OL13 ....64 B1
BRFD/BLYE BB10 ....27 F3
CLI BB7 ....15 J2
GTH/LHO BB6 ....22 D5
RAW/HAS BB4 ....54 D4
Thornton Cl ACC BB5 ....34 C5
BBNW BB2 ....49 K1
Thornton Crs BRFD/BLYE BB10 ....27 K6
Thornton Rd BRFD/BLYE BB10 ....27 K6
Thornwood Cl BBN BB1 ....31 J4
Thornylea BBNW BB2 ....49 H2
Throstle Cl
PDHM/BLYW BB12 * 26 E4
Throstle St BBNW BB2 ....2 B6
NLSN BB9 * 8 E6
Throup Pl NLSN BB9 ....8 E5
Thursby Pl NLSN BB9 * 9 F5
Thursby Rd BRFD/BLYE BB10 ....27 H2
NLSN BB9 ....9 F5
Thursby Sq BRFD/BLYE BB10 ....27 F3
Thursden Av
BRFD/BLYE BB10 * 19 F6
Thursden Pl NLSN BB9 ....9 H6
Thursfield Rd BRFD/BLYE BB10 ....5 K5
Thurston St BLY BB11 ....5 J2
Thwaites Av BBNW BB2 ....30 C3
Thwaites Cl BBN BB1 ....42 D5
Thwaites Rd ACC BB5 ....43 J3
Thwaites St ACC BB5 ....43 J4
Tiber Av BLY BB11 ....37 G1
Timber St ACC BB5 ....44 E2
BCUP OL13 ....64 A2
NLSN BB9 * 18 B3
Timbrills Av CLI BB7 ....15 H1
Tinedale Vw
PDHM/BLYW BB12 ....25 G2
Tintagell Cl BBNW BB2 ....48 A2
Tintern Cl ACC BB5 ....45 G4
PDHM/BLYW BB12 ....24 A2
Tintern Crs BBN BB1 ....32 B5
Tippet Cl BBNW BB2 ....42 A6
Tiverton Dr BBNW BB2 ....49 G1
BRFD/BLYE BB10 ....19 F6
Tockholes Rd DWN BB3 ....49 F4
DWN BB3 ....58 E2
Todd Carr Rd RAW/HAS BB4 ....62 E2
Todd Hall Rd RAW/HAS BB4 ....53 J6
Todmorden Old Rd BCUP OL13 ....57 G5
Todmorden Rd BCUP OL13 ....57 G6
BLY BB11 ....5 K5
BRFD/BLYE BB10 ....19 G6
Tom La RAW/HAS BB4 ....62 E1
Tong La BCUP OL13 ....57 G6
Tontine St BBN BB1 ....2 E3
Top O' Th' Cft BBNW BB2 * 49 H1
Topaz St BBN BB1 ....31 K3
Top Barn La RAW/HAS BB4 ....62 C2
Top La COL BB8 ....10 E3
Tor End Rd RAW/HAS BB4 ....60 C5
Toronto Rd BBNW BB2 ....31 G5
Torquay Av BRFD/BLYE BB10 ....27 H1
Torridon Cl BBNW BB2 ....40 D6
Torver Cl PDHM/BLYW BB12 ....26 A3
Tor Vw RAW/HAS BB4 ....61 K2
Tor View Rd RAW/HAS BB4 ....61 F2
Tottenham Rd DWN BB3 ....49 K3
Tottleworth Rd BBN BB1 ....33 J3
Tower Hi CLI BB7 ....6 E2
Tower Rd BBNW BB2 ....40 D5
DWN BB3 ....59 G3
Tower St ACC BB5 ....43 H2
BCUP OL13 ....64 A1
Tower Vw DWN BB3 ....59 H2
Towneley Av ACC BB5 ....35 H3
Towneleyside BLY BB11 ....38 B3
Towneley St BRFD/BLYE BB10 ....27 G1
Townfield Av BRFD/BLYE BB10 ....28 A5
Town Hall St BBNW BB2 ....2 E4
GTH/LHO BB6 ....22 D6
Town Hill Bank
PDHM/BLYW BB12 ....25 G2
Town House Rd NLSN BB9 ....19 H1
Townley St BRFD/BLYE BB10 ....19 F6
COL BB8 ....10 A2
NLSN BB9 ....18 B4
Townsend St RAW/HAS BB4 ....53 J6
RAW/HAS BB4 ....62 E3
Townsley St NLSN BB9 ....18 E3
Town Vw BBN BB1 ....3 G5
Town Wk BBN BB1 ....3 G5
Trafalgar St BLY BB11 ....4 D3
Trapp La PDHM/BLYW BB12 ....15 H5
Travis St BRFD/BLYE BB10 ....27 F3
Trawden Cl ACC BB5 ....44 E3
Trawden Rd COL BB8 ....10 D2
Tremellen St ACC BB5 ....44 C1
Trent Rd NLSN BB9 ....19 G1
Tresco Cl BBNW BB2 ....41 F6
Trevor Cl BBN BB1 ....31 K6
The Triangle ACC BB5 ....35 G5
Trillium Wy DWN BB3 ....50 A2
Trinity Cl PDHM/BLYW BB12 ....25 G5
Trinity Ct BBN BB1 ....3 H2
Trinity St ACC BB5 ....43 K4
BBN BB1 ....3 H3
Troon Av BBN BB1 ....42 C4
Trout Beck ACC BB5 ....34 B1
Troutbeck Cl
PDHM/BLYW BB12 ....26 A3
Trout St BRFD/BLYE BB10 ....27 F5
Troy St BBN BB1 ....31 K6
Tucker Hl CLI BB7 ....6 D2
Tudor Cl DWN BB3 ....59 F1
GTH/LHO BB6 ....21 H2
Tunnel St PDHM/BLYW BB12 ....4 B2
Tunstall Dr ACC BB5 ....34 D4
Tunstead Av
PDHM/BLYW BB12 ....24 B3
Tunstead Crs BCUP OL13 ....63 H2
Tunstead La BCUP OL13 ....63 F2
Tunstead Rd BCUP OL13 ....63 H3
Tunstill St BRFD/BLYE BB10 ....27 G2
Turf St BLY BB11 ....5 H4
Turkey St ACC BB5 ....35 F6
Turncroft Rd DWN BB3 ....59 G3
Turner Fold PDHM/BLYW BB12 ....24 A1
Turner Rd NLSN BB9 ....18 C1
Turner St CLI BB7 ....6 D4
Turness Av PDHM/BLYW BB12 ....24 A2
Turn La DWN BB3 ....58 E2
Turnpike RAW/HAS BB4 ....62 D2
Turton Gv BRFD/BLYE BB10 ....27 J5
Turton Hollow Rd
RAW/HAS BB4 ....54 E1
Tuscan Av BLY BB11 ....26 B6
Tuscany Gv GTH/LHO BB6 ....12 C3
Tweed St BBNW BB2 ....49 H1
NLSN BB9 ....19 G1
Two Gates Dr DWN BB3 ....59 G1
Tynwald Rd BBNW BB2 ....41 J6
Tythebarn St DWN BB3 ....59 G2

U

Uldale Cl NLSN BB9 ....18 E3
Ullswater Av ACC BB5 ....35 F4
Ullswater Cl BBN BB1 ....3 H2
BBN BB1 ....33 G4
Ullswater Rd BRFD/BLYE BB10 ....27 K6
Ullswater Wy RAW/HAS BB4 ....46 E6
Ulpha Cl PDHM/BLYW BB12 ....26 A3
Ulster St BLY BB11 ....4 B5
Ulverston Cl BBNW BB2 ....42 A6
Ulverston Dr BBN BB1 ....33 G4
Underbank Cl BCUP OL13 ....57 F6
Underbank Rd ACC BB5 ....53 J2
RAW/HAS BB4 ....53 H6
Underbank Wy RAW/HAS BB4 ....53 H6
Under Billinge La BBNW BB2 ....40 C3
Underley St BRFD/BLYE BB10 ....18 C6
Union Rd ACC BB5 ....43 K3
RAW/HAS BB4 ....61 G1
Union St ACC BB5 ....44 D1
BBNW BB2 ....41 J4
BCUP OL13 ....63 H3
BCUP OL13 ....64 A1
CLI BB7 ....6 B3
COL BB8 ....10 A2
DWN BB3 ....59 F2
NLSN BB9 ....18 B4
RAW/HAS BB4 ....54 E6
Unity St BBNW BB2 ....41 J4
Unity Wy RAW/HAS BB4 ....54 D6
Unsworth St BCUP OL13 ....63 J4
Up Brooks CLI BB7 ....6 E2
Uplands Dr PDHM/BLYW BB12 ....17 H2
Upper Cliffe (Bersham Dr)
GTH/LHO BB6 ....22 D5

V

Vale Ct ACC BB5 ....35 H4
Vale House Cl CLI BB7 * 13 J4
Vale St BCUP OL13 ....57 G6
DWN BB3 ....58 E2
NLSN BB9 ....19 F2
RAW/HAS BB4 ....53 K5
Valley Dr PDHM/BLYW BB12 ....25 G3
Valley Gdns BLY BB11 ....36 D1
Valley Rd BBN BB1 ....20 E6
Valley St BLY BB11 ....37 F1
Valli Ga BBN BB1 ....32 A6
Vancouver Crs BBNW BB2 ....31 G5
Vandyck Av BLY BB11 ....37 J3
Vardon Rd BBNW BB2 ....41 F5
Varley St COL BB8 ....10 A1
DWN BB3 * 59 F2
Vaughan St NLSN BB9 ....19 F2
Vauxhall St BBNW BB2 * 41 F4
Veevers St BLY BB11 ....5 F3
NLSN BB9 ....18 A3
PDHM/BLYW BB12 ....25 G3
Velvet St BBNW BB2 * 49 H1
Venables Av COL BB8 ....10 B1
Venice Av BLY BB11 ....37 G1
Venice St BLY BB11 ....4 A5
Ventnor Rd RAW/HAS BB4 ....61 F2
Venture Ct ACC BB5 ....24 A6
Venture St BCUP OL13 ....57 G6
Verax St BCUP OL13 ....64 A2
Verbena Cl DWN BB3 ....50 A2
Vernon Rd COL BB8 ....11 F1
Vernon St BBNW BB2 ....2 E5
DWN BB3 ....59 G2
NLSN BB9 ....18 E2
Verona Av BLY BB11 ....26 B6
Veronica St DWN BB3 ....49 J5
Vicarage Av
PDHM/BLYW BB12 ....24 E3
Vicarage Dr DWN BB3 ....59 H3
Vicarage Fold CLI BB7 ....14 A2
Vicarage La ACC BB5 ....45 G6
BBN BB1 ....20 E5
Vicar St BBN BB1 * 3 G4
GTH/LHO BB6 * 33 J1
Victoria Av ACC BB5 ....45 F5
BBNW BB2 ....40 C6
NLSN BB9 ....18 B3
Victoria Bank DWN BB3 * 59 F1
Victoria Cl CLI BB7 ....13 G2
Victoria Ct BBN BB1 ....2 E4
Victoria Dr RAW/HAS BB4 ....60 E1
Victoria Gdns NLSN BB9 ....8 C5
Victoria Ldg
PDHM/BLYW BB12 ....24 A1
Victoria Pde RAW/HAS BB4 62
Victoria Rd PDHM/BLYW BB12 25
Victoria St ACC BB5 34
ACC BB5 43
ACC BB5 44
ACC BB5 44
BBN BB1 3
BBN BB1 33
BCUP OL13 63
BLY BB11 5
CLI BB7 6
DWN BB3 59
GTH/LHO BB6 22
NLSN BB9 8
NLSN BB9 18
RAW/HAS BB4 53
RAW/HAS BB4 62
Victoria Wy RAW/HAS BB4 62
Victory Cl NLSN BB9 18
Viewfield Ms BBNW BB2 * 41
View Rd DWN BB3 49
Vihiers Cl CLI BB7 13
Viking Pl BRFD/BLYE BB10 27
Villiers St BLY BB11 26
PDHM/BLYW BB12 25
Vincent Ct BBNW BB2 49
Vincent Rd NLSN BB9 19
Vincent St BBNW BB2 49
COL BB8 10
Vincit St BRFD/BLYE BB10 27
Vine St ACC BB5 43
ACC BB5 44
Violet St BRFD/BLYE BB10 27
Viscount Av DWN BB3 50
Vivary Wy COL BB8 9
Vulcan St BLY BB11 5
NLSN BB9 9

W

Wackersall Rd COL BB8 9
Waddington Av
BRFD/BLYE BB10 27
Waddington Rd ACC BB5 35
CLI BB7 6
Waddington St
PDHM/BLYW BB12 25
Waddow Gn CLI BB7 6
Wade St PDHM/BLYW BB12 25
Waidshouse Cl NLSN BB9 18
Waidshouse Rd NLSN BB9 18
Waingate Cl RAW/HAS BB4 55
Waingate La RAW/HAS BB4 55
Walden Rd BBN BB1 31
Wales Rd RAW/HAS BB4 62
Walker Av ACC BB5 44
Walker Rd BBN BB1 50
Walker St BBN BB1 3
CLI BB7 6
Walk Mill Pl BRFD/BLYE BB10 38
Wallace Hartley Ms COL BB8 9
Wallhurst Cl BRFD/BLYE BB10 28
Wallstreams La
BRFD/BLYE BB10 28
Wall St RAW/HAS BB4 62
Walmsley Av BBN BB1 33
Walmsley Brow CLI BB7 13
Walmsley Cl ACC BB5 44
Walmsley St BBN BB1 33
DWN BB3 59
GTH/LHO BB6 22
Walney Gdns BBNW BB2 41
Walnut Av RAW/HAS BB4 54
Walnut St BBN BB1 31
BCUP OL13 57
Walpole St BBN BB1 3
BRFD/BLYE BB10 27
Walsden Gv BRFD/BLYE BB10 27
Walshaw La BRFD/BLYE BB10 27
Walsh St BBNW BB2 41
Walter St ACC BB5 35
ACC BB5 43
ACC BB5 44
BBN BB1 3
DWN BB3 * 59
NLSN BB9 18
Waltham Cl ACC BB5 45
Walton Cl BCUP OL13 64
Walton Crs BBNW BB2 42
Walton La NLSN BB9 9
Walton St ACC BB5 34
COL BB8 9
NLSN BB9 8
Walverden Crs NLSN BB9 19
Walverden Rd
BRFD/BLYE BB10 19
NLSN BB9 18
Wansfell Rd CLI BB7 6
Warcock La BCUP OL13 57
Ward Av ACC BB5 43
Warde St NLSN BB9 18
Wardle St BCUP OL13 * 63
Ward St BLY BB11 4
GTH/LHO BB6 22
Wareham Cl ACC BB5 34
Wareham St BBN BB1 32
The Warings NLSN BB9 18
Warmden Av ACC BB5 45
Warmden Gdns BBN BB1 32
Warner St ACC BB5 44
RAW/HAS BB4 53
Warren Dr BCUP OL13 64
NLSN BB9 8
Warrenside Cl BBN BB1 32
The Warren BBNW BB2 30
Warrington St BBN BB1 32
Warth La RAW/HAS BB4 62
Warwick Av ACC BB5 34
ACC BB5 34
Warwick Cl ACC BB5 34
Warwick Dr CLI BB7 6
NLSN BB9 18

PDHM/BLYW BB12 25 G4
Warwick St ACC BB5 34 B6
NLSN BB9 18 E2
RAW/HAS BB4 53 K6
Wasdale Av BBN BB1 42 C4
Wasdale Cl PDHM/BLYW BB12 25 F2
Washington St ACC BB5 44 E1
Waterbarn La BCUP OL13 * 63 G3
Waterbarn St
BRFD/BLYE BB10 27 G2
Waterfield Av DWN BB3 59 G5
Waterford St NLSN BB9 9 F6
Waterfront BBN BB1 * 3 H7
Waterloo Cl BBNW BB2 49 F1
Waterloo Rd BLY BB11 5 J6
CLI BB7 6 E3
Waterloo St ACC BB5 34 C4
Water Mdw BBNW BB2 49 H2
Waters Edge BBN BB1 3 G7
CLI BB7 13 J5
Waterside Ms
PDHM/BLYW BB12 25 F3
Waterside Rd COL BB8 9 K3
RAW/HAS BB4 60 D1
Water St ACC BB5 44 E1
BRFD/BLYE BB10 28 C6
GTH/LHO BB6 22 D6
NLSN BB9 18 E1
PDHM/BLYW BB12 36 A1
RAW/HAS BB4 54 E2
Watery La DWN BB3 59 G5
Watford St BBN BB1 2 E3
Watkins Cl BRFD/BLYE BB10 18 C5
Watling Cl BBNW BB2 50 A1
Watling Ga GTH/LHO BB6 * 12 C3
Watson St ACC BB5 44 A3
BBNW BB2 41 F5
Watt St CLI BB7 15 H2
PDHM/BLYW BB12 26 B4
Wavell Cl ACC BB5 45 H5
Wavell St PDHM/BLYW BB12 26 B5
Waverledge Rd GTH/LHO BB6 33 H1
Waverledge St GTH/LHO BB6 33 J1
Waverley Cl NLSN BB9 18 D5
PDHM/BLYW BB12 24 A2
Waverley Pl BBNW BB2 41 F2
Waverley Rd ACC BB5 45 G4
BBN BB1 31 J1
BBN BB1 42 E3
Waverley St BLY BB11 4 C3
Weatherhill Crs NLSN BB9 18 E4
Weber St RAW/HAS BB4 62 C2
Wedgewood Rd ACC BB5 35 H4
Weir La BCUP OL13 57 G2
Weir St BBNW BB2 2 E6
Welbeck Av BBN BB1 32 B5
Weldon St BLY BB11 * 4 C4
Wellesley St
PDHM/BLYW BB12 25 J5
Well Fld ACC BB5 34 C3
Wellfield Dr PDHM/BLYW BB12 26 B3
Wellfield Rd BBNW BB2 41 F1
Well Fold CLI BB7 6 E3
Wellgate CLI BB7 6 E3
Wellington Ct BLY BB11 5 J4
Wellington Rd BBNW BB2 41 G4
Wellington St ACC BB5 34 B3
ACC BB5 44 E2
BBN BB1 2 D2
GTH/LHO BB6 * 33 J1
NLSN BB9 8 D6
Wells St RAW/HAS BB4 53 K6
Well St BBN BB1 33 H3
PDHM/BLYW BB12 24 E2
RAW/HAS BB4 55 K6
Well Ter CLI BB7 6 E2
Wenning St NLSN BB9 19 F2
Wensley Cl BLY BB11 37 J2
Wensley Dr ACC BB5 45 F1
Wensley Rd BBNW BB2 41 F3
Wesley Gv PDHM/BLYW BB12 4 A1
Wesley Pl BCUP OL13 63 K2
Wesley St ACC BB5 44 B1
BBN BB1 31 K6
CLI BB7 15 H1
NLSN BB9 18 B3
Wessex Cl ACC BB5 35 G5
Westbourne Av BLY BB11 4 B7
Westbourne Av South
BLY BB11 37 H2
Westbury Cl BRFD/BLYE BB10 27 K1
Westbury Gdns BBN BB1 42 C3
Westcliffe GTH/LHO BB6 22 C5
West Close Av
PDHM/BLYW BB12 16 D4
Westcote St DWN BB3 59 G5
West Crs ACC BB5 34 D5
Western Av BLY BB11 4 C6
Western Ct BCUP OL13 63 G3
Western Rd BCUP OL13 63 H3
West Exchange St COL BB8 * 9 K3
Westfield NLSN BB9 8 D6
Westfield Av
PDHM/BLYW BB12 24 A2
Westfield Cl CLI BB7 13 F2
Westgate BLY BB11 4 D3
PDHM/BLYW BB12 23 K2
West Hl NLSN BB9 8 D3
Westland Av DWN BB3 58 E3
West Leigh Rd BBN BB1 31 G5
Westminster Cl ACC BB5 45 G4
PDHM/BLYW BB12 24 A2
Westminster Rd DWN BB3 * 49 J6
Westmoreland St NLSN BB9 18 C1
Westmorland Cl DWN BB3 59 H5
Westmorland St BLY BB11 4 B4
West Park Rd BBNW BB2 2 A2
West Rosser Ct NLSN BB9 * 18 E1
West St BRFD/BLYE BB10 27 H3
COL BB8 10 A3
NLSN BB9 8 D6
PDHM/BLYW BB12 24 E3
RAW/HAS BB4 62 D3
West Vw ACC BB5 44 A3
BBNW BB2 2 A6
CLI BB7 6 C4
RAW/HAS BB4 53 K5
West View Pl BBNW BB2 41 F1
West View Rd RAW/HAS BB4 55 K5
West View Ter
PDHM/BLYW BB12 25 F4
Westway BLY BB11 4 B3
Westwell St DWN BB3 49 J5
GTH/LHO BB6 * 22 D6
Westwood Av BBN BB1 33 G4
Westwood Ct BBN BB1 * 3 K1
Westwood Rd BBN BB1 42 B3
PDHM/BLYW BB12 26 B3
Westwood St ACC BB5 34 D6
Whalley Banks BBNW BB2 2 C6
Whalley Crs DWN BB3 59 G2
Whalley Dr RAW/HAS BB4 54 E5
Whalley New Rd BBN BB1 31 K2
CLI BB7 13 F6
Whalley Old Rd BBN BB1 3 F2
CLI BB7 13 H6
GTH/LHO BB6 21 K3
Whalley Range BBN BB1 3 F2
Whalley Rd ACC BB5 34 D5
ACC BB5 44 E1
BBN BB1 21 F4
BBNW BB2 30 A2
CLI BB7 6 D4
CLI BB7 13 J5
CLI BB7 13 K1
CLI BB7 14 E4
GTH/LHO BB6 21 J2
GTH/LHO BB6 23 G4
Whalley St BBN BB1 3 F1
BRFD/BLYE BB10 27 F2
CLI BB7 6 C3
Wham Brook Cl ACC BB5 43 H2
Wharfdale Av
BRFD/BLYE BB10 18 B5
Wharfedale Cl BBNW BB2 48 B2
Wharf St BBN BB1 3 H4
BBN BB1 33 H4
Wheatcroft Av
PDHM/BLYW BB12 17 H1
Wheatfield St BBN BB1 33 H3
Wheatholme St RAW/HAS BB4 62 A1
Wheatley Cl
PDHM/BLYW BB12 17 H2
PDHM/BLYW BB12 26 C4
Wheatley Gv NLSN BB9 8 C4
Wheatley Lane Rd
PDHM/BLYW BB12 17 H2
Wheat St ACC BB5 44 C1
PDHM/BLYW BB12 25 F4
Whelan Cl BBNW BB2 49 H2
Whinberry Av RAW/HAS BB4 61 K2
Whinfield Pl BBNW BB2 40 E1
Whinfield St ACC BB5 34 C4
Whinney Hill Quarry ACC BB5 * 34 E4
Whinney Hill Rd ACC BB5 34 D4
Whinney La BBNW BB2 31 G5
GTH/LHO BB6 21 J3
Whins Av CLI BB7 15 G2
Whins La PDHM/BLYW BB12 23 K1
Whipp Av CLI BB7 6 C4
Whitaker Gn RAW/HAS BB4 61 H1
Whitaker St ACC BB5 34 D6
Whitby Dr BBNW BB2 41 K6
Whiteacre La CLI BB7 13 K1
White Acre Rd ACC BB5 45 G6
White Ash La ACC BB5 43 K3
Whitebirk Dr BBN BB1 32 C6
Whitebirk Rd BBN BB1 42 D2
White Bull St
PDHM/BLYW BB12 * 26 B5
Whitecroft Av RAW/HAS BB4 60 E1
Whitecroft Cl RAW/HAS BB4 60 E1
Whitecroft La BBNW BB2 30 C4
Whitecroft Mdw
RAW/HAS BB4 60 E1
Whitecroft Vw ACC BB5 45 G5
Whitefield St
PDHM/BLYW BB12 36 A1
Whitefield Ter BLY BB11 5 H7
Whitegate Cl
PDHM/BLYW BB12 25 H4
White Gv COL BB8 9 J1
Whitehalgh La GTH/LHO BB6 21 H2
Whitehall Rd BBNW BB2 31 F6
DWN BB3 59 F6
Whitehall St DWN BB3 59 G6
NLSN BB9 19 F1
Whitehaven Cl BBNW BB2 42 A6
Whitehaven St BLY BB11 * 4 C5
Whitehead St BBNW BB2 2 A3
RAW/HAS BB4 54 E6
White Lee Av COL BB8 10 E5
Whitendale Crs BBN BB1 3 J7
White Rd BBNW BB2 41 F1
White St COL BB8 9 H3
PDHM/BLYW BB12 26 A5
White Walls Cl COL BB8 9 F4
Whitewalls Dr COL BB8 9 G4
Whitewell Dr CLI BB7 6 B4
Whitewell Pl BBN BB1 3 F1
Whitewell Rd ACC BB5 35 F5
Whittaker Cl
PDHM/BLYW BB12 26 A3
Whittaker St BBNW BB2 2 B3
Whittam Crs CLI BB7 13 G3
Whittam Rd CLI BB7 13 G3
Whittam St BLY BB11 4 E4
Whittle Cl CLI BB7 6 E2
Whittles St BCUP OL13 64 C3
Whittle St RAW/HAS BB4 54 E6
Whittycroft Av NLSN BB9 8 E1
Whittycroft Dr NLSN BB9 8 E1
Wickliffe St NLSN BB9 8 E6
Wickworth St NLSN BB9 19 G2
Widow Hill Rd
BRFD/BLYE BB10 27 J2
Wilfield St BLY BB11 * 4 C3
Wilfred St ACC BB5 44 E3
Wilkie Av BLY BB11 37 J3
Wilkinson St BLY BB11 47 F3
NLSN BB9 8 C4
NLSN BB9 * 18 E2
PDHM/BLYW BB12 16 D4
RAW/HAS BB4 53 K5
Wilkin Sq CLI BB7 6 D3
William Herbert St BBN BB1 3 G1
William Hopwood St BBN BB1 3 K5
Williams Dr BBNW BB2 42 A6
Williams Pl NLSN BB9 19 F1
Williams Rd BRFD/BLYE BB10 27 G2
William St ACC BB5 34 C4
ACC BB5 34 E6
BBNW BB2 41 J5
BCUP OL13 64 D3
COL BB8 10 A3
DWN BB3 * 59 F2
NLSN BB9 8 E6
NLSN BB9 18 B3
Willis Rd BBNW BB2 40 D5
Willis St BLY BB11 4 D5
Willoughby St BBN BB1 2 E2
Willow Av RAW/HAS BB4 54 E5
Willow Bank DWN BB3 59 F5
Willow Cl NLSN BB9 8 B6
Willow Dr CLI BB7 13 K1
Willow Mt BBN BB1 32 A6
Willow Pk ACC BB5 43 J5
Willows La ACC BB5 44 C2
The Willows BBNW BB2 30 A2
Willow St ACC BB5 34 A2
ACC BB5 44 D1
BBN BB1 32 A6
DWN BB3 58 E2
GTH/LHO BB6 33 J1
PDHM/BLYW BB12 4 D2
RAW/HAS BB4 62 D3
Willow Tree Av RAW/HAS BB4 61 H1
Willow Trees Dr BBN BB1 31 G5
Wilmore Cl COL BB8 9 J2
Wilpshire Banks BBN BB1 31 K1
Wilpshire Rd BBN BB1 21 H6
Wilson St BBNW BB2 41 H5
CLI BB7 6 C4
Wilton Cl BBNW BB2 30 D5
Wilton St BRFD/BLYE BB10 27 G2
NLSN BB9 8 D4
NLSN BB9 18 B4
Wiltshire Av
PDHM/BLYW BB12 26 A4
Wiltshire Dr RAW/HAS BB4 60 E3
Wilworth Crs BBN BB1 31 J4
Wimberley Banks BBN BB1 31 J6
Wimberley Gdns BBN BB1 2 E1
Wimberley Pl BBN BB1 * 2 E1
Wimberley St BBN BB1 2 E1
Winchester Av ACC BB5 * 34 E6
Winchester Rd
PDHM/BLYW BB12 25 G5
Winckley Rd ACC BB5 34 B3
Windermere Av ACC BB5 35 F4
BRFD/BLYE BB10 27 F1
CLI BB7 6 B4
COL BB8 10 B1
Windermere Cl BBN BB1 3 H2
Windermere Dr BBN BB1 33 G4
DWN BB3 50 C6
Windermere Rd BCUP OL13 57 G6
PDHM/BLYW BB12 25 F2
Windsor Av ACC BB5 34 C5
CLI BB7 6 B4
RAW/HAS BB4 60 D2
RAW/HAS BB4 62 D2
Windsor Cl BBN BB1 42 B4
PDHM/BLYW BB12 24 A1
Windsor Rd BBN BB1 42 E2
BBNW BB2 41 F1
DWN BB3 49 K6
GTH/LHO BB6 22 E6
Windsor St ACC BB5 * 44 E1
COL BB8 10 A2
NLSN BB9 19 F2
PDHM/BLYW BB12 26 B5
Windy Bank COL BB8 10 A2
Winewall La COL BB8 10 E2
Winmarleigh St BBN BB1 42 C2
Winmarleigh Wk BBN BB1 42 C3
Winnipeg Cl BBNW BB2 31 F5
Winster Ct ACC BB5 * 34 A3
Winston Rd BBN BB1 31 H6
Winterburn Rd BBNW BB2 49 G2
Winterley Dr ACC BB5 35 G4
Winterton Rd DWN BB3 59 F1
Wiseman St BLY BB11 4 D3
Wisteria Dr BBN BB1 50 B2
Wiswell Cl BRFD/BLYE BB10 27 K1
RAW/HAS BB4 54 E5
Wiswell La CLI BB7 13 K3
Wiswell Shay CLI BB7 14 A2
Withers St BBN BB1 3 H5
Within Gv ACC BB5 35 G5
Witney Av BBNW BB2 48 C1
Wittlewood Dr ACC BB5 34 C4
PDHM/BLYW BB12 25 G3
Witton Pde BBNW BB2 2 A7
Witton Weavers Wy
BBNW BB2 40 B3
Woburn Cl ACC BB5 45 G4
Wolfenden Gn RAW/HAS BB4 62 E3
Wolseley St BBNW BB2 41 H6
Woodale Laithe NLSN BB9 8 C4
Woodbank Av DWN BB3 * 58 D1
Woodbine Gdns
PDHM/BLYW BB12 26 A4
Woodbine Rd BBNW BB2 41 F1
PDHM/BLYW BB12 26 B5
Woodburn Cl BBNW BB2 30 E5
Woodbury Av BBNW BB2 41 H6
PDHM/BLYW BB12 17 H2
Wood Cl NLSN BB9 8 A2
Wood Clough Platts
NLSN BB9 18 A4
Woodcourt Av BLY BB11 37 H2
Woodcrest BBN BB1 20 E6
Woodcroft Av RAW/HAS BB4 54 D4
Woodcroft St RAW/HAS BB4 54 D4
Wood End PDHM/BLYW BB12 17 K6
Woodfield Av ACC BB5 45 F4
Woodfields PDHM/BLYW BB12 15 G6
Woodfield Vw CLI BB7 13 J5
Woodfold Pl BBNW BB2 41 F2
Woodgates Rd BBNW BB2 40 D2
Woodgrove Rd BLY BB11 5 K7
Woodhead Cl RAW/HAS BB4 63 F1
Woodhead Rd
PDHM/BLYW BB12 24 A1
Woodland Av BCUP OL13 57 F4
Woodland Dr ACC BB5 23 G6
Woodland Pk CLI BB7 13 K4
Woodland Pl DWN BB3 49 K3
Woodlands Av BBNW BB2 40 C6
Woodlands Dr CLI BB7 13 J4
Woodlands Gv DWN BB3 58 C1
PDHM/BLYW BB12 24 E3
Woodlands Rd NLSN BB9 19 F1
The Woodlands GTH/LHO BB6 12 C3
Woodland Ter BCUP OL13 57 F4
Woodland Vw BCUP OL13 57 F5
Woodlea Gdns NLSN BB9 18 D4
Woodlea Rd BBN BB1 42 B3
Wood Lea Rd RAW/HAS BB4 62 D3
Woodley Av ACC BB5 44 E3
Woodpecker Hl BLY BB11 * 26 B6
Woodplumpton Rd BLY BB11 37 K3
Woodsend Cl BBNW BB2 50 A1
Woodside RAW/HAS BB4 61 F1
Woodside Av BBN BB1 33 F5
Woodside Crs RAW/HAS BB4 62 C2
Woodside Gv BBNW BB2 48 E1
Woodside Rd ACC BB5 35 H4
PDHM/BLYW BB12 24 B1
Woodstock Crs BBNW BB2 * 48 C1
Wood St ACC BB5 44 A2
BRFD/BLYE BB10 27 F3
COL BB8 10 A3
DWN BB3 58 E2
GTH/LHO BB6 23 F6
NLSN BB9 18 B4
PDHM/BLYW BB12 36 A1
Wood St Livesey Fold
DWN BB3 58 E1
Wood Vw BBNW BB2 40 D6
Woodville Rd BBN BB1 32 A6
NLSN BB9 18 B3
Woodville Ter DWN BB3 59 G5
Wooley La ACC BB5 45 H5
Woolwich St BBN BB1 3 K3
Woone La CLI BB7 6 D4
Worcester Av ACC BB5 34 C6
Worcester Rd BBN BB1 42 C2
Wordsworth Av
PDHM/BLYW BB12 25 H4
Wordsworth Cl ACC BB5 43 J3
Wordsworth Dr GTH/LHO BB6 22 C6
Wordsworth Rd ACC BB5 44 C3
Wordsworth St
BRFD/BLYE BB10 * 19 F6
PDHM/BLYW BB12 26 B5
PDHM/BLYW BB12 36 A1
Worsley St ACC BB5 53 J2
Worsten Av BBNW BB2 41 G6
Worston Cl ACC BB5 44 B3
RAW/HAS BB4 54 E5
Worston La GTH/LHO BB6 23 F5
Worston Pl BBNW BB2 41 F2
Wraith St DWN BB3 59 F3
Wren St NLSN BB9 19 F1
PDHM/BLYW BB12 26 B5
Wright St BCUP OL13 57 F2
Wroxham Cl BRFD/BLYE BB10 27 J1
Wycollar Cl ACC BB5 44 E3
Wycollar Dr BBNW BB2 40 E1
Wycollar Rd BBNW BB2 40 E1
Wycoller Av BRFD/BLYE BB10 27 J6
Wyfordby Av BBNW BB2 30 D6
Wynotham St
BRFD/BLYE BB10 27 G1
Wyre Crs DWN BB3 49 H5
Wyresdale Av ACC BB5 34 C5
Wyre St PDHM/BLYW BB12 25 G3
Wytham St PDHM/BLYW BB12 25 G4
Wythburn Av BBNW BB2 48 C1
Wythburn Cl
PDHM/BLYW BB12 26 A3

Y

Yare St RAW/HAS BB4 62 E3
Yarmouth Av RAW/HAS BB4 61 F1
Yarm Pl BLY BB11 5 G2
Yarraville St RAW/HAS BB4 61 K1
Yates Fold BBNW BB2 41 K5
Yerburgh Rd BBNW BB2 30 C3
Yewbarrow Cl
PDHM/BLYW BB12 26 B2
Yewlands Dr BRFD/BLYE BB10 18 B6
Yew St BBN BB1 32 A6
Yew Tree Cl BBN BB1 20 D5
Yew Tree Dr ACC BB5 44 B4
BBNW BB2 30 D5
Yew Tree Gv RAW/HAS BB4 61 J3
Yew Tree Ter WHIT OL12 * 65 F5
York Av RAW/HAS BB4 60 D3
York Cl ACC BB5 34 B2
York Crs BBN BB1 31 K2
Yorke St BLY BB11 5 F4
York La GTH/LHO BB6 21 J3
York Pl ACC BB5 34 D6
York Rd BBN BB1 21 J6
Yorkshire St ACC BB5 35 G3
ACC BB5 44 E3
BCUP OL13 57 F6
BLY BB11 5 J3
NLSN BB9 18 E1
York St ACC BB5 * 43 J4
ACC BB5 44 A1
BBN BB1 * 33 G4
BBNW BB2 41 J4
CLI BB7 6 E2
COL BB8 10 B2
GTH/LHO BB6 22 E6
NLSN BB9 19 F1
RAW/HAS BB4 54 E2
York Ter BBNW BB2 48 B1
Young St BBNW BB2 41 F5

Z

Zebudah St BBNW BB2 41 G5
Zion Rd BBN BB1 32 A5
Zion St BCUP OL13 57 G6
COL BB8 9 K3

Index - featured places

Accrington Business Centre
ACC BB5 44 D1
Accrington Cemetery
ACC BB5 35 F5
Accrington Crematorium
ACC BB5 35 F5
Accrington CC
ACC BB5 34 E5
Accrington & District Golf Club
ACC BB5 43 H1
Accrington Huncoat
Primary School
ACC BB5 35 G3
Accrington & Rossendale College
ACC BB5 44 D2
RAW/HAS BB4 61 J1
Accrington Stanley FC
ACC BB5 34 D5
Accrington Victoria Hospital
ACC BB5 34 D6
Admiral Shopping Centre
NLSN BB9 18 D1
Adult Education Centre
BBNW BB2 2 B3
Al-Asr Primary School
BBNW BB2 41 F1
Alder Grange
High School
RAW/HAS BB4 54 E5
Al-Islah Private School
BBN BB1 3 J6
Alliance Business Park
ACC BB5 44 C2
All Saints CE
Primary School
ACC BB5 34 A3
All Saints RC High School
Language College
RAW/HAS BB4 61 G2
Altham Business Park
ACC BB5 24 C5
Altham CE
Primary School
ACC BB5 24 A5
Altham Industrial Estate
ACC BB5 24 B5
AMF Bowling
BLY BB11 5 G5
Anchor Retail Park
BLY BB11 5 F2
Apollo Five Cinema
BBNW BB2 2 E3
Arndale Shopping Centre
ACC BB5 44 E1
Ashleigh Primary School
DWN BB3 59 F5
Audley J & I School
BBN BB1 42 A4
Audley Junior School
BBN BB1 3 K7
Audley Sports &
Neighbourhood Centre
BBN BB1 3 J5
The Avenue Hotel
GTH/LHO BB6 12 C4

Avondale Primary School *DWN* BB3 49 J6
Bacup FC *BCUP* OL13 57 F5
Bacup Golf Club *BCUP* OL13 63 K1
Bacup Leisure Hall *BCUP* OL13 57 F6
Bacup & Rawtenstall Grammar School *RAW/HAS* BB4 62 E3
Balladen Community School *RAW/HAS* BB4 61 J3
Barden High School *BRFD/BLYE* BB10 27 F1
Barden Junior School *BRFD/BLYE* BB10 27 F2
Barden Lane Athletics Track *BRFD/BLYE* BB10 27 F2
Barnfield Business Centre *NLSN* BB9 19 F3
Barrowford Clinic *NLSN* BB9 8 D4
Barrowford CP School *NLSN* BB9 8 D4
Baxenden CE Primary School *ACC* BB5 45 G6
Baxenden & District Golf Club (Top o' th' Meadows) *ACC* BB5 45 H4
BBC Radio Lancs *BBNW* BB2 3 F5
Beardwood Hospital *BBNW* BB2 40 E1
Beardwood School *BBNW* BB2 40 E1
Beech Industrial Estate *BCUP* OL13 57 G6
Belmont School *RAW/HAS* BB4 61 H1
Belthorn Primary School *BBN* BB1 51 F3
Belvedere & Caldervale Sports Club *BRFD/BLYE* BB10 18 B6
Benjamin Hargreaves CE Primary School *ACC* BB5 45 F1
Bentgate School *RAW/HAS* BB4 61 G3
Blackburn Arena (Ice Rink) *BBN* BB1 3 F7
Blackburn Cemetery *BBN* BB1 32 A4
Blackburn College *BBNW* BB2 2 A2
BBNW BB2 2 D3
Blackburn Golf Club *BBNW* BB2 31 F6
Blackburn Museum & Art Gallery *BBN* BB1 2 E3
Blackburn Ragged School *BBNW* BB2 2 C5
Blackburn RFC *BBN* BB1 31 H3
Blackburn Rovers FC (Ewood Park) *BBNW* BB2 49 H1
Blackburn Royal Infirmary *BBNW* BB2 41 H5
Blackburn Shopping Centre *BBN* BB1 2 E4
Bradley Primary School *NLSN* BB9 8 E5
Briercliffe Business Centre *BRFD/BLYE* BB10 19 F6
Briercliffe County Primary School *BRFD/BLYE* BB10 19 F6
Briercliffe Shopping Centre *BRFD/BLYE* BB10 27 G2
Brierfield Health Centre *NLSN* BB9 18 B3
Britannia Community Primary School *BCUP* OL13 64 D3
Broadfield School *ACC* BB5 44 B5
Broad Oak Industrial Estate *ACC* BB5 44 E2
Broadway Primary School *RAW/HAS* BB4 61 F3
Brookhouse Business Centre *BBN* BB1 3 G1
Brookhouse Primary School *BBN* BB1 31 K6
Brookside Business Park *RAW/HAS* BB4 54 D3
Brookside Primary School *CLI* BB7 6 E3
Brunshaw CP School *BRFD/BLYE* BB10 38 D1
Burnley Business Centre *BLY* BB11 5 H3
Burnley Cemetery *BLY* BB11 36 E1
Burnley College *BLY* BB11 5 H1
Burnley College Higher Education Centre *BLY* BB11 5 H1
Burnley County Court *BLY* BB11 5 F4
Burnley Crematorium *BLY* BB11 36 E1
Burnley CC *BRFD/BLYE* BB10 5 K3
Burnley FC (Turf Moor) *BRFD/BLYE* BB10 5 K3
Burnley General Hospital *BRFD/BLYE* BB10 27 G1
Burnley Golf Club *BLY* BB11 37 K3
Burnley Lawn Tennis Club *BRFD/BLYE* BB10 5 K2
Burnley Road Medical Centre *COL* BB8 9 H4
Burnley Sixth Form Centre *PDHM/BLYW* BB12 25 J4
Burnley Wood Health Centre & CP School *BLY* BB11 5 J6
Burnley Youth Theatre *BRFD/BLYE* BB10 27 H3
Calderstones Hospital *CLI* BB7 13 G2
Calder View School *PDHM/BLYW* BB12 26 E3
Carrs Industrial Estate *RAW/HAS* BB4 53 J5
Castercliff *NLSN* BB9 9 J6
Casterton County School *BRFD/BLYE* BB10 18 C6
Cathedral *BBN* BB1 3 F4
The Cedars Infant School *BBN* BB1 31 K5
Charter Walk Shopping Centre *BLY* BB11 5 G3
Cherry Tree CC *BBNW* BB2 40 D6
Christ Church CE Primary School *COL* BB8 10 D2
Christ the King RC Primary School *BLY* BB11 37 J2
Clarion Hotel *CLI* BB7 13 F6
Clayton Business Park *ACC* BB5 34 B3
Clayton-le-Moors Industrial Park *ACC* BB5 34 A4
Clayton Street Industrial Estate *NLSN* BB9 8 D6
Clitheroe Castle *CLI* BB7 6 D4
Clitheroe CC *CLI* BB7 6 E2
Clitheroe Health Centre *CLI* BB7 6 D2
Clitheroe Hospital *CLI* BB7 7 F1
Clitheroe Royal Grammar School *CLI* BB7 6 E2
Cloughfold CP School *RAW/HAS* BB4 62 B1
Coal Clough CP School *BLY* BB11 4 B5
Colne CC *COL* BB8 10 C2
Colne Gibfield School *COL* BB8 9 H5
Colne Health Centre *COL* BB8 9 K2
Colne & Nelson RUFC *COL* BB8 9 J1
Colne Primet High School *COL* BB8 9 H4
Constable Lee CE School *RAW/HAS* BB4 54 E5
Copper House School *BBN* BB1 33 G4
Crawshawbooth CP School *RAW/HAS* BB4 54 E1
Cribden House Community School *RAW/HAS* BB4 61 G2
Croasdale School of Dance *BLY* BB11 4 E4
Crosshill Special School *BBN* BB1 42 C5
Crown Prosecution Service *BLY* BB11 4 E4
Crown Wood Health & Leisure Club *PDHM/BLYW* BB12 26 D3
Daisyfield Business Centre *BBN* BB1 3 K2
Daisyfield Primary School *BBN* BB1 3 K1
Daisyfield Swimming Pool *BBN* BB1 3 H1
Daisyhill Industrial Estate *BBN* BB1 33 H4
Daneshouse Community Health Centre *PDHM/BLYW* BB12 26 E3
Darwen Cemetery *DWN* BB3 59 G6
Darwen CC *DWN* BB3 49 J5
Darwen FC *DWN* BB3 49 K4
Darwen Golf Club *DWN* BB3 49 H6
Darwen Leisure Centre & Pool *DWN* BB3 58 E2
Darwen Market *DWN* BB3 59 F2
Darwen Moorland High School *DWN* BB3 50 B6
Darwen Tennis Club *DWN* BB3 58 D1
Darwen Vale High School *DWN* BB3 49 H4
Dewan Industrial Estate *RAW/HAS* BB4 60 E3
Dunkenhalgh Hotel *ACC* BB5 33 K4
Eastern Cemetery *DWN* BB3 59 H6
Eastgate Retail Park *ACC* BB5 44 E1
East Lancashire CC *BBNW* BB2 2 A2
East Lancashire Railway *RAW/HAS* BB4 61 H4
Edge End High School *NLSN* BB9 18 C3
Edgeside School *RAW/HAS* BB4 55 J6
Edisford Primary School *CLI* BB7 6 B4
Empire Theatre *BCUP* OL13 64 B1
Ernest Street School *ACC* BB5 44 A1
Euro Trading Estate *BBN* BB1 31 K6
Fearns High School *RAW/HAS* BB4 63 F2
Feniscowles Primary School *BBNW* BB2 48 A1
Fernhurst School *BBNW* BB2 49 G2
Fort Street Industrial Estate *BBN* BB1 3 J2
Furthergate Industrial Park *BBN* BB1 42 A2
Gannow Business Park *PDHM/BLYW* BB12 26 A5
Garden Vale Business Centre *COL* BB8 9 H3
Gawthorpe County High School *PDHM/BLYW* BB12 25 H3
Gawthorpe Hall (NT) *PDHM/BLYW* BB12 25 J2
Gec Business Park *ACC* BB5 34 A4
General Hospital *RAW/HAS* BB4 61 F2
Glenfield Business Park *BBN* BB1 32 B6
Glenfield Park Industrial Estate *BBN* BB1 32 B5
NLSN BB9 9 G6
The Globe Centre *ACC* BB5 44 D2
Grand Cinema *CLI* BB7 6 E2
Grapevine Fitness & Leisure Centre *BLY* BB11 4 E3
Great Harwood CC *GTH/LHO* BB6 22 C4
Great Harwood Golf Club *GTH/LHO* BB6 23 G4
Great Harwood Primary School *GTH/LHO* BB6 22 C6
Greenbank Business Park *BBN* BB1 42 C1
Green Bank Industrial Estate *BBN* BB1 42 B1
Green Haworth CE Primary School *ACC* BB5 44 D6
Green Haworth Golf Club *ACC* BB5 44 D6
Griffin Park Primary School *BBNW* BB2 41 F4
Grimshaw Retail Park *BBN* BB1 3 F7
Habergham High School *PDHM/BLYW* BB12 25 J4
Hannah Street School *ACC* BB5 44 D2
Hapton CE Methodist Primary School *BLY* BB11 36 A1
Hardmans Business Centre *RAW/HAS* BB4 61 H2
Hargher Clough Junior School *BLY* BB11 26 B6
Haslingden Baths *RAW/HAS* BB4 60 E1
Haslingden CC *RAW/HAS* BB4 61 F3
Haslingden High School *RAW/HAS* BB4 60 E3
Haslingden Primary School *RAW/HAS* BB4 60 E1
Haslingden Sports Centre *RAW/HAS* BB4 60 D2
Hawthorne Industrial Park *CLI* BB7 7 F2
Healey Wood Infant School *BLY* BB11 5 F6
Healey Wood Road Industrial Estate *BLY* BB11 5 F5
Heasandford Industrial Estate *BRFD/BLYE* BB10 27 J3
Heasandford Primary School *BRFD/BLYE* BB10 27 G3
Helmshore Primary School *RAW/HAS* BB4 60 D4
Helmshore Textile Museum *RAW/HAS* BB4 60 C3
Henrietta Street Industrial Estate *BCUP* OL13 64 A1
Highfield Industrial Estate *CLI* BB7 6 D3
Hippings Methodist Primary School *ACC* BB5 44 A4
Hodge Bank Business Park *NLSN* BB9 8 D5
Holker Business Centre *COL* BB8 9 H3
The Hollins Technology College *ACC* BB5 45 F5
Hollywood Park Cinema *BLY* BB11 5 F5
Holy Saviour RC Primary School *NLSN* BB9 8 E5
Holy Souls RC Primary School *BBN* BB1 31 J4
Holy Trinity CE School *BLY* BB11 4 C4
Holy Trinity RC Primary School *NLSN* BB9 18 C4
Holy Trinity Stacksteads CE Primary School *BCUP* OL13 63 H2
Holy Trinity VC School *DWN* BB3 59 F2
Horse & Bamboo Theatre *RAW/HAS* BB4 62 C3
Hud Hey Industrial Estate *RAW/HAS* BB4 53 K3
Hugh Business Park *BCUP* OL13 63 H3
Huncoat Business Park *ACC* BB5 35 F4
Huncoat Industrial Estate *ACC* BB5 34 E5
Hyndburn Park Primary School *ACC* BB5 44 C1
Hyndburn Sports Centre *ACC* BB5 44 B1
Ightenhill County School *PDHM/BLYW* BB12 26 B4
India Mill Business Centre *DWN* BB3 59 F3
Inland Revenue Office *ACC* BB5 44 D1
Intack Primary School *BBN* BB1 42 D1
Ivy Bank Business & Enterprise College *PDHM/BLYW* BB12 25 J4
J Nelson War Memorial Sports Club *NLSN* BB9 19 F2
Joint Cemetery *ACC* BB5 34 C5
Junction 7 Business Park *ACC* BB5 34 A3
Kenyon Business Centre *NLSN* BB9 18 B2
Kestrels Leisure Centre *BLY* BB11 47 H1
Kiddrow Health Centre *PDHM/BLYW* BB12 25 K5
King Georges Hall *BBNW* BB2 2 D4
Knowsley Road Industrial Estate *RAW/HAS* BB4 60 E2
Kunzden St Oswalds CEVA Primary School *BBN* BB1 42 E3
Lammack Primary School *BBNW* BB2 31 G4
Lancashire Pupil Reintegration Service *ACC* BB5 44 A3
Laneshawbridge Primary School *COL* BB8 11 F1
Lomeshaye Business Village *NLSN* BB9 18 C1
Lomeshaye Industrial Estate *NLSN* BB9 18 A1
Longshaw Infant School *BBNW* BB2 49 J1
Longshaw Junior School *BBNW* BB2 41 J6
Lord Street Primary School *COL* BB8 9 J2
Lower Audley Industrial Estate *BBN* BB1 3 F6
Lowerhouse CC *PDHM/BLYW* BB12 25 K5
Lowerhouse County Junior School *PDHM/BLYW* BB12 25 K5
Mansfield High School *NLSN* BB9 18 B3
Marl Pits Sports Centre *RAW/HAS* BB4 55 F6
Marsden Community Primary School *NLSN* BB9 18 D2
Marsden Hall *NLSN* BB9 9 H6
Marsden Park Public Golf Course *NLSN* BB9 19 H1
Marsh House Industrial Estate *DWN* BB3 59 J2
Meadowhead Infant School *BBNW* BB2 41 F6
Meadowhead Junior School *BBNW* BB2 40 E6
Mellor St Mary CE Primary School *BBNW* BB2 30 B3
Mercer Hall Leisure Centre *GTH/LHO* BB6 22 D6
The Millstone Hotel *BBNW* BB2 30 B3
Moor End Primary School *ACC* BB5 43 J4
Moorfield Industrial Estate *ACC* BB5 34 D2
Moorhead County High School *ACC* BB5 34 C5
Moorhouses Brewery *BLY* BB11 26 B6
Moorland School *CLI* BB7 6 D1
Mount Carmel RC High School *ACC* BB5 44 C3
Mount Pleasant Primary School *ACC* BB5 34 C3
Myrtle Bank Infant School *BLY* BB11 4 A6
National College of Hypnosis & Psychotherapy *NLSN* BB9 18 D1
Nelson AFC *NLSN* BB9 18 B1
Nelson Bowling & CC *NLSN* BB9 8 C6
Nelson Castercliff City School *NLSN* BB9 9 G6
Nelson & Colne College *COL* BB8 9 G2
NLSN BB9 8 C5
Nelson Golf Club *NLSN* BB9 19 F4
Nelson Health Centre *NLSN* BB9 8 E6
Network 65 Business Park *BLY* BB11 36 C1
Newchurch CE School *RAW/HAS* BB4 62 C2
Newfield School *BBN* BB1 50 B1
New Hall Hey Business Park *RAW/HAS* BB4 61 J2
New Line Industrial Estate *BCUP* OL13 64 B3
Norden High School *BBN* BB1 33
North Cliffe School *GTH/LHO* BB6 22
Northcote Manor Hotel *GTH/LHO* BB6 21
Northern Primary School *BCUP* OL13 57
North Valley Retail Park *COL* BB8 9
Oakhill College *CLI* BB7 13
Oaks Hotel *BRFD/BLYE* BB10 18
Old Barnabys School *DWN* BB3 59
Our Lady of Perpetual Succour RC Primary School *BBNW* BB2 49
Our Lady & St Huberts RC Primary School *GTH/LHO* BB6 23
Our Lady & St John Catholic Arts College *BBN* BB1 42
Padiham Cemetery *PDHM/BLYW* BB12 25
Padiham CP School *PDHM/BLYW* BB12 25
Padiham CC *PDHM/BLYW* BB12 24
Padiham FC *PDHM/BLYW* BB12 24
Padiham Green CE Primary School *PDHM/BLYW* BB12 25
Padiham Leisure Centre *PDHM/BLYW* BB12 25
Padiham Town Hall *PDHM/BLYW* BB12 25
Park High School *COL* BB8 10
Park Primary School *COL* BB8 10
Park Road Industrial Estate *BCUP* OL13 64
Path Industrial Estate *DWN* BB3 50
Peel Park Primary School *ACC* BB5 35
Pendle Business Centre *NLSN* BB9 18
Pendle Community Hospital *NLSN* BB9 8
Pendle Forest Sports Club *PDHM/BLYW* BB12 17
Pendle Heritage Centre *NLSN* BB9 8
Pendle Industrial Estate *NLSN* BB9 19
Pendle Leisure Centre *COL* BB8 9
Pendle Primary School *CLI* BB7 6
Pendle View Medical Centre *NLSN* BB9 18
Plantation Mill Industrial Estate *BCUP* OL13 64
Pleasington Cemetery & Crematorium *BBNW* BB2 40
Pleasington Crematorium *BBNW* BB2 40
Pleasington Golf Club *BBNW* BB2 40
Pleckgate High School *BBN* BB1 31
Porter Brewery *RAW/HAS* BB4 53
Premier Business Park *BBN* BB1 32
GTH/LHO BB6 22
Premier Travel Inn *BRFD/BLYE* BB10 27
DWN BB3 50
Primet Business Centre *COL* BB8 9
Primetime Leisure Centre *BBN* BB1 33
Primet Primary School *COL* BB8 9
Primrose Bank Medical Centre *BBN* BB1 3
Primrose Hill School *BRFD/BLYE* BB10 27
Queen Elizabeths Grammar School *BBNW* BB2 2
Queens Park Hospital *BBNW* BB2 42
Queen Street Mill *BRFD/BLYE* BB10 28
Railway Road Industrial Estate *DWN* BB3 59
Rawtenstall CC *RAW/HAS* BB4 62
Read Congregational School *PDHM/BLYW* BB12 24
Read CC *PDHM/BLYW* BB12 24
Read Hall Golf & Country Club *PDHM/BLYW* BB12 23
Read St Johns CE Primary School *PDHM/BLYW* BB12 24
The Redbrick Theatre *BBNW* BB2 41
Reedley CP School *BRFD/BLYE* BB10 18
Rhyddings Business Enterprise *ACC* BB5 44
Ribble Business Park *BBN* BB1 32
Ribblesdale High School *CLI* BB7 6
Ribblesdale Pool *CLI* BB7 6

mmond Industrial Estate *ACC* BB5 ..... 44 D2
nton CC *BBN* BB1 ..... 33 G5
nton Golf Club *BBN* BB1 ..... 33 H5
nton Methodist Primary School *BBN* BB1 ..... 33 H4
erside Business Centre *NLSN* BB9 ..... 8 E6
erside Industrial Estate
BBN BB1 ..... 33 K3
DWN BB3 ..... 49 K2
efield Leisure Centre *CLI* BB7 ..... 6 A3
e Lee Industrial Estate *BBN* BB1 ..... 31 J4
e Lee Park Primary School *BBN* BB1 ..... 31 K3
nan Road Industrial Estate *BBN* BB1 ..... 50 B2
nan Road Leisure Centre *BBNW* BB2 ..... 49 K1
segrove Infant School *PDHM/BLYW* BB12 ..... 25 K5
sehill County Infant School *BLY* BB11 ..... 37 K2
sehill County Junior School *BLY* BB11 ..... 37 K2
sehill House Hotel *BLY* BB11 ..... 4 D7
ssendale Golf Club *RAW/HAS* BB4 ..... 61 F4
ssendale Museum Whitaker Park *RAW/HAS* BB4 ..... 61 J1
ssendale Road Industrial Estate *BLY* BB11 ..... 37 F2
ssendale United FC *RAW/HAS* BB4 ..... 62 D2
oden Primary School *CLI* BB7 ..... 15 H1
oden RC School *CLI* BB7 ..... 15 H2
cred Heart RC Primary School
ACC BB5 ..... 44 B1
BBNW BB2 ..... 41 F1
dler Street Industrial Estate *ACC* BB5 ..... 44 A2
Aidans CE Primary School *BBNW* BB2 ..... 41 F5
Albans RC Primary School *BBN* BB1 ..... 3 H2
Andrews Bowling & CC *BRFD/BLYE* BB10 ..... 27 H2
Andrews CE Primary School *ACC* BB5 ..... 43 K3
Andrews CE School *BBNW* BB2 ..... 49 F1
Annes CE Primary School *RAW/HAS* BB4 ..... 62 E1
Annes & Josephs RC Primary School *ACC* BB5 ..... 45 F2
Annes RC Primary School *BBNW* BB2 ..... 2 D5
Antonys RC Primary School *BBN* BB1 ..... 42 C4
Augustines RC High School *CLI* BB7 ..... 13 G5
Augustines RC Primary School *PDHM/BLYW* BB12 ..... 26 A5
Barnabas CE Primary School *DWN* BB3 ..... 59 H5
Barnabas & St Pauls CE Primary School *BBNW* BB2 ..... 2 B5
Bartholomews CE School *BBNW* BB2 ..... 49 H1
Bartholomews Parish CE Primary School *GTH/LHO* BB6 ..... 22 D5
Bedes RC High School *BBNW* BB2 ..... 48 E1
St Charles RC Primary School *BBN* BB1 ..... 33 G4
St Christophers CE High School *ACC* BB5 ..... 34 C5
St Cuthberts CE Primary School *DWN* BB3 ..... 49 J6
St Edwards RC Primary School *DWN* BB3 ..... 49 J5
St Francis CE Primary School *BBNW* BB2 ..... 40 C6
St Gabriels CE Primary School *BBN* BB1 ..... 31 J3
St Hildas RC Girls High School *BLY* BB11 ..... 37 H1
St Ives Business Park *BBN* BB1 ..... 42 D3
St James CE Primary School
BBN BB1 ..... 31 J6
CLI BB7 ..... 6 D4
DWN BB3 ..... 59 G1
RAW/HAS BB4 ..... 53 J5
St James Clinic *BLY* BB11 ..... 5 F3
St James CE School
ACC BB5 ..... 34 B4
BBNW BB2 ..... 50 A2
St James Lane Head CE Primary School *BRFD/BLYE* BB10 ..... 27 J1
St James the Less RC Primary School *RAW/HAS* BB4 ..... 54 D6
St Johns CE Primary School
GTH/LHO BB6 ..... 33 J1
ACC BB5 ..... 34 E6
NLSN BB9 ..... 19 H2
St John Southworth RC Primary School *NLSN* BB9 ..... 18 D2
St Johns Primary School *PDHM/BLYW* BB12 ..... 16 E3
St Johns RC Junior School *BRFD/BLYE* BB10 ..... 18 C6
St Johns Stonefold CE Primary School *RAW/HAS* BB4 ..... 53 J2
St Johns the Baptist RC Infant School *BRFD/BLYE* BB10 ..... 27 G1
St John the Baptist RC Primary School *PDHM/BLYW* BB12 ..... 25 F4
St John with St Augustine CE Primary School *ACC* BB5 ..... 34 E6
St John with St Michael Primary School *WHIT* OL12 ..... 65 F6
St Josephs Convent School *PDHM/BLYW* BB12 ..... 25 K3
St Josephs RC Primary School *DWN* BB3 ..... 59 F4
St Josephs School *BCUP* OL13 ..... 63 J2
St Leonards CE Primary School
PDHM/BLYW BB12 ..... 25 F2
GTH/LHO BB6 ..... 12 E6
St Luke & St Phillips CE Primary School *BBNW* BB2 ..... 41 G4
St Mary & Josephs RC Primary School *BBNW* BB2 ..... 41 K4
St Mary Magdalene's RC Primary School *PDHM/BLYW* BB12 ..... 26 C3
St Mary Magdalens CE Primary School *ACC* BB5 ..... 34 D6
St Marys CE School *RAW/HAS* BB4 ..... 54 D6
St Marys RC Sixth Form College *BBN* BB1 ..... 31 J6
St Marys RC Primary School
ACC BB5 ..... 34 B2
ACC BB5 ..... 44 B3
BBNW BB2 ..... 30 B1
BCUP OL13 ..... 64 B1
BRFD/BLYE BB10 ..... 27 H5
GTH/LHO BB6 ..... 21 H2
RAW/HAS BB4 ..... 61 F1
St Matthew's Primary School *BBN* BB1 ..... 3 H5
St Michael & St Johns RC Primary School *CLI* BB7 ..... 6 D3
St Michael with St John CE Primary School *BBN* BB1 ..... 3 F2
St Nicholas CE Primary School *ACC* BB5 ..... 34 B6
St Nicholas Health Centre *BLY* BB11 ..... 5 G4
St Oswalds RC Primary School *ACC* BB5 ..... 44 C4
St Pauls CE Primary School
ACC BB5 ..... 44 A3
NLSN BB9 ..... 18 D2
St Pauls RC Primary School *BBNW* BB2 ..... 48 B1
St Peter & St Pauls CE Primary School *BBN* BB1 ..... 33 G4
St Peters CE Primary School
ACC BB5 ..... 44 C5
DWN BB3 ..... 59 G3
BLY BB11 ..... 5 G2
St Peters RC Primary School *BBNW* BB2 ..... 41 F5
St Peters RC School *RAW/HAS* BB4 ..... 62 D1
St Philips CE Primary School *NLSN* BB9 ..... 18 E1
St Silas CE Primary School *BBNW* BB2 ..... 41 F2
St Stephens CE Infant School *BBN* BB1 ..... 32 B6
St Stephens CE Junior School *BBN* BB1 ..... 32 B6
St Stephens CE School *BLY* BB11 ..... 38 C1
St Theodores RC School *BRFD/BLYE* BB10 ..... 27 H4
St Thomas CE Primary School
BBN BB1 ..... 42 B2
NLSN BB9 ..... 8 C4
St Veronicas RC Primary School *RAW/HAS* BB4 ..... 60 E4
St Wilfreds CE School *BBNW* BB2 ..... 2 D6
St Wilfrids CE GM High School & Technology College *BBNW* BB2 ..... 2 B7
St Wulstans RC Primary School *GTH/LHO* BB6 ..... 22 D6
Salesbury CE Primary School *BBN* BB1 ..... 20 C5
Salthill Industrial Estate *CLI* BB7 ..... 7 F2
Science Park *BBN* BB1 ..... 3 K3
Scotshaw Brook Industrial Estate *DWN* BB3 ..... 49 J2
Scoutbottom Industrial Estate *RAW/HAS* BB4 ..... 55 K6
Seedhill Athletics Stadium *NLSN* BB9 ..... 8 C5
Shadsworth Industrial Park
BBN BB1 ..... 42 D5
DWN BB3 ..... 50 B3
Shadsworth Infant School *BBN* BB1 ..... 42 D3
Shadsworth Junior School *BBN* BB1 ..... 42 C5
Shadsworth Leisure Centre *BBN* BB1 ..... 42 C5
Sharneyford County School *BCUP* OL13 ..... 57 J4
Simonstone Business Park *PDHM/BLYW* BB12 ..... 24 C3
Simonstone CE School *PDHM/BLYW* BB12 ..... 24 C2
Ski Rossendale *RAW/HAS* BB4 ..... 54 C6
Smallshaw Industrial Estate *BLY* BB11 ..... 26 B6
Sparrow Hawk Hotel *BLY* BB11 ..... 5 H2
Sparth House Hotel *ACC* BB5 ..... 34 B1
Springfield Community Primary School *BLY* BB11 ..... 5 J4
Spring Hill Primary School *ACC* BB5 ..... 44 C2
Springvale Business Park *DWN* BB3 ..... 59 G5
SS John Fisher & Thomas More High School *COL* BB8 ..... 9 H5
Station Road Industrial Estate *GTH/LHO* BB6 ..... 23 F6
Stoneholme Industrial Estate *RAW/HAS* BB4 ..... 54 D2
Stoneyholme CP School *PDHM/BLYW* BB12 ..... 26 E3
Sudell Primary School *DWN* BB3 ..... 59 G2
Sunny Bank Preparatory School *BLY* BB11 ..... 4 D6
Swimsafe Swimming Pool *PDHM/BLYW* BB12 ..... 25 K6
Tauheedul Islam Girls High School *BBN* BB1 ..... 2 D2
Taylor Holme Industrial Estate *BCUP* OL13 ..... 63 F3
Thompson Street Industrial Estate *BBNW* BB2 ..... 2 B6
Three Point Business Park *RAW/HAS* BB4 ..... 60 C1
Tockholes CE Primary School *DWN* BB3 ..... 48 E6
Toll Bar Business Park *BCUP* OL13 ..... 63 H3
Towneley Golf Club *BLY* BB11 ..... 38 B2
Towneley Hall Art Gallery & Museum *BLY* BB11 ..... 38 C3
Towneley High School *BLY* BB11 ..... 38 C1
Townhouse Special School *NLSN* BB9 ..... 9 J6
Townsmoor Retail Park *BBNW* BB2 ..... 2 E7
Trans Britannia Enterprise Estate *BLY* BB11 ..... 37 F2
Travelodge
BLY BB11 ..... 4 B3
DWN BB3 ..... 49 K4
Trawden CP School *COL* BB8 ..... 10 E5
Turkey Red Industrial Estate *ACC* BB5 ..... 45 H6
Unity Trading Estate *BBNW* BB2 ..... 2 D6
Up-Brooks Industrial Estate *CLI* BB7 ..... 7 F2
Valley Shopping Centre *RAW/HAS* BB4 ..... 54 E6
Victoria Business Centre *ACC* BB5 ..... 44 D2
Victoria Works Industrial Estate *BLY* BB11 ..... 26 A6
Walker Industrial Estate *BBN* BB1 ..... 50 C2
Walshaw High School *BRFD/BLYE* BB10 ..... 27 J2
Walter Street Community Primary School *NLSN* BB9 ..... 18 B4
Walverden Primary School *NLSN* BB9 ..... 19 F1
Walverden Secondary Modern School *NLSN* BB9 ..... 19 F1
Water CP School *RAW/HAS* BB4 ..... 56 A1
Waterfoot Business Centre *RAW/HAS* BB4 ..... 62 E1
Waterfoot CP School *RAW/HAS* BB4 ..... 62 E3
Waterfoot Health Centre *RAW/HAS* BB4 ..... 62 E3
Waterside Industrial Estate *COL* BB8 ..... 10 A3
Watery Lane Industrial Estate *DWN* BB3 ..... 59 G5
Waverledge Business Park *GTH/LHO* BB6 ..... 33 H1
Waves Leisure Centre *BBNW* BB2 ..... 2 D4
Weavers Triangle Visitor Centre *BLY* BB11 ..... 5 F4
Wellfield Methodist & Anglican Church School *PDHM/BLYW* BB12 ..... 26 C3
Wensley Business Park *BBNW* BB2 ..... 2 A5
Wensley Fold CE Primary School *BBNW* BB2 ..... 41 F2
West End Business Park *ACC* BB5 ..... 43 H2
West End Primary School *ACC* BB5 ..... 43 H2
Westholme Junior School *BBNW* BB2 ..... 40 E2
Westholme School *BBNW* BB2 ..... 40 C1
West Pennine Business Park *BCUP* OL13 ..... 56 E4
West Street Primary School *COL* BB8 ..... 9 K3
Westway School *PDHM/BLYW* BB12 ..... 26 E3
Whalley Abbey *CLI* BB7 ..... 13 J4
Whalley Bank Trading Estate *BBNW* BB2 ..... 2 C6
Whalley CE Primary School *CLI* BB7 ..... 13 J4
Whalley CC *CLI* BB7 ..... 13 H3
Whalley Golf Club *CLI* BB7 ..... 14 B4
Whalley Industrial Park *CLI* BB7 ..... 13 K1
Wheatley Lane Methodist Primary School *PDHM/BLYW* BB12 ..... 17 J1
White Ash School *ACC* BB5 ..... 43 J3
Whitewalls Industrial Estate *COL* BB8 ..... 9 G4
Whittlefield Infant School *PDHM/BLYW* BB12 ..... 4 A1
William Thompson Recreation Centre *BLY* BB11 ..... 5 H4
Wilpshire Golf Club *BBN* BB1 ..... 21 F5
Windsmoor House School *BBNW* BB2 ..... 41 F5
Witton Country Park *BBNW* BB2 ..... 40 D4
Witton Park Athletics Track *BBNW* BB2 ..... 40 E4
Witton Park High School *BBNW* BB2 ..... 40 E3
Woodnook Primary School *ACC* BB5 ..... 44 E3
Wood Top CE School *BLY* BB11 ..... 4 A4
Worsthorne CP School *BRFD/BLYE* BB10 ..... 28 B5
Yorkshire Street Medical Centre *BLY* BB11 ..... 5 J3

Acknowledgements

e Post Office is a registered trademark of Post Office Ltd. in the UK and other countries.

hools address data provided by Education Direct.

trol station information supplied by Johnsons

ne-way street data provided by © Tele Atlas N.V. Tele Atlas

e statement on the front cover of this atlas is sourced, selected and quoted
m a reader comment and feedback form received in 2004

Notes

AA **Street by Street** QUESTIONNAIRE

Dear Atlas User
Your comments, opinions and recommendations are very important to us. So please help us to improve our street atlases by taking a few minutes to complete this simple questionnaire.

You do not need a stamp (unless posted outside the UK). If you do not want to remove this page from your street atlas, then photocopy it or write your answers on a plain sheet of paper.

Send to: The Editor, AA Street by Street, FREEPOST SCE 4598, Basingstoke RG21 4GY

ABOUT THE ATLAS...

Which city/town/county did you buy?

____

Are there any features of the atlas or mapping that you find particularly useful?

____

____

____

Is there anything we could have done better?

____

____

____

Why did you choose an AA Street by Street atlas?

____

____

____

Did it meet your expectations?

Exceeded ☐ **Met all** ☐ **Met most** ☐ **Fell below** ☐

Please give your reasons

____

____

____

____

____

continued overleaf

Where did you buy it?

For what purpose? (please tick all applicable)

To use in your own local area ☐ **To use on business or at work** ☐

Visiting a strange place ☐ **In the car** ☐ **On foot** ☐

Other (please state)

LOCAL KNOWLEDGE...

Local knowledge is invaluable. Whilst every attempt has been made to make the information contained in this atlas as accurate as possible, should you notice any inaccuracies, please detail them below (if necessary, use a blank piece of paper) or e-mail us at *streetbystreet@theAA.com*

ABOUT YOU...

Name (Mr/Mrs/Ms)

Address

Postcode

Daytime tel no **Mobile tel no**

E-mail address

Please only give us your e-mail address and mobile phone number if you wish to hear from us about other products and services from the AA and partners by e-mail or text or mms.

Which age group are you in?

Under 25 ☐ **25-34** ☐ **35-44** ☐ **45-54** ☐ **55-64** ☐ **65+** ☐

Are you an AA member? **YES** ☐ **NO** ☐

Do you have Internet access? **YES** ☐ **NO** ☐

The information we hold about you will be used to provide the product(s) and service(s) requested and for identification, account administration, analysis, and fraud/loss prevention purposes. More details about how that information is used is in our Privacy Statement, which you will find under the heading "Personal information" in our Terms and Conditions and on our website. Copies are available from us by post, by contacting our Data Protection Manager at AA, Fanum House, Basing View, Hampshire, Basingstoke RG21 4EA.

We may want to contact you about other products and services provided by us or our partners but please tick the box if you DO NOT wish to hear about such products and services from us by mail or telephone. ☐

Thank you for taking the time to complete this questionnaire. Please send it to us as soon as possible, and remember, you do not need a stamp (unless posted outside the UK).

ML204z